W9-BYV-849

A DELUSION OF SATAN

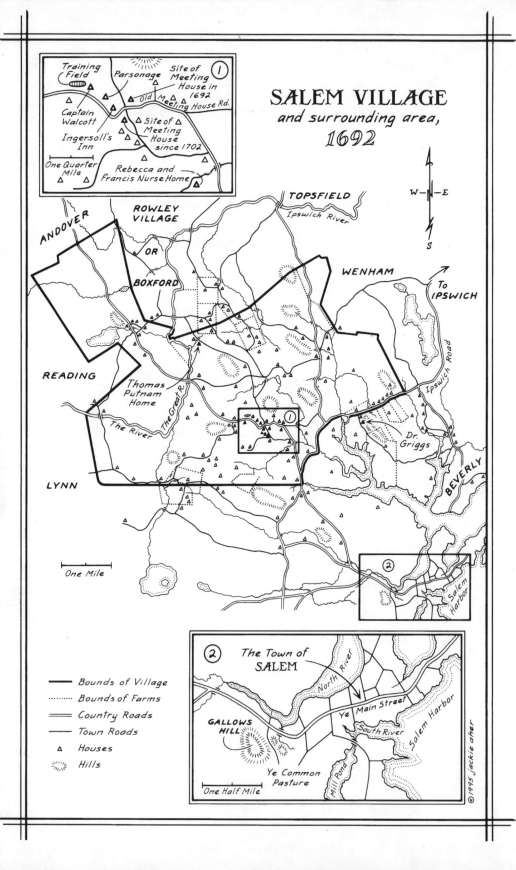

SALEM VILLAGE
and surrounding area,
1692

Inset 1:
- Training Field
- Parsonage
- Site of Meeting House in 1692
- Old Meeting House Rd.
- Captain Walcott
- Ingersoll's Inn
- Site of Meeting House since 1702
- Rebecca and Francis Nurse Home
- One Quarter Mile

ANDOVER
ROWLEY VILLAGE
OR
BOXFORD
TOPSFIELD
Ipswich River
WENHAM
To IPSWICH
READING
Thomas Putnam Home
The River
The Great R.
Ipswich Road
Dr. Griggs
LYNN
BEVERLY

W–N–E
S

One Mile

Inset 2:
The Town of SALEM
- GALLOWS HILL
- North River
- Ye Main Street
- South River
- Salem Harbor
- Mill Pond
- Ye Common Pasture
- One Half Mile

© 1995 Jackie Aher

Legend:
- ▬▬ Bounds of Village
- ···· Bounds of Farms
- ═══ Country Roads
- ─── Town Roads
- △ Houses
- ☼ Hills

A
Delusion
OF
Satan

The Full Story of the
Salem Witch Trials

FRANCES HILL

Doubleday

New York   London   Toronto   Sydney   Auckland

PUBLISHED BY DOUBLEDAY
a division of Bantam Doubleday Dell Publishing Group, Inc.
1540 Broadway, New York, New York 10036

DOUBLEDAY and the portrayal of an anchor with
a dolphin are trademarks of Doubleday, a division of
Bantam Doubleday Dell Publishing Group, Inc.

Library of Congress Cataloging-in-Publication Data
Hill, Frances, 1943–
A delusion of Satan: the full story of the Salem witch trials / Frances Hill.
p.   cm.
Includes bibliographical references and index.
1. Trials (Witchcraft)—Massachusetts—Salem.   2. Witchcraft—Massachusetts—
Salem—History.   3. Salem (Massachusetts)—Social conditions.   I. Title.
KF2478.8W5H55   1995   95-12900
133.4'3'097445—dc20   CIP

ISBN 0-385-47255-2
Copyright © 1995 by Frances Hill

NOVEMBER 1995
1   3   5   7   9   10   8   6   4   2
FIRST EDITION

FOR MY FATHER,
GEORGE HILL,
AND MY DAUGHTER,
TAMARIN ARDEN

Acknowledgments

I would like to thank the staff of the Essex Institute, Salem, Massachusetts, for their patient help. I would also like warmly to thank Vicki Itzkowitz for giving generously of her time in finding some elusive materials for me; Stevie Davies for reading and commenting most helpfully on the passages about Calvinism; Kate Fahy, the actress, for describing to me her experience of developing the part of a "possessed" evangelist; David Bridland, the magician, for explaining some of the psychological tricks of his trade; Leon Arden for reading the manuscript as I wrote it, chapter by chapter, and preventing me from veering off course; and David de Keyser for reading the completed manuscript and smoothing out rough patches. My very warm thanks to all of them, together with Shari Benstock, Deborah Moggach, Philippa Ingram, and Anne MacArthur, for their generous support and encouragement. I have modernized the spelling and punctuation of the contemporary records to prevent annoyance and confusion; however, I have been careful never to alter the meaning. Needless to say, all mistakes and infelicities are my own.

Contents

CONTENTS

Introduction

by Karen Armstrong

PEOPLE on both sides of the Atlantic have long been fascinated by the Salem witch-hunts. They have instinctively attributed to them an importance that is surprising, considering that they lasted only a short time and were fortunately quickly contained. Thousands of witches died during the great witch-hunts that devastated Europe during the sixteenth and seventeenth centuries, afflicting Catholic and Protestant countries alike. In some Swiss villages, there were scarcely any women left alive after the frenzy had finally burned itself out. Yet this catastrophe is almost too large to grasp. Precisely because the Salem disaster was on a much smaller scale, victims and perpetrators alike can become intimately known to us. By studying what happened in Salem in detail, we can learn some valuable but painful lessons about the darkness and perversity of the human heart, and about some of the particular dilemmas that continue to afflict the Western spirit.

Arthur Miller memorably illustrated the emblematic nature of the Salem tragedy in *The Crucible,* pointing to the parallel with the McCarthy trials of the 1950s. For nearly a thousand years, the peoples of Western Europe and America have been periodically convulsed by a murderous fear of enemies whom they have fashioned in their own image and likeness. Jews, Muslims, heretics, Communists, and women have all at times been presented as the enemies of society. Often they were described in ways that revealed a profound disturbance in the Western psyche. In Europe, the fantasies that showed Jews as child-slayers displayed an almost oedipal fear of the parent faith; the conviction that women had sex with demons and flew through the air to worship Satan in orgiastic parodies of the Mass showed a truly diabolic terror of sexuality and the female. Crusaders and inquisitors sought out these imaginary foes and killed them. Some of the people who had been terrorized in this way left Europe, fleeing religious persecution to find a new and better world in America. But, as Salem shows, they brought their phobias and frustrations with them. They also brought from Europe an inadequate conception of religion. Instead of seeing compassion as the primary religious virtue, the Puritans of New England—latter-day Crusaders—cultivated a harsh, unyielding righteousness that was quick to judge and condemn. Instead of seeing God as all-powerful and all-forgiving, the Puritans saw Satan everywhere. Western Christianity is unique among the monotheisms in the power it has attributed to the Devil. In Judaism, Satan is firmly subservient to God, and evil is never allowed to attain such near-omnipotent status. In Islam, Satan is either a trivial creature, not to be taken seriously, or he will be forgiven on the Last Day; he can never be an ultimate threat and is no match for Allah. But Western Christians have not always attained that degree of confidence in their God. From the start, religion was often experienced as a struggle and a strain.

All these traits can be seen in the story of Salem. Yet until now there has been no easily accessible account of the witch-hunt there. When I visited Salem in 1992, I looked in vain in the bookstore for a serious study. I found many books about the occult, New Age theology, and modern "pagan" movements, but nothing to explain in depth what had happened in that New England village in 1692. It is incorrect to class the "witches" of Salem with the so-called "white witches" beloved by modern feminists. There is nothing healing or spiritual about the Salem story. It teaches something far more uncomfortable about the ills that afflict our own society and that plague our own hearts. That is why Frances Hill has performed such a valuable service. Her carefully researched and compelling account helps us to enter into Salem life in such a way that the protagonists become real individuals, with mundane concerns and frustrations familiar to each one of us. As we read, we learn how boredom, envy, a sense of injustice or of being marginalized—trivial ills that we have all experienced—can fester and explode into a destructive violence that assumes truly diabolic proportions.

Salem happened in the New World. The Protestant reformation—of which the Puritans were the proud vanguard in the seventeenth century—claimed to have thrown aside the medieval shibboleths of Catholic Europe. The American Revolution would be fueled by the ideals of the Enlightenment, its Constitution inspired by the Age of Reason. Yet, like Europe, the United States would continue to be plagued by the primitive terrors that lie beyond the control of rationality. It is a reminder that, however modern and scientific our society, we can still be haunted by inner demons, which we project outward onto others with abhorrent effect. During the twentieth century in both Europe and America, we have seen—and continue to see—some of the most savage "witch-hunts" of all time.

People sometimes say that the decline of religion is to blame for such catastrophes. What Frances Hill's book shows so clearly is that bad religion can be as destructive as the most virulent atheism. Like any other human activity, religion can be abused and made to exacerbate our frightened egoism instead of helping us to transcend it. We must learn from past mistakes if we are to avoid such disasters in the future; and where better to begin than Salem? Frances Hill's scholarly reconstruction does not allow us to glamorize these sad events, but helps us to understand exactly what happened, balancing critical insight with a sympathy that was sorely lacking in the Puritan community of Salem. When we read this story of a community alienated from its roots, struggling for survival in an uncharted realm, riddled with tension, jealously, and resentment, we will find ourselves in familiar terrain and learn some valuable lessons about the modern predicament.

The Putnam Family
of Salem Village

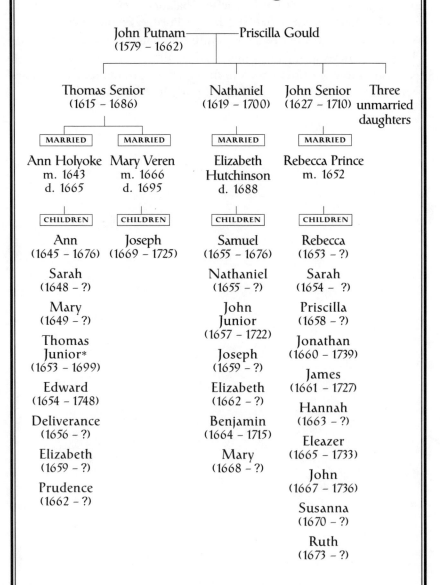

John Putnam ———————— Priscilla Gould
(1579 – 1662)

| Thomas Senior (1615 – 1686) | | Nathaniel (1619 – 1700) | John Senior (1627 – 1710) | Three unmarried daughters |

MARRIED	MARRIED	MARRIED	MARRIED
Ann Holyoke m. 1643 d. 1665	Mary Veren m. 1666 d. 1695	Elizabeth Hutchinson d. 1688	Rebecca Prince m. 1652

CHILDREN	CHILDREN	CHILDREN	CHILDREN
Ann (1645 – 1676)	Joseph (1669 – 1725)	Samuel (1655 – 1676)	Rebecca (1653 – ?)
Sarah (1648 – ?)		Nathaniel (1655 – ?)	Sarah (1654 – ?)
Mary (1649 – ?)		John Junior (1657 – 1722)	Priscilla (1658 – ?)
Thomas Junior* (1653 – 1699)		Joseph (1659 – ?)	Jonathan (1660 – 1739)
Edward (1654 – 1748)		Elizabeth (1662 – ?)	James (1661 – 1727)
Deliverance (1656 – ?)		Benjamin (1664 – 1715)	Hannah (1663 – ?)
Elizabeth (1659 – ?)		Mary (1668 – ?)	Eleazer (1665 – 1733)
Prudence (1662 – ?)			John (1667 – 1736)
			Susanna (1670 – ?)
			Ruth (1673 – ?)

SOURCE: Sidney Perley, *The History of Salem, Massachusetts* (Salem, 1924–28, 2:109–11.
*Husband of Ann Carr Putnam and father of Ann Putnam, one of the afflicted girls.

"Man seeks for drama and excitement; when he cannot get satisfaction on a higher level, he creates for himself the drama of destruction."

– Erich Fromm,
The Anatomy of Human Destructiveness

"It doesn't matter what you believe, so long as you don't believe it completely."

– Bertrand Russell

"Fear is the enemy of love."

– St. Augustine

Preface

WITCH-HUNTS are still with us. There is one gaining momentum today: In the minds of many Americans, evil is embodied by practitioners of Satanic sexual abuse. Rumors of ritual rape, incest, and murder are spreading, not just among unstable private individuals but also among apparently sane therapists, social workers, and police officers. These latter are people in a position to take action against those they believe to be guilty, and they have taken such action. Yet the FBI has investigated hundreds of Satanic sexual abuse claims without ever finding a single piece of evidence.

Court cases in Edenton, South Carolina, and elsewhere have led to the conviction of alleged abusers on nothing but the shaky testimony of very young children resulting from highly suggestive questioning by therapists, parents, and prosecutors. No one has yet been sentenced to death, but men and women have been jailed for life for crimes that were never committed.

This current witch-hunt has been dubbed the "third wave." Salem was the first, McCarthyism the second. In the 1950s a notorious U.S. senator, Joseph R. McCarthy, armed with the powers of the Senate permanent investigations subcommittee, sought out members and supporters of the Communist Party, mostly men and women living productive, respectable lives, and caused them to be stripped of their employment. Some who refused to cooperate went to prison.

Witch-hunts flourish in a climate of intolerance. Today the growing zeal of the "religious right" is both a cause and an effect of such a climate. So is the left's "political correctness." Doctors who perform abortions go in fear of their lives. Equally threatened are scientists who experiment on animals. The bombing of the federal administration building in Oklahoma in April 1995, as a result of which more than one hundred and fifty lost their lives, shows the terrifying depths of the far right's paranoid rage. Given this ethos it is no wonder the "third wave" is ferocious and deadly.

But none of the American witch-hunts was more ferocious and

deadly than the first. Arthur Miller's *The Crucible,* the source of most
people's knowledge of the Salem hysteria of 1692, is an extraordinarily
powerful piece of theater, but the real story is more agonizing as well
as more intricate. The suffering was on a vast scale, comprising not
only spectacular anguish but ongoing daily despair.

How did it happen? How did a small group of girls, the youngest
nine, the oldest nineteen, convince almost a whole population that
scores of largely respectable farmers, tradesmen, and matrons were in
league with the devil? How did they turn husbands against wives,
children against parents, servants against masters? *Why* did they do so?
What forces drove them to send nineteen men and women they had
known since childhood up Gallows Hill to be hanged? These young
girls jeered and laughed as necks broke and bodies went limp. We
might ask, as the Salem villagers asked at the time, What possessed
them? And we might ask too, What possessed those clergy and
magistrates and pillars of the local church and militia who believed
their accusations, or pretended to believe them, or prompted them,
and played their parts in sending the accused to their deaths?

No up-to-date work tells the story in full and answers these questions
satisfactorily. The only popular account written this century is Marion
Starkey's *The Devil in Massachusetts.* Published in 1949, it often lapses
into fiction and has been overtaken by very many new historical and
psychological findings. It was after visiting Salem, when I wanted to
learn all I could about what really happened, that I discovered the gap.
I have here undertaken to fill it.

Readers may wonder why an Englishwoman should feel herself
fitted for the task. The answer is that the settlers of Massachusetts were
English. The area was founded as a colony in 1630. By 1692 it was a
royal province. But whether colony or province, its inhabitants were by
law as wholly English as if they lived in London. The only "Americans"
were the native inhabitants, though of course the word "American" as
a noun was not yet in use. Many of the participants in the Salem
drama, including a great number of the accused witches, were born in
the old country. More than half of those hanged were English-born. As
we shall see, this was not so by chance.

The England of my childhood just after the Second World War was
closer to the New England of the seventeenth century than is anywhere
in the multicultural, multiethnic United States. The population was
made up almost entirely of white Anglo-Saxons, with a sprinkling of
immigrants from Ireland, Eastern Europe, and elsewhere. The
national ethos was one of self-control and repression. Pleasure and self-
indulgence were suspect. The individual conscience was schooled to
perpetual self-doubt.

This ethos of discipline and control spread over the social and political as well as the personal arena. Class deference was strong. The notion of the "gentleman" was still fully alive. He might be a minister or doctor or politician, but he had attained his rank not because of his position, but through being born into an upper-middle-class family and raised to believe that he owned natural authority. He inspired respect, even awe, in less high-born beings. The tones of class deference and authority are heard everywhere in the witch-hunt's primary sources.

Not only the social but also the physical conditions of life in my childhood resembled more closely those of the seventeenth century than anything known to most modern Americans. Central heating was unheard of. It was normal in winter to go to bed in an unheated bedroom. The temperature might be only a degree or two higher than that of the night air outside. Often in the morning the bristles of one's toothbrush were iced. Hot water came in limited quantities. Outside lavatories were still not unknown. Food rationing was in force and many foodstuffs that are commonplace today were scarce or unavailable.

As a result of all these factors, I can begin to imagine the emotional and physical hardships endured by the Puritans. And having spent every summer, and some winters, of the last fifteen years in New England, I have come to know well the landscape and climate the Puritans lived in and to meet some of their descendants. A close neighbor in Connecticut, Dorothy Averill, who died recently at the age of a hundred and one, was directly descended from one of the nineteen people hanged for witchcraft, Sarah Averill Wildes. She did not much like to discuss her doomed ancestor, rightly believing that only lesser people on the social scale were hanged. Those higher up, though sent to prison on suspicion of witchcraft, managed one way or another to escape with their lives. For a woman of her background, born in the nineteenth century, the Puritan sense of shame or pride in one's origins was still very strong. Younger members of the Averill family are rightly proud of an ancestor who was killed as a result of her heroism. She was hanged because she refused to confess to crimes she had not committed.

It is important that the story of Salem be retold. There is an urgent need to understand the social and psychological mechanisms that make witch-hunting possible. In searching for the truth about the devils of Salem we shall investigate the demons in all human societies and all human souls.

CHAPTER ONE

Sowing the Dragon's Teeth

ALMOST thirty died. Well over a hundred languished for months in cramped, dark, stinking prisons, hungry and thirsty, never moving from the walls they were chained to, unsure if they would ever go free. Some were tortured by the strange method known as "tying neck and heels," their bodies forced into hoops, necks roped to feet. Others were made to stand without rest during interminable sessions of questioning. Many were even more exquisitely tortured by knowing that their children were left unprovided for when they were seized. Mothers wondered if their babies still lived.

By the spring of 1693 despair lay almost as heavy outside the prisons as in. Farms had been neglected while families traveled long distances, on horseback or foot, to visit their relatives in prison and to attend their examinations and trials. Some of those families had been impoverished or bankrupted by the disruption of work and the need to pay for the upkeep of their jailed mothers and fathers, brothers and sisters, husbands and wives. It seems incredible today, but prisoners were responsible for prison fees for their board and lodging, their fetters and chains. Many were without income or assets. Some had been poor, even destitute, before they were accused. Others had their estates and possessions seized by the sheriff on imprisonment, at times so vindictively that cattle were killed, beer poured out of barrels, and broth tossed from pots. Children were left to shift for themselves or to be saved from starvation by the mercy of neighbors.

The witchcraft hysteria, which had begun in Salem Village a year before, had wrecked eastern Massachusetts as would a civil war.

It had started in the unlikeliest setting. Salem Village parsonage was a good-sized house by the standards of seventeenth-century New England, though it would seem to us small. It had four rooms, two upstairs, two on the ground floor, and a "lean-to" structure built on the back, used as a dairy and brewery. Excluding this addition, the house was forty-two feet long and twenty feet wide. Inside the heavy wooden front door was an entranceway from which steps led down to a cellar. Beyond them stood a massive brick chimney providing a fireplace in each of the rooms, even those upstairs.

The huge hearth in the main room or hall was equipped with a spit for roasting pigs, chickens, and sides of beef, hooks to hang caldrons for stews, and an oven in the wall for overnight bread-baking. In winter most of the life of the house went on near its warmth. The other ground-floor room was probably used as a bedroom

Dwellings of this size in New England sometimes housed twelve or thirteen. This one contained only eight. However, the tensions were extreme. Samuel Parris, the pastor, was a man obsessed with the sinfulness he saw everywhere and with his own importance and status. He believed himself ill-treated by a faction in the village. His great terror was of Satan arming his foes to destroy both him and his church. He has gone down in history as the person most responsible for the coming calamity, and fundamentally this is true, not just because when events got under way he helped drive them on, but because at the deepest level his own fears created them. He looked for evil everywhere but in his own life and heart. Out of his denial came the devils that destroyed the very community he strove to keep safe. It was no accident that Satan strode forth from God's house.

Parris had come to Salem Village three years before with his wife, three children, eleven-year-old niece Abigail Williams, and a Caribbean slave couple, Tituba and John Indian. Among the children was an impressionable nine-year-old daughter, Elizabeth, called Betty, steeped in her father's Puritan theology that made terrifying absolutes of good and evil, sin and saintliness and heaven and hell. Unsurprisingly, she was full of anxiety. Abigail seemed on the surface a tougher personality, but in her own way she was as fragile. When Parris's wife was unwell or out visiting, the two girls were left in Tituba's care. Their relationship with the slave must have been uneasy. It was unusual for New Englanders to own slaves and as Caribbean Indians, rather than Negroes, Tituba and John Indian were especially suspect even to the people they lived with. The Puritans believed that native Americans were servants of the devil or devils themselves. It is unlikely that even close daily contact could eliminate such prejudice. The girls would have despised and half-feared Tituba as well as feeling dependent on her. Parris may sometimes have anxiously wondered what his young charges were up to when alone in her company. As it happened, he had cause for concern. In the atmosphere of fear, guilt, and suspicion he had created, they indulged in pastimes that gradually led to catastrophe.

The family included two other offspring, a ten-year-old boy and a five-year-old girl. The family was unusual not only for owning slaves but for having only three children. The norm in Puritan New England was for one child to follow another at intervals of about two years until there were between five and ten. This was so much the case that the Parris's small number of children indicate that Elizabeth Parris, the pastor's wife, was not in good health. The four-year gap between Betty and her sister, Susannah, and the failure to produce a fourth child suggest difficulties with conception or a series of miscarriages. Samuel Parris was to father several more offspring by a second wife after Elizabeth died. Elizabeth's death in 1696, at forty-eight, gives added strength to the suspicion of chronic poor health. Her epitaph suggests a long illness: "Thou hast thy longed wish, within Abraham's Breast." She is a shadowy figure in our story, lauded on her tombstone as an excellent wife, mother, neighbor, and friend but otherwise left undescribed.

What was *not* unusual in the Parris household was the presence of a young person who was not the parents' daughter or son. It was very common among New England Puritans for children to live in families other than their own. Historians have speculated that the Puritans were so terrified of the overindulgence of earthly affections that they often removed from their homes the major temptation: their offspring. But there were usually more practical reasons, economic or social. Abigail was probably taken in by the Parrises for the simple reason that she was an orphan. There is no mention of her parents in any contemporary records. All we know of her background is that she had almost certainly come with the Parrises three years before she and Betty made history.

It seems probable that the adults slept in one upstairs room and Parris used the other as his study. The children may have slept in the smaller room downstairs, and the slave couple by the remains of the fire in the living room. A rope bed may have been set against the wall in the daytime and lowered at night, or the couple may have simply lain on the hay strewn on the floorboards.

Betty and Abigail and the other two children spent their days and nights in this small house, which in winter was as icy indoors as out. Heat dissipated within feet of the fire. When the temperature dropped to well below freezing, water froze on the hearth. The winter of 1692 was a particularly cold one. On those frigid January mornings the girls would be awoken by the creaking of floorboards or the rumble of Reverend Parris's voice or the sound of Tituba pumping the bellows to breathe new life into the fire. The girls rose in the dark, scrambled into several layers of shifts, skirts, and bodices, and hurried to the hearth, there to chorus the "Amens" of the family prayers led by the pastor. Breakfast was by candlelight even if daybreak had come and Tituba had slid open the shutters, for the little windows with their tiny panes of dark glass let in so little light that in deep winter candles were needed all day. After clearing the table the girls began sewing, spinning, helping with the cooking, or washing and cleaning. There was always plenty of work since the family, like any other in that time and place, made their own bread, butter, cider, ale, clothes, candles, and virtually everything else they used or consumed. At midday there was dinner; in the evening, supper, then prayers, including a reading from the scriptures and psalm singing, then bed. If the weather warmed a little, and the deep snow lay glimmering in the pale, brief sunshine, the girls might walk the few hundred yards to Captain Jonathan Walcott's house, where seventeen-year-old Mary Walcott lived, or the half-mile to Dr. and Mrs. Griggs's residence to see the old couple's great-niece, Elizabeth Hubbard, also seventeen. Another friend, twelve-year-old Ann Putnam, and a seventeen-year-old servant girl, Mercy Lewis, lived a mile away at farmer Thomas Putnam's. Perhaps Betty and Abigail sometimes went farther to visit other acquaintances. But given the harsh weather, rough terrain, and dirt roads, they cannot have done so too often, if ever. There were other obstacles as well: Visits for mere pleasure would have been regarded by adults as dubious activities, bordering on the sinful.

Some recent historians claim that the American Puritans were not the grim-faced killjoys of popular tradition but relished pleasures such as food, drink, and conjugal sex. At hearty meals they ate venison and other game from the forest, fish from the rivers, meat and poultry raised on their homesteads, and vegetables grown in their fields. Spices imported from the West Indies and herbs grown at home flavored recipes brought from England such as salmon in ale and a pie of pork and apples. A variety of sauces to accompany roast veal and venison included a wine, vinegar, and nutmeg sauce and another with orange juice and lemon slices. As in medieval England, cooks habitually mixed sweet and savory flavors, not just within the same course but in the same dish. Chicken was eaten with fruit, venison with maple syrup. A typical first course at dinner included chicken, soup, meat, vegetables, and a sweet and savory pudding; a second course may have consisted of fish, meat, or game pie, game, and fruit or custard pies. There was no sweet course as such. Everyone drank wine, beer, or alcoholic cider with the meal. Alcohol was not at all disapproved of, though drunkenness, like any disorderly behavior, certainly was.

Strict decorum, rather than abstinence, was the order of the day regarding physical needs. This applied to sex as to food. Though sexual relationships outside marriage were outlawed, sex within marriage was seen as a blessing from God. Anne Bradstreet, one of the first settlers and the only poet among the New England Puritans, wrote of her love for her husband in a way that leaves no doubt that it was sensual as well as deep and tender. These lines are taken from a poem called "A Letter to Her Husband, Absent upon Public Employment":

> *I, like the Earth this season, mourn in black,*
> *My Sun is gone so far in's zodiac,*
> *Whom whilst I 'joyed, nor storms, nor frost I felt,*
> *His warmth such frigid colds did cause to melt.*
> *My chilled limbs now numbed lie forlorn;*
> *Return, return, sweet Sol, from Capricorn.*

The Puritans wore colored clothes, not just black, and played simple instruments. They did not celebrate the religious festivals, even Christmas, but they socialized at harvests and roof raisings. This revised picture rightly reminds us of the historical context of New England Puritanism, between the roisterous age of Elizabeth and the urbane eighteenth century. The first American Puritans had been born in a land and an era famed for its lusty enjoyment of living. Their descendants a hundred years later were to relish the material rewards of hard work and enterprise. All the same, the picture of the seventeenth-century Puritans happily indulging in moderate pleasure is misleading. Despite the fact that they drank cider and ale with their meals and were free of the neurotic horror of sex we associate with Low Church Victorians, they were not displaced Merrie Englanders. Their diaries, letters, and sermons leave no doubt that they regarded all activities besides work and prayer as potentially sinful distractions and believed they should be extremely wary of impulses that led to fun or amusement.

A useful guide to their stern outlook can be found in the list made in the 1590s by William Perkins, an English Puritan preacher of huge influence in seventeenth-century New England. He itemizes various attitudes toward religion held by ordinary Englishmen that he finds utterly shocking. Such attitudes might seem eminently sensible today, but to Perkins and the New England Puritans they demonstrated a lax, slothful approach instead of a properly zealous one. Most English people believe, Perkins says, with an incredulous dismay he assumes his readers will share:

That God is served (merely) by the rehearsing of the ten commandments, the Lords Prayer, and the Creed.

That none can tell whether he shall be saved or no certainly.

That it is the safest to do in religion as most do.

That merry ballads and books, as *Scoggin, Bevis of Southampton, etc.,* are good to drive away the time, and to remove heart-qualms.

That you know all the preacher can tell you.

That drinking and bezzling in the ale-house or tavern, is good fellowship, and shows a good kind nature, and maintains neighbourhood.

That it was a good world, when the old religion was, because all things were cheap.

The delightful good humor of such an approach was invisible to New Englanders such as the Reverend Parris.

The New Englanders expected as much of the young as of adults. After earliest childhood there was little play or amusement. There were few dolls or toys. Nathaniel Hawthorne, nineteenth-century descendant of a leading magistrate in the witch trials and lifelong resident of Salem, describes in his novel *The Scarlet Letter* seventeenth-century children "disporting themselves in such grim fashion as the Puritanic nature would permit; playing at going to church, perchance; or at scourging Quakers; or taking scalps in a sham-fight with the Indians; or scaring one another with freaks of imitative witchcraft." This may be fiction, but it is well-informed fiction.

Such childhood as there was ended early. At seven or younger, children were expected to share fully in the chores of the household. Samuel Sewall, a respected Boston clergyman, makes clear in his diary that he expected his five- and seven-year-old daughters to help upholster chairs as well as to make curtains and counterpanes.

As girls grew older, there were no entertainments or hobbies or even gatherings of young people in a village green or town center. Salem Village, today the independent town of Danvers, was inland of Salem Town and in 1692 legally part of it. But the village and town were separated from each other by rivers and inlets and a two-to-three-hour walk. They were quite different places in appearance and style. The town was a prosperous port containing fine merchants' houses, municipal buildings, and shops. The village comprised widely scattered farms with forest beyond. Its official population was five hundred and fifty people in about ninety households, though slaves, indentured servants, and the homeless often went uncounted, so the real numbers were greater.

At the village center the parsonage stood between a tavern at a crossroads and a training field for the local militia. Opposite the tavern, at the highest point in the area, was the watchhouse, fortified against Indian raids. Salem Village had not yet been attacked, but there were constant fears that it might be. A few hundred yards down the road was the meetinghouse. At some distance, on the road leading to the bordering township of Ipswich, were the dwellings of tradesmen such as potters, shoemakers, and carpenters. Apart from farmhouses there were no other buildings. On the horizon were the treetops of unchartered wilderness.

The only books to be had were religious ones. It is true that these included graphic accounts by various clergymen of strange supernatural occurrences. They are reminiscent in their credulity and sensationalism of today's paperbacks, embossed with red lettering, on paranormal phenomena. Their authors wrote them with the conscious intention of countering a growing tendency in late-seventeenth-century New England toward rationalism and skepticism. They played a vital part in promoting the witch-hunt. But there was almost no secular writing. Few children read anything but the Bible and a primer or catechism. Some might occasionally see a hymnbook or almanac.

It is not certain that Betty and Abigail could read. There were few schools for girls in New England and none at all in Salem Village. Parents were urged by society's leaders to teach their children enough reading to enable them to study the Bible. But the Reverend Parris may have been too preoccupied, and Mrs. Parris lacking the energy, to tutor their young. As we know from the documents to which they put their "marks," neither girl could write.

Young women in that time and place had nothing to feed the imagination, to expand understanding or heighten sensitivity. There were no fairytales or stories to help order and make sense of experience. There was no art or theater or any but the simplest music to express and give form to chaotic emotion. Boys enjoyed hunting, trapping, and fishing, carpentry, and crafts. For girls there were no such outlets for animal high spirits or mental creativity.

The only break in the weekly routine was on Sundays. Then, instead of work, there were three hours of church in the morning, two in the afternoon, and religious reading, prayers, and contemplation at home for the rest of the day. The Puritan Sabbath was similar to the Jewish one, strictly observed and lasting from sundown to sundown. Any activities but religious were regarded as sinful. Observance was even enforceable by law.

In 1647 a man in New Haven who was tried for absence from public worship pleaded that he had fallen into the water late on Saturday, could not light a fire on Sunday to dry his only suit of clothes, and stayed in bed to keep warm. He was found guilty of "slothfulness" and whipped.

In 1656 a Boston man sat in the stocks for two hours because of behavior that on the Sabbath was "lewd and unseemly." It consisted of kissing his wife in public on returning from three years at sea.

Church services cannot have afforded young people, or anyone but the most pious, much enjoyment. The meetinghouse was a plain wooden structure without decoration. Psalms were sung in a manner guaranteed to destroy any possible pleasure to be had in the singing: The deacon chanted a line; the congregation repeated it. There were no musical instruments, the first note was struck on a pitch pipe, and the singing was execrable. The tunes the psalms were set to were dull. And to fit these tunes, the psalms' words were rewritten, to doleful effect. The exquisite King James version of the Twenty-Third Psalm became

> The Lord to me a shepherd is want therefore shall not I.
> He in the fields of tender grass doth make me down to lie.

After the psalms came a prayer, then one of the Reverend Parris's interminable, menacing sermons. A "tithing man" walked up and down the aisles and prodded people with a stick if they dared fidget or doze. Subtle flirtations during services were ruled out by the seating arrangements: men on the west side of the meetinghouse, women on the east. Children and servants were relegated to the galleries built around the walls. A strict seating plan placed people according to age, status, and wealth, starting at the front. The Puritans were as class-conscious as their forebears in England. Though there were few "Lords" and "Sirs" in the colonies, there were people of standing called "Mr." and "Mrs." in contrast to mere ordinary folk termed "Goodman" and "Goodwife."

There was no heating in church. Samuel Sewall wrote in his diary in January 1686, "This day is so cold that the Sacramental Bread is frozen pretty hard, and rattles sadly as broken into the plates." On the coldest days some of the shutters over the windows stayed closed and the pastor read out his sermon by the light of a candle. At least the congregation was allowed to bring in blankets and, to warm their feet, pans filled with hot coals or hot bricks wrapped in cloth. They were even allowed, also for foot warming, well-behaved dogs. But sometimes the extreme cold forced them to evacuate the meetinghouse and continue the service in the tavern. This seems strange to us today but appeared natural to the Puritans. Their society was so permeated by its religious beliefs that there was virtually no distinction between sacred and secular. Besides, for the Puritans, holiness resided in the soul, not in any aspect of the material world. To invest a building with sanctity would have been tantamount to committing the sin of idolatry. The meetinghouse was used for village committee meetings and legal examinations just as the tavern was sometimes used for services.

When all church members were present, the small meetinghouse was crammed. In summer the stench of so many closely packed bodies, even with the windows open, must have been almost overpowering. No one in the seventeenth century washed very often, as water had to be carried from rivers or wells. In any case, cleanliness and hygiene were given far lower priority than today, with our understanding of their importance for health. Since the meetinghouse was on the edge of a swamp, mosquitoes caused further discomfort.

The meetinghouse—or tavern—was always filled on Thursday afternoons as well as on Sundays. Thursday was "lecture day," when the population was expected to attend a long midweek sermon.

The lives of young girls were monotonous past bearing and also full of anxiety. They lived, as did everyone, with the constant danger of Indian attacks, serious illness, and political upheaval. They also felt the continual need to repress feelings of rebelliousness and rage. The Puritans saw human nature in the starkest possible terms. A person was saintly or sinful, godly or devilish. For a young girl to exhibit anything but docility in the face of her dreary existence would have been to stir fears she was thoroughly evil.

The Calvinist doctrine embraced by the Puritans maintained that every human being is predestined from before birth, indeed from the beginning of time, for paradise or the pit. But this did not lead them to feel they could do as they pleased on the grounds that no action of theirs would make any difference. They assumed that the people they called "saints," that is, those chosen by God to spend eternity in heaven, would by their nature live godly, well-ordered lives. This seems reasonable but is not logical. According to the Calvinist theory of election, God selected the saved for His own inscrutable reasons, not because of His foreknowledge of their future behavior. But New England Calvinism was not noted for logic. At its very heart was a paradox. On the one hand, it assumed that it was possible to know, from outward and visible signs, who was saved and destined for heaven. On the other hand, it conceded that in the final analysis only God knows who is chosen. What was more, the age-old Christian view that it is good behavior that gains a person admission to heaven, though in complete contradiction to the theory of election, was never totally jettisoned. Children were taught that sinfulness is punished with hellfire. In other words, doctrine was flexible, bent one way or another according to need. The coexistence of the contradictory notions of certainty as to who was saved, and ultimate *uncertainty* on the subject, helped produce that characteristically New England Puritan mix of smugness and fear.

Given this ethos, it is hardly surprising that those who transgressed were given no quarter. Tolerance was not a virtue but laxity. The many servants and hirelings and freemen who emigrated from England to improve their present lives, not their future ones, were expected to worship in Puritan meetinghouses whatever their faiths. The "church," in the sense the word was used by the Puritans, meaning those worshipers allowed to partake of communion, was highly exclusive. Made up of the "visible saints," that is, people judged by their peers to be destined for heaven, it formed an elite whose members filled all the political and judicial positions in the colony. ("Invisible saints" were all those souls already in heaven or going there, whether other people knew it or not.) Membership of the church was attained by means of a speech known as a conversion narrative, to the pastor and other church members, describing spiritual experiences which proved that the speaker had been granted God's grace. Other requirements were to be sober, law-abiding, hardworking, and, if possible, prosperous. Few new recruits were made, or indeed sought, outside Puritan families. The New England Puritans were not evangelists, having little interest in the salvation of anyone beyond their own fold. Yet they forbade all forms of worship but theirs. And they expected everyone who lived in New England to conform to their rules.

Those wretches who broke those rules, more often servants and the poor than better-off citizens, were punished in ways intended to humiliate as well as to hurt physically. Transgressors had eggs thrown at them in the pillory or stocks, were made to stand in the marketplace with notices attached to their foreheads describing their offenses, and were publicly whipped. To read through the court records is to be overwhelmed with a sense of human vulnerability in the face of implacable authority. Page after page lists crimes such as fornication, "railing and scolding," stealing food, "unseemly practices" on the part of a young woman "betwixt her and another maid," breaking off an engagement, "unseemly speeches against the rule of the Church," and sleeping during a service and "striking him who awaked him." Almost no offense against the Puritans' rigid code of belief and behavior was too trivial for punishment.

Well-meaning folk with different beliefs were thought not misguided but evil. Without qualms the Puritans whipped and hanged Quakers. For them, common humanity shown to transgressors was blasphemy: it placed the mere human creature above God and His laws. As a consequence, those in the wrong seemed to them in effect *less* than human.

Soon they were to demonstrate all the ferocity of judgment and punishment such thinking can lead to.

Terror and shame were used to encourage conformity even in the youngest. It was made clear to small children that they were in as much danger of hellfire as adults. They were reminded that, however young they were, they might sicken and die at any time. The thoughtful ones agonized incessantly over the state of their consciences. The leading Boston minister, Cotton Mather, wrote, "Are the souls of your children of no value . . . they are not too little to die, they are not too little to go to hell." In a preface to a children's book, he thundered, "Do you dare to run up and down upon the Lord's day? Or do you keep in to read your book? . . . They which lie, must go to their father the devil, into everlasting burning; they which never pray, God will pour out his wrath upon them; and when they beg and pray in hell fire, God will not forgive them, but there [they] must lie forever. Are you willing to go to hell to be burnt with the devil and his angels? . . . Oh, hell is a terrible place, that's worse a thousand times than whipping."

One of the few books to be found in ordinary households, besides the Bible and a catechism, was a long poem called *The Day of Doom* written by a minister called Michael Wrigglesworth. One of its verses makes clear that even unbaptized infants were damned. However, God would allow them a measure of mercy.

> *A crime it is; therefore in bliss,*
> *You may not hope to dwell,*
> *But unto you I shall allow*
> *The easiest room in hell.*

It is hardly surprising that a sensitive child such as Samuel Sewall's young daughter Elizabeth was subject to terrified weeping fits.

Samuel Parris's niece Abigail and little daughter Betty may not have been especially thoughtful or sensitive; Abigail's role in coming events suggests this. But they were under the care of a man who was as fanatical a Puritan as any and would have taught them accordingly. The Reverend Parris's sermons make clear that he was foremost in viewing human beings as either irreproachably good or dangerously evil. He preached constantly of the vileness of sinners and of their deserving their punishment.

"I am to make difference between the clean and unclean," he preached, "so as to labour to cleanse and purge the one and confirm and strengthen the other." And "Sinners see no hell, and therefore they fear none. Oh sinners! time enough, time enough, have but a little patience, and you shall see an hell time enough, wrath will overtake you time enough, if you prevent it not by true repentance."

His dark brown eyes gaze guardedly out from his portrait, hiding the feelings that caused him repeatedly to exhort his parishioners to award him his due in love, respect, firewood, and pay. The long nose, large jaw, and jutting underlip in a fairly handsome face show no cruelty or malice, but neither do they show any kindness or humor. In his sermons Parris reveals bottomless depths of envy, insecurity, and greed. He harps on the nobility of his calling and the baseness of those who pursue it for profit. But his attempts at convincing himself of his own lack of interest in money are belied by his constant references to the price of things. He estimates that Judas's thirty pieces of silver was the equivalent in the money of the time of about three pounds, fifteen shillings, a "small, poor and mean price." Even Christ's blood becomes a commercial commodity: "Men highly value their own blood. Nay God sets an high price upon man's blood. How much more will he prize his own blood?"

In speaking of Christ's suffering, he emphasizes the shame, reproach, and degradation of his crucifixion as well as his birth in humble circumstances. These are constant Christian themes, but Parris's preoccupation with them seems excessive. It is as though the most important issue in the New Testament were the Son of God's fragile ego. In reality, of course, the fragile ego was Parris's. He was obsessed with his standing in other people's eyes. His father had left him less than he might have expected of his estate in England and business in Barbados, and young Samuel had left Harvard without a degree. He had failed in the business; he was now a mere village pastor in a backwater community. Parris's low self-esteem fed his frightened self-importance. The proof of this is in his actions as well as his words. He demanded gold candlesticks for the altar and made a complicated issue out of the simple rite of ordaining a deacon.

Parris's deep inner terrors made him rigid and merciless, and he attracted much hatred and enmity. After only four years in Salem Village he was the focal point for bitter wrangling between two opposing factions. (We shall learn more of that later.) He cannot but have filled his daughter and niece with terrible anxieties, religious and personal. If Abigail told herself she need have no concern for the state of her soul, it was at the expense of awareness of very deep fears. In cutting off that awareness, she may have cut off the ability to share others' pain. This perhaps was not all that difficult for one reared to believe in a pitiless God. That is, of course, speculation. What is certain is that in the coming events she was, like her uncle Samuel Parris, quite without mercy.

The two girls of the parsonage, that January, found one way to relieve boredom. They dabbled in fortunetelling. The rumor has come down to us that Tituba, with her West Indian background of voodoo and magic, was the instigator. That rumor is probably untrue. The sorcerers' methods the girls employed were thoroughly English ones, using "sieves and keys, and peas, and nails, and horseshoes." Another common technique was to break the white of an egg in a glass of water to see what shapes it flowed into.

A second rumor has reached us, through the nineteenth-century chronicler of the witchcraft hysteria Charles Upham, that Betty and Abigail were part of a circle of girls who met at Reverend Parris's house to practice all manner of palmistry, necromancy, and magic. But this too is almost certainly false. The girls he names as constituting this circle lived at distances from the parsonage of up to three and a half miles. It seems incredible that they should have habitually walked so far in that deep winter of 1692.

These rumors passed down through the years may have sprung out of prejudice against Tituba's Caribbean Indian background together with the psychological need to find an alien source for the witchcraft hysteria. Upham himself, though an impressive historian, clearly felt such a need. Throughout his book *Salem Witchcraft* he, a Salemite, exhibits defensiveness about the hysteria having happened in his much-loved hometown. It is significant that he lists as members of the circle most of the girls who were to become the "afflicted children," or witchcraft accusers. It is as though he cannot believe that anyone could be responsible for the evil to come who had not been influenced by Tituba's West Indian magic. In fact, everything about the witchcraft accusations and trials was homegrown, that is, transplanted from England and then taking on a New England flavor. All that was unusual about them was their scale and ferocity. And the reasons for these were also homegrown.

Even if there was no regular spiritual "circle," it may be that one or two friends joined Abigail and Betty in using the egg-and-glass and other methods of telling their fortunes. It could be that one of the older girls who lived nearby—Mary Walcott, Elizabeth Hubbard, or Ann Putnam—instigated the activity. Perhaps the parsonage was a convenient place to conduct it since the Reverend Parris was often out on church business and Mrs. Parris would have delegated many motherly duties to Tituba. If both Parrises were absent, the children would have had an unusual measure of freedom since Tituba could hardly be expected to share a Puritan's view of what was forbidden.

One or more of the older girls may have huddled by the fire with the younger ones, the eggs and glass on the floor or on a table before them, Tituba among them or else on the sidelines but having given her word not to tell.

Whoever was present, they would have shared frightening moments. In the winter silence, by the light of a candle and the flames of the fire, they watched the strands of shining egg white hang suspended in the dark glass and then gradually settle. The girls were asking their improvised crystal ball what their husbands' callings would be. All of them knew they were doing something unlawful, something to invoke evil powers, something that might call up the devil himself. And for these girls the devil was no abstract notion but a physical being. His black clothes and complexion were as familiar characteristics as the long face or dark eyes of a brother or uncle.

It must have been terrifying indeed when the egg white went still and they realized, or one of them whispered, that it was shaped like a coffin.

There is reason to believe it was this turn of events that brought on the girls' first hysterical fits. John Hale, a pastor in nearby Beverly who was soon closely involved in the witchcraft, wrote, "I knew one of the afflicted persons, who (as I was credibly informed), did try with an egg and a glass to find her future husband's calling; till there came up a coffin, that is, a spectre in likeness of a coffin. And she was afterward followed with diabolical molestation to her death."

It seems likely that the "afflicted person" was Abigail. The other girls lived for many years afterward, whereas her fate is unknown. In any case, it was "divers young persons belonging to Mr. Parris's family," that is, Betty and Abigail, together with "one or more of the neighbourhood," who were identified as first behaving strangely "by getting into holes, and creeping under chairs and stools, and to use sturdy odd postures and antic gestures, uttering foolish, ridiculous speeches, which neither they themselves nor any others could make sense of."

The drama had begun.

CHAPTER TWO

A Witch Cake

THERE was nothing unfamiliar to late-seventeenth-century New Englanders about fits involving violent bodily contortions and meaningless babbling, with no natural cause. Several sensational cases had been chronicled by two Boston clergymen, a father and son with the odd names of Increase and Cotton Mather.

Increase was himself the son of a prominent English Puritan minister who had come to the Massachusetts Bay Colony five years after its founding, in 1635. In those early days there was a vogue for giving children bizarre-sounding names of religious or political significance. One family's five children were dubbed Truegrace, Reform, Hoped for, More Mercy, and Restore. Another family's three were Return, Believe, and Tremble. Increase, born four years after his father's arrival in the colony, was so called "because of the never-to-be-forgotten increase, of every sort, wherewith God had favoured the country, about the time of his nativity."

Cotton, born in 1663, was named, more traditionally, for his maternal grandfather, John Cotton, another of the first religious leaders.

Father and son were both prominent members of the Massachusetts theocracy. The Massachusetts Bay Colony was governed by a secular body called the General Court, but its laws were based on the edicts of the Old Testament and only male church members had the vote. In practice it was a dictatorship by an elite of Puritan politicians and clergymen. Within that elite, Increase and Cotton were foremost in power and influence.

Or such was the state of affairs till 1684. In that year the English Crown revoked the charter granting the colony its powers of self-rule and in 1686 appointed an English governor, Sir Edmund Andros. He was loathed by the Puritans and, a year after the Glorious Revolution in England in 1688, when William and Mary succeeded James II on the throne, he was deposed. This event plunged the colony into legal and political limbo. In 1692 Increase Mather was in London trying to negotiate, with little success, a new charter as much like the old one as possible.

Before the start of this political upheaval, the versatile clergyman had had time to compose the first work of its day to give detailed accounts of paranormal occurrences. Called *An Essay for the Recording of Illustrious Providences,* or, more usually though inaccurately, *Remarkable Providences,* it quickly became hugely influential and popular. This was intended: Its publication was a move calculated to encourage belief in things supernatural among the ordinary populace. Not that such belief was by any means lacking. But by the end of the seventeenth century leading American Puritans were beginning to fear the subtle effects on feeling and thought of scientific developments, increasing commercialism, and greater individualism. They felt strong anxieties about the colony's failure to hold to the original Puritans' ideals. In their eyes the ferocious war with the Indians in 1675 and several smallpox epidemics were judgments from God on the colony's moral decline. On the all-important New England battleground in the cosmic war between good and evil, evil seemed to be winning. *Remarkable Providences* was intended as a graphic reminder of the forces involved and of what was at stake.

One of its most sensational tales was that of Elizabeth Knapp, a sixteen-year-old living in the house of a clergyman in Groton, who "was taken after a very strange manner, sometimes weeping, sometimes laughing, sometimes roaring hideously, with violent motions of and agitations of her Body, crying out 'money, money.' "

Mather's account was cribbed from a much longer one by the Reverend Samuel Willard. Elizabeth Knapp had lived with him and his family as a servant for two or three months when, at the end of October 1671, she began to suffer violent, inexplicable pains in her legs and breasts and to feel as though someone were trying to strangle her.

"In November following," says Mather, "her tongue for many hours together was drawn like a semicircle up to the roof of her mouth, not to be removed, though some tried with their fingers to do it. Six men were scarce able to hold her in some of her fits, but she would skip about the house, yelling and looking with a most frightful aspect. . . . Her tongue was drawn out of her mouth to an extraordinary length."

In December, a voice spoke through her closed lips, the words seeming to form in her throat. They were terrible words, consisting of "railings and revilings of Mr. Willard" and "most horrid and nefandous blasphemies." It was assumed, by Samuel Willard and everyone else on the scene, that the voice was a demon's.

Elizabeth accused a local woman of causing all this by witchcraft. The woman was sent for; Elizabeth touched her, eyes closed, and her sufferings temporarily ceased. This supposedly proved that the woman was a witch by showing that the evil possessing the victim had flowed back whence it came. But the woman was "very sincere" and "holy" and, despite the success of the "touch test," the accusation lost credibility. Common sense had not in this case been entirely destroyed by fear and hysteria, as was to happen in Salem. Elizabeth retracted the accusation, saying Satan had deluded her.

Remarkable Providences was published in 1684. Five years later Increase's son Cotton wrote of a whole family of afflicted children in his own, similar work, called *Memorable Providences Relating to Witches and Possessions.*

Cotton had been brought up to follow his father's example in all things. However, despite precocity as a child, he had a less-balanced intellect and character than his sire. This may have been at least partly the result of having to match up to two revered grandfathers as well as to the illustrious Increase himself. As a youth Cotton had a terrible stutter, so bad that for a time it seemed he might not be able to enter his intended career of the ministry. He trained as a doctor, but eventually the stutter improved and he joined his father as a clergyman at the South Church of Boston. To his huge disappointment he never achieved, as his father had, success as a diplomat or the presidency of Harvard. Perhaps as compensation, he became an amazingly copious writer.

He wrote well. His prose is often graphic and sometimes compelling. But it is always shot through with a half-disguised boastfulness caused by deep insecurity. Nothing Mather says can ever be completely trusted. He was incapable of genuine detachment since he always had something to prove regarding his abilities or integrity. His habitual self-delusion made him mistrust himself, increasing his anxiety and reducing his acuity further. He was a dangerous man to have on the scene when evil was sifted from good. But that time was not yet.

Meanwhile, his account of the Goodwin family's troubles is long and dramatic and far from impartial. According to him, Martha Goodwin, the thirteen-year-old daughter of a "sober and pious" mason and his wife, began to have "strange fits," worse than "those that attend an epilepsy or a catalepsy," after she accused the woman who did the family's laundry of stealing some linen. This provoked the woman's mother, who had a modest reputation for witchcraft, to "bestow very bad language upon" her, in other words, to curse her out. Soon one of Martha's sisters, and then two of her brothers, started having fits too. The doctors who were called in concluded that the whole family were bewitched.

"The variety of their tortures increased continually" Mather writes.

They slept well at night but in the daytime they would be deaf or dumb or blind, or all at once. Sometimes their tongues would be "drawn down their throats" and sometimes pulled down their chins to "a prodigious length." Sometimes their mouths opened so wide that "their jaws went out of joint," to be clapped together again with the force of a spring lock. The same would happen to their shoulder blades, elbows, and wrists. The four children would lie as though numb, then be drawn into hoops as though "tied neck and heels." They would be "stretched out" and "drawn backwards" till it seemed as though the "skin of their bellies" would crack.

"Their necks would be broken, so that the neck-bone would seem dissolved unto them that felt after it," Mather continues, "and yet on the sudden, it would become again so stiff that there was no stirring of their heads; yea, their heads would be twisted almost round; and if main force at any time obstructed a dangerous motion which they seem'd to be upon, they would roar exceedingly."

All this went on for weeks. Eventually four ministers of Boston, who must have included Cotton though he does not say so, spent a day of prayer at the Goodwins' house, which resulted in the youngest of the children being cured. It also resulted in the magistrates being told of the case—by the ministers themselves, Mather implies, self-approvingly. After making inquiries of the mason, the magistrates jailed and prosecuted the laundress's mother for witchcraft.

This woman was named Mary Glover but is referred to by Cotton as "the hag." An Irish Catholic, she damned herself in court by uttering what the magistrates considered a confession, though her meaning might not have been clear since she spoke in Irish through interpreters. And, besides, she talked in so wandering and incoherent a fashion that the court appointed six physicians to examine whether she was "craz'd in her intellectuals." Sadly for her, they decided she was not, though it is apparent to the reader, from Cotton's account of her ravings about hearing the voices of spirits or saints and of her rage when questioned more closely, that she was schizophrenic or senile.

She was sentenced to death. By this time the certainty of the clergy and magistrates on the subject must have wholly convinced her she was guilty. But as she was going to her execution she claimed that others as well as herself were responsible for bewitching the children and that her demise would not help them. In this prediction she proved quite correct.

Far from coming to an end, the Goodwin family's sufferings became more extreme and bizarre. Cotton reports that the children began to bark and purr, to see specters, to sweat as though in an oven and shiver as though doused with cold water, to cry out that they had been hit and show red streaks on their flesh, to be roasted on invisible spits, pierced with invisible knives, and have their heads pinned to the floor with invisible nails. They flew "like geese," their toes just touching the ground, their arms flapping. On one occasion one of them flew the length of the room, about twenty feet, coming to land in a high chair.

Cotton is aware that his readers may wonder if the children were achieving their effects by a mixture of acting and trickery. He claims that this is impossible because they were unusually religious. This argument carries little conviction today if we consider only Cotton's own reasoning, which is that their pious "temper and carriage" precluded a "design to dissemble." But another line of argument, unimaginable to the author of *Memorable Providences,* may incline us to think that their behavior was genuine. Their extreme piety, with its inevitable repression of human impulse and feeling, might well have predisposed them to fits. In any case the stiff limbs, locked joints, extended tongues, sweating, and shivering would have been hard to produce by sheer histrionics.

Cotton unwittingly provides further clues to the nature of their troubles when he says they "could never assay the doing of any harm, unless there were some-body at hand that might prevent it." They tried to hit people or throw them downstairs but only after giving due warning so no one would be hurt. Similarly they came close to burning or drowning but always called out in time.

This might sound like shamming. But what Cotton's words in their context convey is a degree of control in the children's most uncontrolled moments. The impression is of behavior not wholly involuntary though not consciously faked. Apparently chaotic activities are governed by some inner logic.

The children had more tranquil periods, but these always ended abruptly if their parents reproved them, when they fell into "grievous woeful heart-breaking agonies." And "if there were any discourse of God, or Christ, or any of the things which are not seen and are eternal, they would be cast into intolerable anguishes." Any small accident, such as the tearing or dirtying of a garment or the falling of a cup or the breaking of a glass, would cause them huge pleasure and merriment.

It seems the young Goodwins were experiencing enormous relief in casting off crushing restrictions. It must have been bliss, despite all the agonies, to quell their parents' reproofs, so constant and burdensome. It was surely as joyous to cut off talk of religion, which had been used all their lives to control them. The frustration of their parents' desire for order, through mishaps, must have been delightful enough to induce wild euphoria.

Mather claims that the Goodwin children "had an observable affection unto divine and sacred things . . . their parents kept them to a continual employment, which . . . young as they were, they took a delight in." No wonder, once the fits started, they did not soon end.

Since Cotton, because of the pressure of his work, could not visit the fascinating family as often as he would have liked, he took the eldest daughter, the thirteen-year-old Martha who had started it all, to live with him in his own family. His plan was both to study her and to cure her, though he may also have had in mind the book he would write.

After a respite, when the novelty of the different surroundings subsided, Martha resumed her antic behavior. Now, like Elizabeth Knapp, she also talked without moving her lips in a voice everyone assumed was a demon's. In her "last fit," she claimed she was dying but, when it was over, was restored to normality. Perhaps the sense of imminent death was so frighteningly convincing as to shock her out of her illness.

For illness it was. There can be no doubt that what beset the Goodwin children, Elizabeth Knapp, and all the others described by the Mathers, was clinical hysteria. To read Freud and Breuer's *Studies on Hysteria,* written two centuries later, after reading *Remarkable Providences* and *Memorable Providences,* is to experience déjà vu. The extraordinary body postures, inexplicable pains, deafness, dumbness, and blindness, meaningless babbling, refusal to eat, destructive and self-destructive behavior, always with warnings so no one got hurt, are just the same in all three accounts. So are the exhibitionism, the self-control even in apparent abandonment, and the complete power over parents, caregivers, and everyone else within range.

Freud and Breuer had no doubt that the cause of their patients' maladies was buried emotion. Freud had not yet hit on the theory that all such emotion was induced by sexual trauma, lost to memory. As young medical doctors, he and Breuer had been led almost by chance into the study of mental disturbance through an interest in hypnosis. When first faced with hysterics, they had no theories but were merely observers. Whatever one may think of the edifice of psychoanalytic thought that Freud was eventually to build, there seems no reason to doubt these early descriptions or the view that repressed feeling was the cause of the symptoms he witnessed. This was not a scientist's deduction but a young doctor's perception. The way Freud himself put it later was that the "theory put forward in the book . . . hardly went beyond the direct description of the observations."

One of those observations was that within hysteria there is always "dual consciousness." The hysteric, to varying degrees, observes herself even in her fits and knows what she is about, though for the most part she cannot control herself. Another perception was that the sheer monotony of women's lives at the time *Studies on Hysteria* was written produced mental states from which hysteria easily arose. The two men well knew it was no accident that all their hysterical patients were female. However, they did not understand the main reason for this.

All studies of hysteria, even those preceding Freud's—of Pierre Janet and J. M. Charcot—suggests to the modern reader that what its victims have in common is powerlessness. It is this that ensures that most sufferers are female. The only widespread incidence of hysteria among men occurred during the First World War. Soldiers coming back from the trenches who had experienced inexpressible terror and utter helplessness suffered pain, blindness, mutism, and paralysis similar to that of Freud and Breuer's women patients.

Freud's later theory that all hysteria is caused by traumatic sexual experiences, lost from consciousness till retrieved on the psychiatrist's couch, can be attributed more to the desire to fit his findings into a theoretical framework than to the results of impartial observation. He claimed that all his patients revealed such experiences sooner or later. But he himself renounced the theory several years afterward on the grounds that it was impossible that incest could have been as prevalent in middle-class Vienna as his findings suggested. He replaced the first theory with the one he is famous for, that of infantile sexuality and the Oedipus complex. According to the latter theory, hysteria is the result of the young child's repressed sexual fantasies. But such fantasies cannot always be the cause of hysteria. Soldiers returning from Ypres and the Somme were not suffering from paralysis and mutism primarily because of buried desire for their mothers.

What never occurred to Freud was that it was because he was looking for sexual abuse and, later, repressed sexual fantasies, that he discovered them. His patients told him what unconsciously they realized he wanted to hear. Therapists working with children and adults in Satanic abuse cases often unwittingly suggest notions which their patients believe to be their own rediscovered memories. Despite his later almost mythical status as the founder of psychoanalysis, Freud may have done the same thing.

Some modern psychologists, alarmed by the growing tendency among patients in therapy to "remember" childhood abuse that never took place, have suggested that the whole notion of "repressed memory" is mythical. Others do not go that far but point out that sometimes what the patient believes to be memory may be imaginings born of suggestion. Lawrence Wright, in his book *Remembering Satan,* suggests that "whatever the value of repression as a scientific concept or a therapeutic tool, unquestioning belief in it has become as dangerous as the belief in witches." Patients' accusations are accepted in court, without corroborating evidence, in the same way as were accusations by people such as the Goodwins claiming to be afflicted by witches.

Whatever the truth about repressed memory, few would doubt that repressed *feelings* may give rise to physical symptoms. When an individual's emotions, desires, and will are subjugated almost completely to the demands of society, those symptoms can assume the severity of paralysis and fits.

It is no accident that clinical hysteria is seldom talked of today. Few women are denied self-expression and power to the extent that was common in the nineteenth and earlier centuries. The one hysterical symptom still frequently found is anorexia, which psychologists agree arises mainly among girls who have suffered from too much maternal control. Anorexia may have survived while the fits, pains, babbling, and hallucinations of classic hysteria have gone out of fashion because it is so potent a means for those who feel powerless to exert their will over others. It is particularly effective against those who care most about the sufferers' welfare. There is no weapon in the controlling mother's armory that can match it.

But other hysterical symptoms *are* still occasionally found, more often among children than among adults. A recent American study of mental patients with such symptoms yielded results that for the Salem Village historian seem eerily familiar. Most of the sufferers in the study had lost or felt rejected by their parents and suffered poor self-esteem, a lack of confidence, and a strong sense of their own badness. Yet to all outward appearances they were happy and extremely good and well behaved.

Abigail Williams was separated from both parents, probably an orphan. Among the other girls who were to join the afflicted, only two lived with both mother and father, most with neither. And, as we have seen, Puritan society by its nature produced self-doubt and even self-loathing masked by perfect behavior.

Other recent research suggests that hysteria occurs more often among ill-educated, rural populations than among others. This is presumably because such populations are more likely to live stifling lives. And there is evidence that when epidemics of hysteria break out in an institution such as a boarding school, the atmosphere is usually one of constraint and a number of dissatisfied individuals are usually present.

In Salem Village young women were as rigidly controlled, as powerless, and as dissatisfied as perhaps they have ever been anywhere. In the backwaters of New England, the exercise of the private will was regarded as inherently evil. Men and women were expected to subjugate themselves to the church, the community, and God. Young women had also to subjugate themselves to their elders and to men. Their human urges to express their emotions, fulfill their desires, exercise personal will, and exert control over others were pushed out of sight. But, alas for Massachusetts, they were not destroyed.

Although Abigail Williams and Betty Parris would have known all about Elizabeth Knapp and the Goodwin children, there seems no reason to think they consciously imitated them. Those predisposed to hysteria are highly suggestible. It can reasonably be said that hysterical symptoms are catching. The epidemics of apparent "possession" in the Middle Ages, including the outbreak of widespread wild dancing in Germany following the Black Death, demonstrate this, as do the several known cases of hysteria in boarding schools.

During the few weeks after their fits started, sometime in January, Abigail's and Betty's condition grew worse. The doctors called to the house could do nothing. It was, according to Samuel Parris, some weeks before witchcraft was thought of. But about the middle of February, one of the physicians, probably Dr. Griggs, the great-uncle of seventeen-year-old Elizabeth Hubbard, declared that the girls were "under an evil hand."

As a result of these words, all hell was let loose. In Samuel Parris's opinion, that was literally true. The neighbors seized on the notion that the girls were bewitched, and one of them encouraged Tituba and John Indian to bake a "witch cake" containing Betty's and Abigail's urine. The plan was to feed this to the dog to see if it too would act strangely, thus confirming the witchery. Whether the Parrises' unfortunate pet was actually induced to eat this concoction and, if so, how it reacted has not come down to us through the centuries. But the pastor believed it was the "diabolical" cake-baking, in itself evil since it used the devil's own means to reveal the devil's presence, that worsened his niece's and daughter's condition. By this means, he said, "the Devil hath been raised amongst us."

CHAPTER THREE

The Hand of Satan

SAMUEL Parris felt utter terror when Betty and Abigail progressed from crawling into holes, making odd gestures, and babbling, to seeing visions. Their fits escalated to a violence that twisted their arms, necks, and backs into normally impossible positions. Sometimes they were struck dumb and seemed to be choking. According to the thoughtful though misguided pastor John Hale, their sufferings were as bad as those of the Goodwin children, or worse, since they felt pins invisibly stuck in their flesh.

It had been bad enough when Parris discovered the witch cake. He must have sensed it could only make matters even worse than they were. To come across what seemed an ordinary cake, made of corn-meal, and find it included his relatives' urine, for devilish purposes, at a time when the family was already in uproar, the young people in fits, his wife beside herself and perhaps blaming him, must have deepened his terrible dread of events running out of control and damning them all, both in this world and the next.

He cannot but have rounded on the bakers, Tituba and John Indian. One imagines that he ordered them to dispose of the remains, or did so himself, perhaps burying them in the earth some yards from the parsonage. Then he returned to his diatribe. A few weeks later he bitterly and repeatedly castigated the neighbor and church member who had suggested the baking, as we know from church records. She was Mary Sibley, an aunt of Betty and Abigail's friend Mary Walcott, who was soon to take a major part in events. Parris has left us the exact words he declaimed from the pulpit before the whole Salem Village church membership on March 27: "Diabolical means was used, by the making of a cake by my Indian man, who had his direction from this our sister Mary Sibley: since which [time] apparitions have been plenty, and exceeding much mischief hath followed. But by this means (it seems) the Devil hath been raised amongst us, and his rage is vehement and terrible, and when he shall be silenced the Lord only knows."

On the pretext of proposing a show of hands on whether the unfortunate Mary Sibley should be forgiven her error, he goes on and on lecturing. At last he seems to be winding down, when he says, "Nevertheless, I do truly hope, and believe, that this our sister doth truly fear the Lord, and am well satisfied from her, that what she did, she did it ignorantly, from what she had heard of this nature from other ignorant, or worse, persons." But then he says, "Yet we are in duty bound, to protest against such actions, as being a going to the Devil, for help against the Devil." And he's off again, describing the offense for the second time, at even greater length.

When the show of hands was finally made, it was unanimously in favor of poor Mary Sibley's forgiveness.

Parris ends his account by writing that earlier he had "discoursed said sister in my study about her grand error abovesaid, and then also read to her what I had written as above to read to the Church, and said sister Sibley assented to the same with tears and sorrowful confession." If he treated a respected church member like this, what would he have done to his slaves?

It is hardly surprising that the girls' first hallucinations were of Tituba. They must have seen her shouted at, called "evil" and "devil," threatened, or even inflicted with horrible punishments, possibly beating. If they had not seen it they must have heard it through the thin walls. Their fear of and contempt for her, as a Caribbean Indian, instilled all their lives by Puritan demonology as well as by the universal prejudice against what is alien, would have sharpened and deepened. Previously fear was soothed by familiarity, contempt by affection. Tituba had almost certainly lived in the family since before Betty was born. It is likely she came to New England with Samuel Parris from Barbados in about 1680. Later, when examined by the magistrates, she was to claim she loved Betty. We can never know for certain Betty's and Abigail's feelings for her, but they must have included dependency. Suddenly she must have seemed terrifying. A doctor had told them they were bewitched. Their father—in Abigail's case, surrogate father, but perhaps the only father she had known—was shouting at or beating her for witchcraft.

It is no wonder that in their hysterical state they claimed to know where she was and what she was doing when she was out of their sight. Or that they felt her invisibly pinching and pricking them. Yet the girls did not hallucinate the equally guilty John Indian. They did not accuse *him* of pinching or pricking them. There was no close relationship with him as with Tituba.

It has been argued that the particular hysterical symptoms of feeling pinched, pricked, choked, and bitten are primitive aggressive urges toward an all-powerful mother, turned on the self. The desire to inflict pain in the only way the baby knows or can even imagine is revived in later childhood when maternal power again causes furious resentment. In today's society that resentment is conscious and clearly expressed. But in a repressed society, such as the Puritans, such resentment was not admitted even to oneself. Murderous urges were projected onto others; would-be murderers became victims.

Circumstances made Tituba an even more perfect recipient for repressed fury toward the maternal oppressor than Glover, the despised Irish Catholic neighbor of the Goodwins. Elizabeth Parris, however weak in character or in health, as a mother exerted the automatic, total control invested by a society that allowed children no will of their own. Tituba was, as her proxy, an authority figure yet at the same time despised. Children's sadism toward "inferiors" with power, such as nannies and governesses, or in our day au pairs and babysitters, is an all too familiar phenomenon.

As the weeks passed, the girls' sufferings and accusations did not lessen. This was no doubt inevitable, given the whole neighborhood's, as well as the doctor's, excited conviction that they were bewitched. They were constantly viewed and questioned in their fits by streams of thrilled visitors. Their condition gave them an importance and power they could never have dreamt of. This is not to suggest that they were enjoying themselves. They were profoundly disturbed and unhappy, no doubt frightened, often in pain. But what they were going through fulfilled long unsatisfied cravings to express and assert themselves. Unconsciously they willed themselves on.

Naturally Parris's fury toward Tituba did not abate. It was bad enough that his children were in such a desperate state. It was worse that they were bewitched. But something even more dreadful might be in store. The line between affliction by witchcraft and possession by the devil was narrow. A person seen as an innocent victim could all too easily be transformed in the community's eyes to an agent of Satan. This happened to Elizabeth Knapp when her neighbor, accused of witchcraft, proved innocent. Elizabeth was then suspected of harboring a demon by her own means, not as the result of the acts of another. She could easily have been accused of practicing witchcraft herself. Under pressure from Samuel Willard she confessed to signing a pact with the devil but then, aware of the danger of this, tried to recant. It may have been the stress of maintaining her innocence, without the recourse of shifting the blame for diabolic activity, that caused the climax of her ordeal, a demon's voice speaking through her. Parris would have been all too aware of the risk of events taking a badly wrong turn and his daughter and niece being branded as witches.

The pastor was terrified not only for his relatives' welfare but also for his reputation and standing. There had been bitter infighting in Salem Village for years, with Parris at its center. He had a great many enemies. No doubt he was genuinely afraid for the fate of the souls of the young people under his care. But the threat to his livelihood was far more immediate. He could quickly find himself out of the parsonage if it was known that Satan had moved in.

During the latter part of February he invited some "worthy gentlemen of Salem" and "neighbor ministers" to his house for a consultation, no doubt hoping to keep the local men of power and influence sympathetic toward him as well as to get some advice. The reflective John Hale of Beverly was one of the ministers, as was Salem Town's far less reflective, indeed thoroughly closed-minded, Nicholas Noyes. The gentlemen may have included the magistrates John Hathorne and Bartholomew Gedney. This gathering of worthies agreed with Dr. Griggs that the "hand of Satan" was in the children and advised patience and prayer. They suggested that Parris "wait upon the providence of God to see what time may discover."

But they also questioned Tituba. Parris had told them that Abigail and Betty saw her in visions and accused her of invisibly pricking and pinching them. She denied that she was a witch. But she confessed to baking the witch cake and made the dangerous admission, or ill-advised fanciful claim, that her old mistress in Barbados was a witch and that she had taught her "some means to be used for the discovery of a witch and for the prevention of being bewitched."

It is impossible to know whether she was telling the truth as she understood it or just saying what she thought the gentlemen, pressing her hard, wanted to hear. Perhaps it was she who was the "ignorant or worse" person from whom Mary Sibley had heard about witch cakes. Perhaps Parris had not said this in church since he was afraid of admitting that the source of the trouble was within his own home.

It is sad to imagine Tituba's awe, terror, bewilderment, and helplessness. Her partial admission, meant to mollify, did her no good. It must have confirmed Parris's feeling that it would be highly convenient if she were deemed wholly responsible for his children's afflictions. If she could be made to confess to causing their agonies by witchcraft, the dangers to himself and his relatives—physical, spiritual and political—could be averted. The whole hideous nightmare might be brought to an end.

Over the next few weeks Parris did not fully follow the worthies' advice. He may well have prayed. But he did not "wait upon the providence of God to see what time may discover." He tried to make Tituba confess to being a witch by beating her and "otherways" abusing her. What the "otherways" were we can only conjecture.

CHAPTER FOUR

The Nightmare of a Religion

SOME readers may wonder whether Tituba was perhaps guilty. What, after all, *is* witchcraft? Did it—does it—exist? Could she have practiced it?

The notion of sorcery has existed at all times in all cultures. All through the ages some special people have been thought to be gifted with magical powers. But the Western European concept of witchcraft is something more specific than magic. The historian G. L. Burr wrote in 1890: "Magic itself is actual and universal. But witchcraft never was. It was but a shadow, a nightmare: the nightmare of a religion, the shadow of a dogma. Less than five centuries saw its birth, its vigor, its decay."

However, whatever they may think of its being a shadow or a nightmare, many people claim that witchcraft never decayed. Or that, if it did, it has since been revived. At present there are thousands of covens of witches throughout Europe and America. Their members are the adherents of a religion called Wicca, neopaganism, or the Craft. They talk of their aims in such terms as the search for spiritual fulfillment through a sense of connectedness between themselves and the universe. In their view there is no distinction between the spiritual and material, sacred and secular. They ascribe the highest possible value to the "female" gifts of compassion, nurturing, and empathy; they link the practice of witchcraft with the traditional arts of folk medicine. They believe that these ways of viewing the world were universal in pre-Christian times but then were forced underground.

In fact, Wicca is strongly informed by modern ecological and feminist beliefs, with their twentieth-century concerns for the environment and rejection of patriarchal religions. It draws on the notion of a spiritually sound pre-Christian era rather as the early Romantics drew on the myth of a preindustrialized Eden. However, be their inspiration ancient or modern, members of Wicca view witchcraft as something very different from its popular, Halloween image. For them it is the celebration of humanity as part of the whole natural world, not casting spells or flying or making pacts with the devil. Such activities, they believe, were attributed to witches by their Christian traducers and persecutors.

The belief that witchcraft was essentially paganism gone into hiding and given a very bad press by Christian rulers and clergy has its source in the writings of Margaret Murray, an Egyptologist, folklorist, and anthropologist of the 1920s. She believed that witchcraft was a religion dating to the Stone Age, embracing the worship of the god of the hunt and the goddess of fertility, and that the Christian church took the god, with his hoofs, horns, and tail, and turned him into the devil. But Murray's work has now largely been discredited and many Wiccans accept that it has. In the highly influential 1979 book of Wiccan and neopagan theory and lore, *Drawing Down the Moon,* Margot Adler, herself a member of Wicca, describes Murray's theory as mythical. Her argument is that Wicca has spiritual validity even though what was recently considered its history, literally true, is now known not to be so.

The truth, Adler recognizes, is that the witchcraft of the Middle Ages, leading to the horrific witch-hunts of 1500 to 1650 throughout Europe and in New England from its founding till the late seventeenth century, was a delusion. Certainly there were women who practiced herbal medicine and other "healing arts" and "cunning folk" who seemed to be gifted with second sight and other strange powers. But they did not call themselves witches and were usually seen as distinct from witches.

The mistaken belief on which the folklore of witchcraft was founded was that ill-intentioned people could cause harm to their enemies, or their enemies' children or livestock, by the sheer power of their anger and envy. Their means might be cursing or sticking pins in dolls or giving looks full of malice. They might use the help of supernatural pets called "familiars," which looked like cats, dogs, or toads or bizarre combinations of two or more of these species. Among witches' most frequent activities was causing bread not to rise or beer brewings to fail or butter not to "come" or livestock or children to sicken and die.

Such folklore grew out of the tensions of lives lived in close-knit communities where great pain and disappointment were commonplace. For women constantly pregnant or nursing, often ill, always exhausted, struggling to get through each day with its almost impossible burden of chores, any extra misfortune was bitter indeed. Afflictions and diseases which today can be named and explained were then inexplicable. When babies or children sickened, there was no one to tell distraught mothers that their children had meningitis or kidney disease. If livestock went lame, there was no vet to explain foot and mouth disease. The natural human desire both to cast blame and to find explanations led to the ascribing of mishaps not to chance but to evil intention. The victims would remember black looks or harsh words from a neighbor. If the child or cow died, the suspect would become even more feared and even more likely to come under suspicion next time misfortune occurred.

The ground-breaking study of witchcraft trials in Essex, England, by Alan Macfarlane suggests that most victims of the fear and suspicion of witchcraft were women between fifty and seventy. Whole communities, not isolated individuals, focused on particular suspects. What they had in common, besides gender and age, was that they were less affluent than their neighbors, begged from them, and, if turned down, cursed and grumbled. Macfarlane's theory of the genesis of witchcraft accusations is more specific than that of the need to find cause of misfortune, though it is compatible with it. He believes that the supplicants created guilt in those who refused them; the guilt turned to anger; then the anger was projected back on the supplicants. By this process the women who had asked for assistance became repositories for feelings their neighbors disliked in themselves.

Macfarlane argues that witchcraft prosecutions increased between the mid-sixteenth and mid-seventeenth centuries as a result of sociological changes that made this process of guilt, anger, and projection more likely to happen. As a result of population growth and the collapse of the feudal system, village life was disintegrating. The old ethos of helpfulness toward neighbors was in conflict with the growing emphasis on fulfilling individual needs and desires. At the same time, the traditional sources of support for the poor, the Church and the manor, could no longer be counted on. People still felt a moral obligation to help their neighbors, but the growth of belief in self-help and the increasing demands from those unprovided for made them less willing to give. The less affluent—not the destitute, who were treated as criminals—thus created the feelings of guilt which in due course led the withholders of help to suspect them of avenging themselves by devilish means.

Macfarlane's theory carries considerable conviction as the description of one, if not the sole, process leading to accusations of witchcraft. One aspect of his reasoning seems beyond doubt: that women found guilty of witchcraft were perceived as full of the envy and rage their "victims" despised and denied in themselves. When the witches were hanged and the evil destroyed, their accusers at an unconscious level felt cleansed.

It is possible that certain old women, as aware of the folklore of witchcraft as the rest of the populace, sometimes *did* curse their neighbors or stick pins in dolls, hoping to hurt people. Occasionally the victims may have known of these actions and had hysterical reactions in line with the witches' intentions. But most misfortunes attributed to witchcraft were undoubtedly caused by accident, disease, and mistakes.

Confessions of witchcraft, when not obtained under torture, may be blamed, like the accusations that led to them, on delusion. Strong mental pressures, exacerbated by the physical hardships imposed, then as now, by interrogators—enforced wakefulness, uncomfortable postures, hunger, and thirst—provoke states in which fantasy and reality merge. Even without such harsh treatment, those of weak mind may be brought to think themselves guilty. As we know from twentieth-century research on interrogation techniques, there may be an unconscious desire on the part of the questioned to placate an all-powerful father figure. In Puritan New England a magistrate or minister was nothing if not a powerful father figure.

Many of the accused witches suffered from some form of dementia. Mary Glover, supposed scourge of the Goodwins, heard voices of spirits and saints. It is hardly surprising that she came to believe herself supernaturally empowered to harm.

No one has ever satisfactorily explained why witches have mostly been women. Since witch accusers have also often been women—probably more often than men—the explanation cannot simply be man's fear and hatred of females. Macfarlane's guess is that women, as wives, mothers, and gossips, were more centrally involved in village life than men, more likely to wield power at village level, and more likely to be lenders and borrowers. They were therefore more likely to arouse the guilt, hate, and envy that would lead to accusations.

It may be that postmenopausal women, no longer confined to the childbearing role and inclined to assert themselves, tended to be viewed as aggressive and threatening. And witchcraft was unquestionably an expression of aggression, in the witchcraft accuser if not the witch.

In New England many accused witches were women who were economically independent of men. This is not to say they were affluent; on the contrary, they were more often poor. But they were without fathers, husbands, or brothers and thus in control of their own finances. Such independence was unusual, and those who enjoyed it may have seemed especially dangerous to the established social order. A further theory is that when spinsters and widows increased in number during the later Middle Ages they were seen, in a society in which the patriarchal family was the norm, as an alien element.

All of these views may have some or much truth in them. But it also seems likely that people accuse women, not men, of witchcraft for the reason that, in all Western cultures, girls and women subtly torment each other with words, looks, or silences while boys and grown men physically fight or shout blatant insults. Women's habitually more covert tactics in any struggle for power make them more suspect when the methods of attack are invisible.

In the late Middle Ages, in Europe and Scotland though not in England, the fear of witchcraft among ordinary people became linked to the dread of heresy among the rulers and clergy. The historian Norman Cohn, in *Europe's Inner Demons,* argues that since antiquity European society has tended to locate evil, in the most horrific guises imaginable, within groups seen as posing a religious or political threat. The pagan Romans believed that the obscure sect known as Christians practiced ritual murder and cannibalism and engaged in incestuous orgies. By the fifth century a revivalist group known as the Montanists was accused of those same activities by the Christians, now in power as the upholders of the Roman Empire's official religion.

The dread of evil, secret groups practicing ritual murder and incest persisted through the centuries, focusing in turn on various sects: the Paulicians, the Bogomiles, and a group of mystical canons in Orleans, among others. All were equally innocent. By the Middle Ages ritual murder and incest had become associated with devil worship. The notion had crystallized that nocturnal orgies were supervised by a demon. Meanwhile the Inquisition was developed by the Catholic church to eradicate heresy. Gradually the concept of the devil-worshiping heretic evolved into that of the witch. This invention of the literate, clerical elite was a very different creature from the powerful but earthbound old woman of folklore. The cleric's witch could be man, woman, or child, flew to witches' Sabbaths, held sexual orgies that included incest and mating with demons, and feasted on babies. When the Inquisition began torturing people to make them confess to such practices, most of them did so, often naming associates. Thus was launched the great continental witch-hunts of the sixteenth and seventeenth centuries.

Torture is not used to elicit confessions in today's accusations of Satanic sexual abuse. But the modern equivalents are prolonged police questioning, the denial of bail, years pending trial in jail, and the pressure to plea bargain.

Witch-hunts in the sixteenth and seventeenth centuries did not happen in England on the same scale as on the continent or in Scotland. Fear of heresy had never existed with the same force in England. There was no Inquisition. Though suspected witches were often given rough treatment, torture was employed, on a couple of occasions, only as a result of the zeal of particular witch finders. Otherwise witches were prosecuted in fairly small numbers, for causing harm to their neighbors rather than for devil worship. They were tried under secular laws passed in the reigns of Elizabeth I and James I before judges and juries at the Courts of Assizes. The ecclesiastical courts investigated insignificant cases, often merely with a view to establishing fraud. Four out of five accused witches were aquitted or sentenced to prison or the pillory; the minority who were sent to their deaths were not burned but hanged.

The clerical notion of witches as the devil's disciples, selling their souls for earthly rewards or the power to harm, able to fly through the air, attending Sabbaths and indulging in murder and incest, crossed the English Channel only in modified form and late in the day. But it had arrived by the early seventeenth century, when the Puritans first left England for America. However, this notion continued to be more popular with the clergy than with the ordinary people. In New England, as at home, the clergy's idea of a witch emphasized a pact with the devil while that of the ordinary folk focused on the power to do harm by malice. But even in the minds of the clergy, witches' communal activities were tame compared with those of their counterparts in Europe. Witches were thought to attend meetings led by the devil but without indulging in spectacular horrors.

A peculiarly English feature of witchcraft belief was possession by devils, particularly of children. During the sixteenth century in England, several well-known cases arose presaging those of the Goodwins in Boston and featuring hysterical fits and an accused servant or neighbor. New Englanders knew of the English cases of possession from hearsay and witchcraft pamphlets, the equivalent of today's instant paperbacks on sensational current events, published in England in the reigns of Elizabeth and James.

The Catholic church used rites of exorcism to deal with possession. Leaders of the Church of England, with a pragmatism as characteristic then as now, investigated possible fraud. Puritans, initially advising patience and prayer, later took to searching for witches guilty of sending out demons.

It is surely significant that one of the busiest regions for witchcraft prosecutions in England was Essex and that a disproportionate number of Puritan emigrants came from that county.

All the English Puritans' sixteenth-century witchcraft beliefs, though on the wane in the homeland, were still current in New England in 1692. But all such beliefs were the products of the human imagination with no basis in fact. There is no reason whatsoever to believe Tituba guilty of anything. Apart, that is, from being a Caribbean Indian slave in a New England parsonage at a most unfortunate moment.

CHAPTER FIVE

New England Night-Birds

By the end of February at least two other young girls had joined Betty and Abigail in having fits and seeing visions. It is possible that one or two others had been involved from the beginning, but more likely it was after the baking of the notorious witch cake that Ann Putnam and Elizabeth Hubbard began suffering the symptoms besetting Parris's daughter and niece. Mary Walcott and Mercy Lewis joined in either at the same time or soon afterward.

All these girls would have been constant visitors to the parsonage once the fits started. Ann Putnam was the child of the prosperous farmer Thomas Putnam, the Reverend Parris's most powerful ally. Putnam must have been almost as alarmed as Parris himself by the way things were going. It would badly undermine his position if the daughter and niece of the man he had promoted as minister were possessed by the devil. Ann was, of all the girls living locally, closest in age to Betty and Abigail. She was still only twelve. When Putnam called round to see how things fared he would no doubt bring her along. Perhaps sometimes he also brought Mercy Lewis, the seventeen-year-old orphan who lived in his family. As we know from the Mathers' accounts of the Goodwin children and Elizabeth Knapp, the Puritans did not believe in cases of possession being hidden away. Possessed girls were on show, officially for religious edification, unofficially for diversion. They afforded a wonderful break in the dreary Puritan routine.

Among other visitors was seventeen-year-old Elizabeth Hubbard, niece of the Dr. Griggs who declared the girls "under an Evil Hand." She may have come with her uncle on his calls. Travel in Salem Village was by canoe, horseback, or foot, though mostly foot, since the two rivers ran north–south and most travel was east–west. Horses were expensive. They would have been needed for work on the farms and released most reluctantly for traveling. But Dr. Griggs must have had a horse for visiting patients. The Griggs family had lived close to the parsonage till mid-February but then moved to a larger house three miles away. Very likely Elizabeth begged rides on a pillion, behind the horse's saddle, just as young people in rural areas in the United States today beg rides in relatives' cars. Perhaps she sometimes stayed overnight at the parsonage or with Mary Walcott when her uncle went home. Mary Walcott, also seventeen, lived only a few hundred yards from the Parrises.

At some point Ann and Elizabeth, Mary Walcott and Mercy Lewis, watching Betty and Abigail in their fits, began also to writhe, choke, babble, and suffer deafness and blindness. And they joined in screaming accusations that Tituba tortured them.

No doubt the terrified adults asked the girls if, with their second sight, they saw anyone else besides Tituba. The slave was still denying her guilt; not even by beating her could Parris make her confess. Thomas Putnam, a forceful, aggressive personality, and his wife, a fearful, disturbed woman, would have been desperate. They would have kept trying by all possible means to find the source of their daughter's affliction. Soon the girls began to scream out two other names. Once they did so, Parris tried to make Tituba accuse the named women as "sister-witches," though still unsuccessfully.

The choice of names is no mystery. If there were any witches in Salem, these two were among them. They were middle-aged, assertive, awkward, and so despised as to be virtually outcasts. Sarah Good got her living by begging and borrowing; Sarah Osborne was weak-witted, with a scandalous past.

Good had not always been poor. Her father was a prosperous innkeeper, but he had drowned himself, twenty years earlier, when Sarah was nineteen. She had been cheated of her inheritance by her mother's new husband. Now the wife of a ne'er-do-well and the mother of several young children, Sarah was reduced to begging for food. She did so in an angry, ill-natured spirit. If refused, she would turn away cursing. A kindly neighbor who put her up for a while at last turned her out, defeated by her bad temper and terrified she would set fire to the house with the pipe she smoked.

Sarah Osborne had also once been prosperous, having married Robert Prince, the owner of a hundred-and-fifty-acre farm. But when her husband died, she scandalized Salem Village by buying a young Irish immigrant, Alexander Osborne, for fifteen pounds. That is, she bought his "indenture," the right to own him for a period of time as a servant. Fifteen pounds was a substantial sum in those days but he must have proved worth it because she later married him. The scandal of the transaction lay chiefly in the general belief that the two lived as husband and wife before they actually were so. Such an offense, if proved, could be punished by whipping. The eventual wedding did not lessen its wickedness.

Sarah then made matters worse by contesting her first husband's will to try to keep his lands as her own, though he had left them to her in trust for his sons. This too caused a scandal. In 1692 the dispute, begun fifteen years before, was still unresolved. Sarah and Alexander were no longer as prosperous and Sarah was bedridden. Another factor may have contributed to Sarah Osborne's being viewed as an outcast and named as a witch. She had made an enemy of John Putnam Senior, Thomas Putnam Junior's uncle.

The Putnam family was one of the largest and most powerful in the village. John Putnam Senior had been a neighbor and friend of Sarah Osborne's first husband, Robert Prince; in Prince's will, John and his elder brother Thomas Putnam Senior were appointed executors. An additional, strong reason for the appointment was that John had married Robert Prince's sister Rebecca. In trying to break the will, Sarah Osborne both complicated the executors' task and threatened the welfare of the boys, who were not only her sons but also Putnam nephews. At a stroke, she secured the Putnams' undying hostility.

Osborne was the first of many "witches" who were Putnam family foes. For this reason historian Charles Upham believed that the witch-hunt was engineered by the vengeful Thomas Putnam Junior, and his allies, from the point when the girls accused Tituba. A more recent writer goes further and asserts that the witch-hunt was planned in advance. But Parris's chastisement of poor Mary Sibley has the ring of genuine panic in the face of horrific and unexpected events. And Betty and Abigail's first fits sound, as the Goodwins' do, like hysteria, not fraud.

The belief that Tituba and Sarah Good were chosen by Parris and the Putnams as credible witch suspects, to soften up the populace before they picked off their enemies, does not tally with the evidence as well as does a more complex and subtle pattern of motives and causes.

It seems likely that Ann Putnam, Elizabeth Hubbard, and the rest were as genuinely hysterical as Betty and Abigail. The atmosphere at the parsonage was so charged as easily to spark latent madness. The girls probably all believed that Tituba, Sarah Good, and Sarah Osborne were afflicting them. Or, at the least, they half-believed it. Among the tricks the mind can play on itself in a hysterical state is to believe and not believe simultaneously. But half-belief is quite different from deliberate fraud.

The four girls were emotionally vulnerable, and not just for the many reasons affecting all girls in that time and place. The only one of them who lived with both parents was Ann Putnam. And there is ample evidence that Ann's mother was deeply disturbed. Ann Putnam Senior, like the pipe-smoking Sarah Good, was a disinherited daughter. Her father was rich but when he died she got nothing. His wife and sons kept control of his wealth, depriving his daughters. The fact that Ann and her husband went to court to try to regain her inheritance testifies to her sense of injustice. When the suit failed, her bitterness increased.

Ann had married Thomas Putnam after coming to Salem Village from Salisbury with her sister, who was the wife of Salem Village's first minister, James Bayley. Her sister's three children died in Salem Village, one after another; in 1688, the sister herself died. During the course of coming events Ann Putnam Senior was to reveal the extent to which these events had adversely affected her.

Mary Walcott had lost her mother when she was eight. Elizabeth Hubbard was an orphan, as was Mercy Lewis. We do not know how Elizabeth's parents died. But we do know that Mercy saw her parents slaughtered by Indians. This happened three years before in Maine. (The area then known as Maine was part of the Massachusetts Bay Colony. It covered roughly the same land area as today's state of that name and was remote, dangerous territory, also known as "the East-ward.") Mercy had been lucky to escape with her life. All these girls, from the loss of one or both parents as well as cultural conditioning, were as susceptible to hysteria as are the physically weak to disease.

And the inhabitants of Salem Village, having endured extreme anxiety and hardship over the past several years, were also susceptible: not to hysteria but to extreme irrational fear. The defenses of common sense, skepticism, and a sense of proportion had been lowered, not only by Puritan fanaticism but also by continual stress, virtually out of existence.

Like the rest of the colonists, the villagers had suffered smallpox epidemics, a political upheaval that threw the ownership of their lands into question, and the constant threat of attacks from the Indians.

For everyone at that time, death was always nearby. The assumption that death comes at the end of a long life except in rare instances belongs to the twentieth century. But epidemics that strike down huge numbers, especially of babies and children, are hard to bear even for those all too accustomed to the notion that life is precarious.

The colonial charter, revoked in 1684, had not yet been restored. Without it the colonists had no legal right to the lands that, for most of them, constituted the bulk of their wealth. The rumors reaching the colony from London about Increase Mather's negotiations were far from encouraging. But the greatest fear was not epidemics or loss of wealth but the Indians.

It would be hard to exaggerate the terror inspired in the settlers by the native Americans. Unsurprisingly, they had responded to the white people's cruelty, treachery, and injustice with merciless fury. When the

English first arrived, the Indians had welcomed and aided them. But the English took their lands, broke treaties, and killed and enslaved them. They also, less culpably, infected them with smallpox and other diseases to which the native people had no immunity, cutting their numbers by three-quarters in less than fifty years.

In 1675 the Indians' gathering rage and desperation broke forth in a countrywide attack. King Philip's War—so named because the Indian leader, Metacomet, was dubbed Philip by the English—lasted only two years but was the bloodiest in American history. One in ten settlers was killed. That figure represents more people dead, per capita, than in any other conflict in which Americans have taken part. Seventy soldiers from Salem Village and adjacent towns died in one battle. Young women such as Mary Walcott and Mercy Lewis grew from infancy to childhood in that war's aftermath and were exposed daily to the grief of its widows and orphans and the innumerable tales of its horrors.

Of the 1676 massacre at Lancaster, only forty miles from Salem Village, Mary Rowlandson wrote, shortly afterward: "It is a solemn sight to see so many Christians lying in their blood, some here and some there, like a company of sheep torn by wolves, all of them stripped naked by a company of hell-hounds, roaring, singing, ranting and insulting as if they would have tore our very hearts out."

The reciprocal hatred of the Puritans for the Indians is dramatically illustrated by an episode in 1677, in which "a group of women emerging from church set upon two Indian prisoners from Maine and with their bare hands literally tore them apart. An eyewitness reported that 'we found the Indians with their heads off and gone, and their flesh in a manner pulled from their bones.' "

In 1692 there were signs that the Indians might be about to launch another full-scale offensive. King William's War, fought between the French and the English but with Indian support for the French, had started three and a half years before. The Indians had already perpetrated those devastating raids in Maine to which Mercy Lewis's parents had fallen victim. The most recent had happened that winter, on January 25, in York. The homes of three or four hundred people were burned, eighty people were captured, and fifty were killed. Inhabitants of Salem Village, living scattered as they did over a largely undefendable area, felt exceedingly vulnerable to an attack that might come at any time.

The Salem villagers had written in 1667, in a petition to Salem Town asking to be allowed not to send men to join the watch there, "The distance of our houses, one from another—some a mile, some further —[is such] that it is difficult sending one neighbor to another in dark nights in a wilderness that is so little cleared and [by] ways unpassable." They showed the degree of their fear of the Indians when they added, " 'Tis probable, if the French or Dutch should come, they will have a convoy of Indians from east or west, and come first upon remote dwellers. The consideration whereof is liable to strike terror into the hearts of women and weak ones, especially considering what dreadful examples former times hath afforded in that respect, in this country, from Indians (and from others also), in the night season, when their husbands have been absent."

Cotton Mather believed that the Indians were the "wretched remnant of a race seduced to the Western hemisphere by the Devil" so that he might rule undisturbed by Christians teaching the gospel. This view of course made them all the more terrifying. The fact that whole tribes had been converted to Christianity by the French made them seem not less sinister but, if anything, more so. Catholicism was to the Puritans as abhorrent as devil worship. The Indians' menace was deepened still further by the fact that they appeared to exert a terrifying attraction over those in their power. Of all the New Englanders taken captive and offered the chance to go home again, between twenty-five and seventy-one percent elected to stay. That at least a quarter of captives should have preferred life with the Indians to their Puritan existence must have seemed threatening indeed.

To read Thomas Hutchinson's mid-eighteenth-century description of Indian life is to glean some idea why so many captives felt loath to relinquish it. The Indians spent their time not in labor and prayer but in leisurely pursuits such as football matches, which could go on for two days before either side scored a goal, and games of chance ending without any clear winner. Their hunting and fishing provided useful food but "served also as diversions." As for religion, "they had as little as can well be imagined. Some notions they had of a future state. A Mahometan paradise, where they were to solace themselves in fruitful cornfields and fine flowery means, with pleasant rivers to bathe in; curious wigwams, provided for them without any labour of their own; hunting, fowling, and fishing without any weariness or pains to molest them." How different from Puritan existence and the Puritan hell.

The New Englanders' fear of the devil was in turn rendered more concrete and powerful by their terror of the flesh-and-blood enemies with whom he was linked. It is hard today to grasp the nature of the Puritans' belief in supernatural beings. Devils and spirits were not abstract ideas but creatures dwelling all around them. It was for this reason that Satan was sometimes referred to as the "Prince of the air." For New Englanders, living as they did on the edge of the wilderness, the sense of such beings, always just out of sight, was even stronger than for their forebears in England. Cotton Mather wrote, "These evil spirits are all around. There is confined unto the atmosphere of our air a vast power or army of evil spirits under the government of a Prince (Satan) who employs them in a continual opposition to the designs of God.''

And here was yet another threat to the colonists, greater than earthly ones. Cotton Mather had for some time been preaching that Satan regarded New England as rightfully his and was determined to conquer it back. Indeed, he was the true source of all the Puritans' troubles. Even Indian attacks were his doing. They were one of his methods of weakening his enemy. Another was witchcraft.

''Go tell mankind, that there are devils and witches,'' Cotton wrote, ''and that tho those night-birds least appear whether the day-light of the Gospel comes, yet New-England has had examples of their existence and operation; and that not only the wigwams of Indians, where the pagan powaws [witch doctors] often raise their masters, in the shapes of bears and snakes and fires, but the houses of Christians, where our God has had His constant worship, have undergone the annoyance of evil spirits.''

By the end of February the devil's threat to the colony, as well as to Salem Village and individuals, must indeed have seemed pressing. In this atmosphere of panic, in a desperate attempt to gain control of a worsening situation, four village leaders—the domineering Thomas Putnam; his brother Edward Putnam; independent-minded Joseph Hutchinson; and another farmer, Thomas Preston, a son-in-law of Rebecca Nurse, who was soon to figure prominently in events—filed a complaint with the Salem magistrates accusing Tituba, Sarah Good, and Sarah Osborne of hurting Betty Parris, Abigail Williams, Ann Putnam Junior, and Elizabeth Hubbard by witchcraft. On February 29 the Salem magistrates issued warrants for the arrest of the three women. On March 1, the constables apprehended them. That morning at ten o'clock they were brought to be examined at the Salem Village meetinghouse.

CHAPTER SIX

A Thing like a Man

THE original plan was for the examinations to decide if there was enough evidence against the accused to bring them to trial, which was to be held at Ingersoll's tavern. The constables arrived with their prisoners at the inn, which was set back from the crossroads at the highest point in the village with a vista of farmlands, scattered buildings, and forest beyond. But the crowd already assembled was too large for the room meant to hold them.

Salem Village had never known such excitement. No one wanted to miss it. Everyone knew of the fits; many had witnessed them. Few doubted that the devil was here, in the village, and that he had enslaved three old women and through them inflicted terrible pain on four girls, three still only children. That the villagers and everyone else referred to the accusers as "the afflicted children" throughout the proceedings, even after many older girls and even grown women joined their ranks, shows the hold on the local imagination of the notion of tortured unsullied innocence.

As the girls arrived, the crowd was agog. Most likely the girls were subdued, full of tension yet overawed at their power. They would soon be chief players in a drama in which lives were at stake. But also at stake were all the sympathy and status they had recently won. Whether they held on to them depended on how they performed. If they lost them, they might also lose all credibility and find themselves outcasts.

People would have been equally keen to see Tituba, Sarah Good, and Sarah Osborne as they were led up, in manacles, by the constables. Tituba would have been docile, perhaps weeping; Sarah Good may have shouted and struggled; Sarah Osborne, in such poor health that she was normally bedridden, had to be supported, even dragged. To the people observing them, they had been transformed from unfortunate old women into evil incarnate. Everything they said or did was transmuted from the merely self-pitying, bad-tempered, or half-crazed to the devilish.

At the sight of that crowd, Samuel Parris, Thomas Putnam, and the two magistrates who had traveled on horseback from Salem engaged in self-important consultations. They decided to transfer the multitude down the road to the meetinghouse, a mere two minutes' walk. No doubt the magistrates, with their accompanying marshals, led the way, followed by the constables and their prisoners, then the men who had lodged the complaints against the accused, the afflicted girls themselves, and the rest of the village population.

The meetinghouse was soon crammed. People squeezed into the tall-sided pews and onto the benches in the galleries or stood, pressed together, at the back and in the aisles. The men wore the Puritans' high-crowned black hats, cloaks, and breeches, the women layers of shifts, skirts, and bodices and hooded cloaks and muffs. A table was brought in and placed at the front for the magistrates to sit at. Only the prisoners stayed outside, with their attendants, awaiting the call.

Parris ascended his pulpit and, in the sudden, deep hush, said a prayer. The words have not come down to us, though we may suppose that he asked for God's help in finding out witches.

The first prisoner was brought in. It was the beggar Sarah Good, who was placed facing the magistrates, flanked by constables. The four girls who claimed she afflicted them were led to the front and told to stand near but looking away from her, also facing the magistrates.

These were John Hathorne and Jonathan Corwin, both members of leading Salem families, successful merchants, and important local officials. Hathorne was to do most of the questioning. Though without legal training, he was one of Salem's most experienced law officials.

The silence in the packed meetinghouse was full of fearful expectation. What the crowd was to witness might prove to be nothing less than a talk with the devil. Hathorne certainly thought so. With his very first query he revealed his assumption of Sarah Good's guilt.

"Sarah Good, what evil spirit have you familiarity with?"

"None," Sarah answered defiantly.

"Have you made no contract with the devil?"

"No."

"Why do you hurt these children?"

"I do not hurt them. I scorn it."

"Who do you employ then to do it?"

"I employ nobody."

"What creature do you employ then?"

"No creature, but I am falsely accused."

"Why did you go away muttering from Mr. Parris his house?"

"I did not mutter but I thanked him for what he gave my child."

"Have you made no contract with the devil?"

"No."

By his repetition of the question "Have you made no contract with the devil?" Hathorne implied not only disbelief in Good's answer but exasperation that she did not confess. At a loss, in the face of her stubbornness, to know what to ask next to break down her defenses and elicit what he assumed was the truth, he turned to the four afflicted girls and asked them to look at Good to see if this was the person who had been hurting them.

The record says, "So they all did look upon her and said this was one of the persons that did torment them" and "presently they were all tormented."

Such dryness of tone belies what occurred. The girls screamed, writhed, twisted their limbs beyond what seemed possible, collapsed, choked, and fainted. Sarah Good, standing before them with an air of defiance and assumed by all present to be the cause of the girls' behavior, must have seemed Satan himself. People rushed to the girls, supported them, soothed them, tried to revive them. Anyone still with doubts about the presence of witchcraft must surely have had them dispelled.

It was only years later that writers speculated that this apparent suffering might have been fraudulent. At the time no one doubted its genuineness. Of course, people were predisposed to believe in what they saw. Yet it does appear that there was something truly awesome about the girls' fits. Thomas Hutchinson, governor of Massachusetts, wrote in the mid-eighteenth century that the opinion "prevailed in New England for many years after the tragedy that there was something preternatural in it and that it was not all the effect of fraud and imposture." Even at the time of his writing, he said, many were still not fully convinced that the accusers were fraudulent but were willing to suppose them "under bodily disorders which affected their imaginations."

The minister Deodat Lawson, an eyewitness at later examinations, directly addressed the issue of whether the fits could have been in any sense voluntary. He writes, "Sometimes, in their fits, they have had their tongues drawn out of their mouths to a fearful length, their heads turned very much over their shoulders; and while they have been so strained in their fits, and had their arms and legs, etc, wrested as if they were quite dislocated, the blood hath gushed plentifully out of their mouths for a considerable time together, which some, that they might be satisfied that it was real blood, took upon their finger, and rubbed on their other hand. I saw several together thus violently strained and bleeding in their fits, to my very great astonishment that my fellow-mortals should be so grievously distressed by the invisible powers of darkness. For certainly all considerate persons who beheld these things must needs be convinced, that their motions in their fits were preternatural and involuntary, both as to the manner, which was so strange as a well person could not (at least without great pain) screw their bodies into, and as to the violence also, they were preternatural motions, being much beyond the ordinary force of the same persons when they were in their right minds."

In other words, there seem to have been forces at work inspiring behavior beyond the girls' normal mental and physical capacities. The Salem villagers thought the forces were those of witches given power by the devil. Today we are more likely to believe they were those of furies in the human unconscious.

However, it must be asked why the girls should conveniently go into fits when confronted by Good. The explanation that they believed her a witch, at that moment bewitching them, could be sufficient. But it seems more likely that the girls had by now learned how to switch on the hysterical state whenever they wanted to. It could be that by experiencing hysteria they had discovered its secrets. They may well have been switching it on, over the past two or three weeks, for neighbors and visiting ministers. "Performing" hysterics are a recognized phenomenon in psychiatric history. J. M. Charcot, who studied hysteria in Paris in the late nineteenth century, had a few patients who displayed a wide repertoire of hysterical symptoms for visiting doctors and students. The most famous, Augustine, was repeatedly photographed in bizarre, theatrical poses. She too was a young girl: thirteen when she came to him, fifteen when she left.

Anyone who has had to "psych themselves up" to perform as actor, teacher, or public speaker understands to some degree the phenomenon of finding something inside oneself "taking over." Sometimes that "something" seems astonishingly at odds with the normal personality. It appears that a more extreme version of this everyday phenomenon may be at work when a hysteric "performs." And under the influence of a powerful emotion a person may feel unable to control herself and, at the same time, as though she is being self-indulgent. This feeling seems similar to the dual consciousness experienced by hysterics, described by Freud and Breuer in *Studies on Hysteria*. There seems to be a fine line between extreme histrionic behavior and full-blown mental illness. Or it may be that there is no line at all but rather a spectrum of behavior, from willful self-display to uncontrollable bodily contortions, along which a sufferer moves in response to inner, involuntary promptings.

Arthur Miller effectively dramatized this aspect of what happened at Salem in *The Crucible*. He portrays the girls turning on fits, the slyest deliberately, the more suggestible without conscious awareness of doing so. He shows the power that a closely knit peer group has over its orphaned or semi-orphaned members. He also shows the power of the ringleader over that group. In the play Abigail, whose age he raises by six years to seventeen, takes the role of leader. In reality it probably belonged at least equally to Ann Putnam. But whichever girl it was, at the examination of Good, the fits were extraordinary.

Hathorne would have had to shout to be heard, when he asked, "Sarah Good, do you not see now what you have done? Why do you not tell us the truth? Why do you thus torment these poor children?"

"I do not torment them."

"Who do you employ then?"

"I employ nobody. I scorn it."

"How came they thus tormented?"

And then Sarah Good, no doubt as frightened by the girls' fits as everyone else, despite her initial defiance, said, "What do I know?" and went on, "You bring others here and now you charge me with it."

Hathorne seized on this.

"Why, who was it?"

"I do not know but it was some you brought into the meeting house with you."

"We brought you into the meeting house."

"But you brought in two more."

"Who was it then, that tormented the children?"

"It was Osborne."

Like any prosecuting lawyer who has tricked the defendant into making the statement he wanted, Hathorne at once changed his questioning. He returned to the subject of Good's muttering when she went "away from persons houses," asking her what she said. He was after an admission that she was uttering curses.

She said, playing for time, "If I must tell, I will tell."

"Do tell us then."

"If I must tell, I will tell. It is the commandments. I may say my commandments, I hope."

"What commandment is it?"

"If I must tell you, I will tell, it is a psalm."

"What psalm?"

The reporter writes, "After a long time she muttered over some part of a psalm."

Having now established that she was not strong in religion, even at the simplest level of knowing the commandments and psalms, Hathorne hoped to trick her again into self-contradiction, if not confession, when he asked, "Who do you serve?"

"I serve God."

"What god do you serve?"

The reporter then writes that Good said, "The God that made heaven and earth" and goes on without break or punctuation, not distinguishing between Good's words and his own, "though she was not willing [to] mention the word God her answers were in a very wicked, spiteful manner reflecting and retorting against the authority with base and abusive words and many lies she was taken in."

The reporter who penned these lines was Ezekiel Cheever, a tailor by profession and a church member. Neither impartiality nor punctuation was his strong point. But his is the only one of the three reports of the examination to give dialogue; the others, by the magistrates and Joseph Putnam respectively, are summaries. Cheever may have been chosen for the role of reporter because, as a tailor, he had nimble fingers and could write quickly, though it says little for the educational level in Salem Village that there was no rapid writer who was also fully literate and capable of apparent neutrality. Admittedly Cheever was scribbling down in a rush what was said; yet he found time to make editorial comments.

What happened next in the meetinghouse was that Sarah Good's husband was questioned about her and said "that he was afraid that she either was a witch or would be one very quickly." But under further questioning he would not concede he had ever seen her perform any witchcraft. What he complained of was "her bad carriage to him." Presumably without intending a pun, he said, "She is an enemy to all good." This must have seemed evidence enough. Still protesting her innocence, Sarah Good was led away.

Next, Sarah Osborne was brought into the meetinghouse and placed before the magistrates. The girls were kept at a greater distance from her than they had been from Good, ostensibly to avoid being afflicted but perhaps in reality to make their affliction, when it came, seem all the more devilish. As before, they did not look at the defendant.

Hathorne followed the same line of questioning as he had with Good, asking what evil spirit Osborne had familiarity with, whether she had made a contract with the devil, and so on. Osborne, like Good, denied everything. But next Hathorne asked Osborne what familiarity she had with Good. Osborne said at first that she had not seen her for two years and had not then known her by name. But when pressed, she admitted that she had addressed her as Sarah. Osborne was clearly trying to distance herself from someone also suspected of witchcraft. The motive for Hathorne's questions about Good remain vague till he states, "Sarah Good saith it was you that hurt the children," shamelessly using the accusation he had tricked out of Good to try to trap

Osborne. Osborne's reply was, "I do not know that the devil goes about in my likeness to do any hurt." She meant that if the devil was putting on her appearance while injuring anyone she did not know of it.

At this, "Mr. Hathorne desired all the children to stand up and look upon her and see if they did know her which they all did and every one of them said that this was one of the women that did afflict them and that they had constantly seen her in the very habit that she was now in." And they duly went into fits.

Sarah, as disturbed by the screaming and choking as Good had been and impelled to try to defend herself by other means than mere denials of Hathorne's accusations, a tactic that seemed useless, said she was more likely to be bewitched than to be a witch. Hathorne asked her why she said this. No doubt still misguidedly attempting to defend herself by allying herself with the accusers, though very likely also saying what was true, she said "she was frighted one time in her sleep and either saw or dreamed that she saw a thing like an Indian, all black, which did pinch her in her neck and pulled her by the back part of her head to the door of the house."

Hathorne asked her if she ever saw anything else and she said no. But then various people in the meetinghouse called out that she had said "she would never be tied to that lying spirit any more." Hathorne pounced on this.

"What lying spirit is this? Hath the devil ever deceived you and been false to you?" he asked.

Osborne said she had never seen the devil and when Hathorne inquired, "What lying spirit was it then?" she replied that it was a voice she thought she had heard. Very likely Osborne, like Mary Glover, was slightly "crazed in her intellectuals," which may have been another reason, besides the scandals in her past and the Putnam family's enmity, that the girls had accused her. Hathorne asked what the voice said and Osborne answered, "That I should go no more to meeting but I said I would and did go the next Sabbath day."

Hathorne then asked if she was ever tempted further and she said "no." Hathorne revealed that he had received prior information about Osborne, no doubt from Parris, by asking, "Why did you yield thus far to the devil as never to go to meeting since?"

Osborne said she had been sick and not able to go. Hathorne must have asked the assembly how long it had been since she went "to meeting," that is, to a religious service, because Cheever reports that her husband and others said she had not been for a year and two months. That information, coming after the vision of the "Indian all black" and the "lying spirit" must have seemed sufficiently damning. Osborne was removed.

Next to be led in was Tituba. Her appearance created even more of a stir than had the appearances of Osborne and Good. Everyone knew it was she the girls had first called a witch. Besides, as an Indian, she was to that roomful of Puritans linked with the devil. It is notable that Osborne had described the apparition that dragged her across the room by the scruff of her neck as "a thing like an Indian all black," merging the notions of demons and Indians.

The girls started to have fits the moment Tituba entered. In their later depositions to the court, they accused her of pinching and pricking them from the beginning of her examination. There is no mention in the record of Hathorne later asking them to look at her, as happened during the interrogations of Osborne and Good. The overwhelming feeling in the place must have been that if anyone was a witch—and somebody undoubtedly was—it was Tituba. The slave, for her part, must have been in a state of stupefied terror.

Our knowledge of her examination is unusually full since as well as the three testimonies by Ezekiel Cheever, Joseph Putnam, and the magistrates, there is a fourth by Jonathan Corwin. This last is more detailed than Cheever's, as well as better punctuated, and conveys particularly strongly the sense of extreme pressure put on Tituba by Hathorne's relentless, emotional questioning. This must have seemed all the more bullying for being shouted over the din made by the girls in their fits. By virtue of being more detailed, Corwin's record brings into focus Hathorne's constant trick of reading self-incriminating meanings into innocent answers.

The interrogation began in the usual way with the query about what evil spirit the accused had familiarity with. Tituba said "none" and Hathorne immediately asked, "Why do you hurt these poor children? What harm have they done unto you?" When Tituba answered, "They do no harm to me, I not hurt them at all," Hathorne shamelessly ignored the denial and asked, "Why have you done it?"

Tituba said, "I have done nothing: I can't tell when the devil works," and Hathorne cried, triumphantly, "What, doth the devil tell you that he hurts them?" Tituba kept her head, saying, "No he tells me nothing," but Hathorne pressed harder, asking, "Do you never see something appear in some shape?"

She said, "No, never see anything."

He kept pressing.

"What familiarity have you with the devil, or what is it that you converse with all? Tell the truth, who it is that hurts them?"

Tituba answered only the last of these questions, saying, "The devil

for ought I know." Hathorne disingenuously took this as meaning she
knew it was the devil. He asked, "What appearance or how doth he
appear when he hurts them, with what shape or what is he like that
hurts them?"

At this Tituba cracked. She could stand the pressure no more. And
she thought she saw a way out. She would tell Hathorne what he
wanted to hear while protesting her innocence. With the words "Like
a man, I think yesterday, I being in the lean-to chamber, I saw a thing
like a man," she began one of the most extraordinary statements ever
heard in a court.

The crowd went very still. They were listening to a firsthand description of the devil himself. Even the afflicted children went quiet. They
too wanted to hear. Hathorne's demeanor utterly changed. The bullying air was replaced by avid interest. Tituba must have felt a relief that
was almost euphoric. Buoyed by that relief, her imagination floated
free, into realms far from kitchen and dairy. Despite her Barbadian
origins, that imagination had been fed for a great many years on Puritan superstitions and folklore.

The man had told her to serve him, she said, but she told him no,
she would not do such a thing. Sarah Osborne and Sarah Good had
hurt the children and would have had her do so too. She had seen four
people, two of whom she did not know. She saw them last night as she
was washing the room; they told her to hurt the children and wanted
her to go to Boston. There were five of them with the man. They told
her if she would not hurt the children they would hurt her. At first she
agreed, but afterward she told them she would not do so anymore.

It is not clear why Tituba confessed to having once hurt the children. Perhaps she felt she had to do so to give the rest of her statement
credibility.

Hathorne began to question her again. He asked whether the people would have had her hurt the children last night. She said yes, but
she said she would do so no more, but would fear God. Hathorne
asked her what first appeared to her to ask her to hurt the children.
She said, "One like a man," just as she was going to sleep. This was
when the children were first hurt. The man threatened to kill the
children and her too if she would not serve him. Hathorne asked if
this was the same man as had appeared last night and she said yes. He
asked if anything else had appeared to her and she said a hog and a
great black dog, who had both told her to serve them. (The implica-
tion was that all these creatures were the devil.)

As Hathorne asks, "What other creatures have you seen?" and
Tituba answers, "A bird," and he asks, "What bird?" and she answers,
"A little yellow bird," the reader gets the impression not only of

Tituba thinking fast on her feet, but of the two of them, the magistrate and the slave, putting on a macabre, thrilling show, feeding a hunger for drama, in themselves and their audience.

Hathorne asked where the bird lived.

"With the man who hath pretty things there besides."

"What other pretty things?"

"He hath not showed them unto me, but said he would show them me tomorrow, and told me if I would serve him, I should have the bird."

"What other creatures did you see?"

"I saw two cats, one red, another black, as big as a little dog."

"What did these cats do?"

"I don't know, I have seen them two times."

"What did they say?"

"They say, 'Serve them.' "

"When did you see them?"

"I saw them last night."

"Did they do any hurt to you or threaten you?"

"They did scratch me."

"When?"

"After prayer . . ."

"What service do they expect from you?"

"They say more hurt to the children."

"How did you pinch them when you hurt them?"

"The others pull me and haul me to pinch the children, and I am very sorry for it."

And so it went on.

Never was the principle of the leading question eliciting the expected information more graphically illustrated. But even as she supplied all the detail Hathorne required and was led by his queries to tell of going to the Griggs's house to pinch Elizabeth Hubbard and to the Putnams' to pinch Ann, Tituba kept remembering to say she was sorry. She never lost sight of her aim to establish her present innocence and negate her previous guilt.

Of all Hathorne's leading questions, one of the most shameless was "How did you go? What did you ride upon?" when Tituba had said nothing yet about riding. Tituba must have thrilled the whole meetinghouse when she answered, "I rid upon a stick or pole and Good and Osborne behind me. We ride taking hold of one another."

Soon afterward she said that the night before Sarah Good and Sarah Osborne told her to cut off Ann Putnam's head with a knife. At hearing her say this in the meetinghouse, Ann Putnam called out that at that time Good and Osborne had urged her to cut off her own head and had said if she would not, then Tituba would do it. She had had the sensation of her throat being cut. This exchange suggests that Tituba knew of Ann Putnam's self-destructive fantasy and was making use of it to give her confession greater credibility.

Hathorne asked Tituba why she had not told her master these things; Tituba said that Good and Osborne had threatened to cut off *her* head if she did so. The magistrate then sought information about Good's and Osborne's familiars; the slave supplied a yellow bird, which she said sucked Good between the fingers, a cat, and two nameless creatures, one with wings and two legs and a head like a woman's, the other "all over hairy, all the face hairy and a long nose and I don't know how to tell how the face looks, with two legs, it goeth upright and is about two or three foot high and goeth upright like man and last night it stood before the fire in Mr. Parris' hall."

This man wore black clothes, Tituba said, though on another occasion he wore a serge coat of a different color. The woman with wings wore a black silk hood with a white silk hood under it, with topknots. Bafflingly, Tituba described the man when he wore his serge coat as tall with white hair. Perhaps she meant that he sometimes changed his height as well as his appearance. There would, after all, be no reason to suppose the devil capable of anything less.

At this point the children had fits again, perhaps as a result of Tituba's testimony dwindling to merely sartorial matters. Hathorne asked her who was afflicting them and she said Goody Good. ("Goody" was the short form of "Goodwife," used of a woman below the status of "Mrs.") The children agreed. But then Elizabeth Hubbard had a worse fit than usual. When Hathorne asked who was causing it, Tituba said she did not know, she was blinded. She then had a fit herself, twice being struck dumb. No doubt she hoped, by joining the girls in their afflictions, to avoid being jailed as a possible afflictor. But her hope was in vain. Hathorne decreed that Good, Osborne, and Tituba must all be examined further and sent them to jail.

CHAPTER SEVEN

Brother against Brother

CHARLES Upham, writing in the mid-nineteenth century, believed that Parris and Thomas Putnam had told Tituba in advance what to say when she confessed. He thought it suspicious that Tituba knew of Ann Putnam's claim that Tituba had tried to cut off Ann's head. He found it equally suspicious that Tituba knew that Elizabeth Hubbard had that morning said she was pinched and that Abigail Williams had claimed she saw a woman with two legs and wings. Tituba "had been fully admitted to their councils," Upham says, suggesting that the girls' claims and Tituba's confession were carefully coordinated. He implies that this was the doing of the parents and guardians.

In Upham's view, Putnam and Parris told Tituba to say she had seen four people with the devil, two of whom were Sarah Good and Sarah Osborne and two of whom were unknown. The men's ruse was to prepare the village population for the next accusations of witchcraft they intended to make.

But there is no reason to suppose that Tituba could not have heard of the girls' hysterical claims by innocent means. She lived in the same house as one of them. Anyone might have told her that morning of the other afflicted girls' fantasies. The stories would have spread like forest fire through the crowd outside Ingersoll's inn. Her giving *four* as the number seen with the devil could well have been arbitrary.

Upham's suspicions are understandable. The amount and intensity of enmity in Salem Village, and particularly the beleaguered position of Parris and the Putnams, make plotting seem very possible. Writing before Freud, Upham had little knowledge of the mind's tricks and fancies, as opposed to deliberate scheming and fraud, by which a widespread delusion may start. But the evidence points to a far less contrived train of events than he thought had occurred. Political and economic conflict played a crucial part in the escalation of the witchcraft hysteria, but more subtly than Upham, writing without the benefit of important twentieth-century psychological and historical findings, could possibly know.

Among such findings are those of two modern historians, Paul Boyer and Stephen Nissenbaum. By carefully studying the Salem church and village records, they have traced the complex issues at the root of the escalation of the witchcraft hysteria to the extraordinary proportions it eventually reached. All previous communal panics about witchcraft had died away after one or two accusations.

The conflict went back a long way. The writers argue in their fascinating and persuasive *Salem Possessed* that its intensity was due to the village's anomalous position as a distinct community from the town yet a unified legal and political entity with it. The village's lack of any legal or religious authority to settle internal disputes meant that all conflicts remained unresolved and became increasingly vicious.

Salem Village had grown up, bit by bit, as a result of Salem Town's need for food. The town was settled in 1626, the Massachusetts Bay Colony's first habitation. It was a superb port but almost cut off from the mainland by rivers and inlets. As the need for farm produce grew greater, grants of land were made north and west of those waterways; trees were felled; dwellings were built; crops were planted. For a time the newly cleared area was called Salem Farms and did not even have its own meetinghouse, though the one in Salem Town was two or three hours' walk away. It was only after much pleading, in 1672, that the town allowed the hinterland's inhabitants to build their own place of worship. Once this was erected, the area became known as Salem Village; but it still had no church in the Puritan sense—a gathering of people judged by a minister likely to be destined for heaven. Anyone who wished to take communion had to join the church either in Salem or in one of the other towns that had grown up nearby. A Salem Village church came into being only in 1689, with the ordination of Reverend Parris.

Back in 1672, the newly formed Village Committee, elected by the whole male village population, appointed a recent Harvard graduate named James Bayley to be the first minister to preach in the newly built meetinghouse. The appointment soon caused dissension. There was nothing wrong with Bayley himself; complaints about his lack of devoutness are less than convincing. The trouble arose, or at least quickly focused on, the matter of how and by whom his appointment had been made.

In the usual way, in New England, a minister was chosen by the members of a church in the Puritan sense. But since Salem Village had no church, the Village Committee, representing all the householders, both church members and nonmembers, made the appointment. Many inhabitants objected, feeling that only villagers belonging to *some* church—in Salem Town or elsewhere—should have a voice in selecting a minister.

What made this quarrel increasingly bitter was that for a very long time no power or authority would settle it. Petitions to the Massachusetts General Court met with evasions. When finally the General Court did pronounce on the issue, in 1679, it came down in favor of the whole body of inhabitants choosing a minister. But by that time great damage was done, and attitudes were hardening. Deep differences of interest underlay the surface dissension over voting. Two powerful factions were drawing up battle lines.

The quarrels continued. For James Bayley the game must have finally seemed not worth the candle. His opponents were still in control of the Village Committee, and the whole village was at odds as a result of his presence. In 1680 he left Salem Village to take a post in Killingworth, Connecticut, though later, perhaps unsurprisingly, he gave up the ministry altogether and set up as a doctor.

The choosing of the next pastor was as contentious as might be expected, and the man chosen was not someone likely by nature to tread carefully around mine fields. George Burroughs was confident, strong-willed, and decisive, a man of action as well as a preacher, unusually athletic and clever enough to do well at Harvard. Short of stature, muscular, dark-complexioned, he was highly attractive to women, as is shown by his winning the hand of a rich widow as his second wife when he was a mere village minister. He had been born in England, brought early to America, and raised by his mother in Roxbury, Massachusetts. After graduating in 1670, he took a post as minister in distant, dangerous Casco, in Maine; he was there when the Indians attacked in 1676, in King Philip's War, killing large numbers. Having escaped with his first wife and their children, he settled in Salisbury, Massachusetts, until taking the step which, unknown to him, was even more risky than going to Casco. Salem Village might be safer from Indians, but its own dangers were to prove, for George Burroughs, deadlier.

When he arrived in 1671, village conflicts had not eased. The deep differences of interest beneath the quarrels of the surface were becoming ever more evident. A faction of which the Putnams were leaders wished to establish a Salem Village church and gain full independence from Salem Town. A second group, in which the Porter family was a less visible but equally powerful force, was indifferent about the founding of a church and wished to retain close ties with the town.

The Putnams and their allies were farmers who had little materially to gain from the connection with Salem and who resented the town's mercantile prosperity and cosmopolitan outlook and values. They formed an old, established elite who for years had dominated village affairs, including the militia that trained in a field near the village center in readiness for Indian attacks. Their most prominent members were men whose names were to appear again and again on the complaints to the magistrates that led to witchcraft arrests: Thomas Putnam, John Putnam Junior, Thomas's brother-in-law Jonathan Walcott, and Walcott's uncle, the innkeeper Nathaniel Ingersoll. They all lived relatively close together, near the village center. Literally losing ground as their farmland was subdivided among the next generation, they clung tenaciously to the old-fashioned Puritan values of community, simplicity, and piety. They were straitlaced, backward-looking, self-righteous, and punitive, even by Puritan standards. It is indicative of their social standing that they were all termed "Mr." or given their military titles, as in the cases of Captain Jonathan Walcott and Lieutenant Nathaniel Ingersoll.

The second group, most of whose members lived east of and closer to the town than the first, was made up largely of farmers with Salem Town links or tradesmen who benefited commercially from intercourse with the town. Less socially secure but rapidly gaining in prestige and prosperity, they espoused the more up-to-date—though still Puritan—viewpoint and attitudes of the well-to-do merchants, promoting self-help and commerce and urbanity.

The hostility between the two groups was fueled by moral disapproval as well as differing needs. It was deepened, on the Putnams' side, by the envious contempt of an old elite for prosperous newcomers. Though the first Porters had arrived in Salem Village, like the first Putnams, in the 1640s, most of their allies were recent arrivals.

We do not know what precise points were at issue between Burroughs and those villagers who opposed him. Indeed, there may not have been any points at issue at all, beyond resentment at the method by which he was chosen, stemming in turn from the deeper village divisions. But there may have been ego clashes. Before the building of the parsonage, in 1680, Burroughs and his wife lived with John Putnam Senior and his wife, Rebecca, for nine months. Such a period of house sharing gives ample time and opportunity, among any two couples, for conflicts to develop and fester. There is evidence that the Putnams and Burroughses lived all too closely. According to John Putnam, Burroughs once asked him and Rebecca to arbitrate between Burroughs and *his* wife. Burroughs wished his wife to sign a covenant promising that she would not reveal any of his secrets, a request she did not appreciate. Putnam's sanctimonious answer was that Burroughs and his wife had once made a covenant before God and men that bound them to keep each other's lawful secrets.

It is hard to know what to make of it all. Perhaps Burroughs's wife was wildly indiscreet; or perhaps Burroughs was paranoid. Or, as Charles Upham suggests, perhaps the Putnams kept pumping Mrs. Burroughs for information about her husband's affairs and this was a method of trying to stop them. Or perhaps Putnam had rewritten history. He can hardly be regarded as a reliable witness to Burroughs's matrimonial affairs. By the time he came to write his account of the strange proposed covenant, his motives were scarcely disinterested, to put it mildly.

Putnam also claimed that all the time Burroughs lived at his house he was "a very sharp man to his wife" though she was "a very good and dutiful wife to him." Perhaps Burroughs's wife put on a good show before others and was nasty in private; or perhaps she was indeed "very good" and Burroughs "very sharp." All that can be said for certain is that the Putnams' reply to the Burroughses about the proposed covenant, if indeed they made it, cannot have endeared them to Burroughs.

By April 1682, a certain Jeremiah Watts was writing to Burroughs complaining that it was impossible that the village should be upgraded in status to a town or a church should be gathered, "when brother is against brother and neighbours against neighbours, all quarrelling and smiting one another." In 1681 the parsonage was built for Burroughs to move into. But by early 1683, Burroughs's salary payments had stopped.

With characteristic firmness of purpose, George Burroughs, when he ceased being paid, ceased holding services. He accepted an offer to go back as minister to Casco, which was in the process of being resettled.

The Salem Village Committee complained to the county court of his sudden departure and threatened to sue him. A man of honor, he came back to settle accounts.

What happened when he attended the May 2 meeting set up for this purpose tells us a great deal not only about Burroughs himself but also about the men of the Putnam family and their modus operandi. It also is an eerie preview of the events to take place nine years later.

Burroughs was on the point of presenting his accounts to the inhabitants of the village in the meetinghouse, when Henry Skerry, the marshal, walked in. He hesitated; then he went up to John Putnam Senior and whispered. Putnam said, loudly, "You know what you have to do: do your office." At that the marshal went to George Burroughs and announced, "Sir, I have a writing to read to you." He proceeded to read out a warrant for Burroughs's arrest. Its first words, addressed to himself, as the marshal, were "You are required in his majesty's name to attach the goods and, for want thereof, the body, of Mr. George Burroughs of Salem Farms in the County of Essex." The warrant had been issued on the complaint of John Putnam. According to an eyewitness account, Burroughs answered, with what seems considerable aplomb, even wit, "that he had no goods to show, and he was now reckoning with the inhabitants, for we know not yet who is in debt, but there was his body."

According to the testimony of one of those present, Burroughs then asked John Putnam what debts he was having him seized for. Putnam listed them. Nathaniel Ingersoll stood up and said he wondered at this list, as "to my knowledge you and Mr. Burroughs have reckoned and balanced accounts two or three times since, as you say, this money was due, and you never made any mention of it when you reckoned with Mr. Burroughs."

John Putnam admitted this was true.

Burroughs asked, "Well, what will you do with me?"

Again the marshal appealed to John Putnam, saying, "What shall I do?"

Putnam answered, "You know your business."

The marshal must have still hesitated, or asked for further instructions, because then Putnam went to his brother Thomas Putnam, pulled him by the coat, and they left the meetinghouse together, soon to come in again. John Putnam said, "Marshal, take your prisoner, and have him up to the ordinary [Ingersoll's inn] and secure him till the morning."

John Putnam's action was extraordinary. He well knew that Salem Village owed Burroughs a considerable amount in back salary. The specific aim of the May 2 meeting was to balance that debt against what Burroughs owed various village inhabitants. Since Burroughs attended the meeting voluntarily, there was no reason to suppose that, when paid, he would not in turn pay.

Besides, one of Burroughs's debts to John Putnam was for credit to buy the customary funeral wine when Burroughs's first wife died in 1681. It had been understood that this credit was an advance on Burroughs's salary: since the salary was in arrears, it was inevitable that the debt was outstanding. And it is clear from Nathaniel Ingersoll's protest that, in previous settlements of debt, John Putnam had failed to mention it. Presumably he had not done so precisely because it was understood to be, in effect, part of Burroughs's pay.

It could be that John Putnam's action was aimed not so much against Burroughs himself as against those who had been withholding what was owed him. If Burroughs were not paid, Putnam would also lose out. But such strong-arm tactics as Burroughs's public arrest and a night spent under guard appear scarcely necessary, in the circumstances, to achieve restitution. If they were needed at all it would surely be only if the debt-settling meeting aborted. Such tactics suggest a bullying nature that is feeling frustrated, threatened, and vengeful. It seems likely, since John Putnam chose to submit him to such a painful, humiliating ordeal, that at least some of those feelings were aroused personally by Burroughs.

We see in this scene the Putnam brothers' habit of working together in an aggressive but underhand manner to take down an enemy, as well as Burroughs's strong character and considerable style. Both Putnams may have felt threatened by Burroughs's superior intellect and poise. After all, the Putnams, though leading lights in the village to whom underlings such as the marshall kowtowed, were merely uneducated farmers. George Burroughs was a man of renowned physical prowess, his courage proven during the Indian attacks, who had also graduated with distinction from Harvard.

After Burroughs's arrest, six villagers came forward to post bail for him. At the Salem county court on June 26, after Burroughs's salary was paid and the outstanding debts were all settled, John Putnam withdrew his case. Such a peaceable conclusion left the Putnams cheated of a triumph. Burroughs returned to Casco Bay, no doubt assuming he would never see Salem Village again. He did not count on the Putnams' long, vengeful memory. He would be arrested nine years later and forcibly returned to the village, accused by Thomas Putnam Junior and his brother-in-law Jonathan Walcott of a far more serious offense than nonpayment of debt and carrying a far graver penalty.

CHAPTER EIGHT

Church of Putnam

AND so the search began for yet another minister. Three separate committees worked on the task during the rest of 1683. They may not have been overwhelmed with candidates. All New England must by this time have heard of the unhappy experiences of Bayley and Burroughs. The pastor they at last approached with an offer might have been expected to seize on it gratefully, for he had suffered a checkered career. In fact, he took some persuading before he accepted.

The Reverend Deodat Lawson of Boston had started life well enough. He was born in England, the son of a dissenting minister, and immigrated to Massachusetts in the 1670s. His unusual Christian name is derived from the Latin *Adeodatus,* meaning "God-given," which St. Augustine had christened his son. Through his father's influence, Lawson was appointed minister of the church at Edgartown on Martha's Vineyard. But he left there, for reasons unknown, and then tried and failed at various secular posts.

When controversy flared up again a couple of years after his appointment at Salem Village, however, it was not centered on Lawson's personal qualities or lack of them but on the issue of whether to press Salem Town for permission to gather a church and ordain Lawson as minister. (None of Salem Village's ministers had been ordained, that is, granted full status as Puritan ministers. They preached not to a covenanted church but merely to a congregation and did not offer communion.)

The records of this controversy clearly reveal the emergence of Salem Village's factions. The Village Committee supporting the move to gather a church and ordain Deodat Lawson included Captain John Putnam Senior and his nephew Thomas Putnam Junior, the father of twelve-year-old Ann Putnam, one of the afflicted girls. The opposition to the ordination was led by a group of four men including Joseph Porter.

Another of the men in the latter group was an independent-minded farmer named Joseph Hutchinson. In 1672 he had given an acre of land to the village as a site for the meetinghouse. He now claimed it as his own again and started fencing it in. When the Village Committee sued him, complaining that he "hath so hedged in our meeting house already that we are all forced to go in at one gate," Hutchinson responded by saying, "They have no cause to complain of me for fencing in my own land. . . . [As] for blocking up the meeting house, it was they did it, and not I, in the time of the Indian wars. . . . I wish they would bring me my rocks they took to do it with, for I want them to make fence with."

Hutchinson's stance against Lawson's ordination may have had a specific as well as a general cause. In 1672 Thomas Putnam Senior had sued Hutchinson and his brother John for operating a dam and saw-mill which, he claimed, flooded the access road to his farm. There can have been no love lost between Hutchinson and the Putnams and no desire on Hutchinson's part to espouse any cause of theirs.

It is interesting to note that Joseph Hutchinson would be one of the complainants against Tituba, Sarah Good, and Sarah Osborne in 1692. Given his enmity to the Putnams, shown both before and after that date, this suggests that the terror of witchcraft unleashed in the village at that early stage must have been severe enough to cross factional lines.

In February 1687, presaging the conflict to come, the dispute over Lawson's ordination had become so heated and intractable that it was laid before a meeting of five Salem Town arbitrators: the two Salem Town parsons, elderly, diplomatic John Higginson and stout, fanatical Nicholas Noyes; two wealthy merchants, Bartholomew Gedney and William Brown Junior; and the magistrate and merchant who was five years later to become so familiar a figure in the Salem Village meetinghouse—John Hathorne.

The five advised against Lawson's ordination because the attempt to bring it about "hath not been so inoffensively managed as might have been." They recommended that the villagers wait "till your spirits are better quieted and composed." It seems the meeting had got somewhat out of control: "To our grief we observe such uncharitable expressions and uncomely reflections tossed to and fro as look like the effects of settled prejudice and resolved animosity."

It was with something close to clairvoyance that the arbitrators added, "[the prejudice and animosity] have a tendency to make such a gap as we fear if not timely prevented, will let out peace and order and let in confusion and every evil work."

Boyer and Nissenbaum argue that Salem Town representatives would in any case hardly have been favorably disposed to the gathering of a Salem Village church, with its bid for greater village autonomy. Be that as it may, the Putnam faction bowed to the arbitrators' advice.

Soon afterward, the ill-starred Deodat Lawson joined his predecessors in making an early departure from a post that had proved yet again to offer more trouble than joy. And so it was that in 1688 Samuel Parris came to Salem Village.

The Putnam faction, now, were determined. They would stop at nothing to gather their church. Private negotiations were held with Parris and an understanding was reached that went beyond anything arranged with his predecessors. In October 1689 at a "general meeting of the inhabitants," Parris "and his heirs" were given the village parsonage with its barn and two acres of land. This broke the resolution made in 1681 that the parsonage would always belong to the village inhabitants and would never be transferred "to any particular persons or person." With a breathtaking disregard for even the appearance of legality, the meeting voted that the previous ruling was "made void and of no effect." Parris was also granted a series of niggling demands, to do with such things as the price at which he bought corn and other provisions, an arrangement that illustrates both the Putnams' keenness to have him and his own grasping nature.

The "general meeting of the inhabitants" had clearly been led by the Putnams. The men chosen to carry out the transfer of property were four Putnam family members: Nathaniel Putnam; John Putnam Senior; Jonathan Walcott, husband of Deliverance Putnam (Thomas Junior's sister); and Thomas Flint, brother-in-law of Elizabeth Putnam (another sister of Thomas Junior). A fifth man involved was the innkeeper Nathaniel Ingersoll.

On November 19, 1689, a Salem Village church at last came into being. Samuel Parris stood in the meetinghouse pulpit before seventeen village farmers, six of their wives and three other women, and began his declaration of intent to form a society to serve the Lord Jesus Christ and edify one another, with the words "We whose names (tho' unworthy of a name in this [Church]) are hereunto subscribed."

Eleven of the twenty-six names Parris proceeded to list were Putnam. There was John Putnam Senior, who had had Burroughs arrested for debt; his brother Nathaniel Putnam; his nephew Thomas, father of Ann; three other nephews, Edward, John, and Benjamin; and his son Jonathan. Among the women were John Senior's wife, Rebecca; Hannah, the nephew John's wife; and Deliverance, his niece.

As Parris went on, "We do, in some measure of sincerity, this day give up ourselves one unto another in the Lord," an impartial observer might have wondered if the bonds being formed had as much to do with solidifying existing connections in this world as with creating new ones for improving the chances of entry to the next. Parris's declamation, beseeching God to help the band keep its covenant, ends with the request that God "at length receive us all into the inheritance of the Saints in Light." An ironic prayer, given the darkness ahead.

Over the next few months, twenty-six more villagers joined the church, making a total, with the Parrises, of fifty-three, almost a quarter of the village's adult population. During the same period moves were afoot to gain political independence for Salem Village from the town. In August 1689 a village meeting had voted to petition the town for a total separation. But the strategy resulted only in an offer from the town to lower village taxes.

Certain villagers who had supported the August petition had no true interest in town-village separation but merely in those lower taxes. But by 1690 they found themselves, as a result of all the political maneuvering, in a weakened position. The church that they had allowed to come into being was a powerful new force for political autonomy.

Parris alluded to these maneuverings in the first sermon he preached after his ordination. No doubt, with his customary touchiness, he was smarting at the lack of true enthusiasm for himself and his purposes on the part of some of the villagers who had ostensibly supported him. The text of his sermon was "Cursed be he that doeth the work of the Lord deceitfully," and he castigated "persons" who "attend any duty, any service or ordinance . . . but yet aim at some private and carnal interest, some by-end of their own." But he may also have had more serious aims than the mere venting of spleen. He may have been trying to influence the waverers who, if they sided with his opponents, could tip the balance of power away from the Putnams and their allies.

Despite—or perhaps because of—his harangues, at least some of those waverers eventually moved over to the opposing side. Almost two years later, in October 1691, the five Parris supporters on the Village Committee were replaced by five leading members of what by now had emerged as the anti-Parris, anti-Putnam faction. Parris's list of their names in the margin of the church record book, next to the date of the Village Committee meeting, speaks of the ominousness of this development all the more eloquently by its absence of comment. The names were Joseph Porter, Joseph Hutchinson, Daniel Andrew, Francis Nurse, and Joseph Putnam.

That last name may at first sight seem surprising. But Joseph was the odd man out in the Putnam clan, his material interests opposed to those of his brothers and sisters. Indeed, his siblings (or rather half-siblings) hated him, and for an excellent reason. Though he was the youngest, their father, Thomas Putnam Senior, had left him most of his estate. Thomas Senior had had eight children by his first wife, of whom the eldest son was Thomas Junior, father of Ann Putnam. When his first wife died, Thomas Putnam Senior married Mary Veren, widow of a well-to-do Salem ship captain. By her he had Joseph.

We cannot know whether the decision to make Joseph his chief inheritor was due to the sheer doting fondness of an old man for his new wife and young son or whether there was conflict between him and his other children. Either way, the result was a severe blow for Thomas Putnam Junior. He had stood to inherit at least three hundred acres and the family homestead. Instead he was bequeathed just a small farm on a small piece of land. He had already been disappointed in his expectations of a substantial bequest to his wife, Ann Carr, from *her* father. This second blow was thus doubly bitter. With his brother Edward and brothers-in-law Jonathan Walcott and William Trask, he did all he could to break the will. But he had no success and was forced to watch, powerless, as young Joseph, through his inheritance and through marriage to a daughter of the powerful Porter family, rose to preeminent wealth and importance. With strong connections to the commercial world of Salem Town through his mother, as well as through the Porters, Joseph was firmly against town-village separation. He was soon a leading light in the anti-Parris/anti-Putnam faction.

Parris's sense of the ominousness of political developments was given clear expression in an entry in the church record book two weeks after the fateful Village Committee meeting in October 1691. To an evening gathering of seventeen church members held at his house, he declared, "I have not much to trouble you with now; but you know what committee, the last town-meeting here, were chosen; and what they have done, or intend to do, it may be, [you know] better than I." They had already done enough to cause him the gravest concern. At the same village meeting a vote had been passed agreeing that no tax would be assessed that year for paying his salary.

Parris and the Putnams were in this position of deep disadvantage when God—or the devil—delivered into their hands a weapon of unexpected and extraordinary power. It took them a while to grasp its significance. By the time Tituba, Sarah Good, and Sarah Osborne were incarcerated, they were beginning to understand.

In all previous cases of New England witchcraft, when a witch or two went to jail or was hanged, that was the end of it. In Salem, with three witches in jail, it was just the beginning. The afflicted girls, far from being encouraged by the adults around them to calm down and resume their normal lives once scapegoats were found, were listened to closely as they continued to complain of the harm being done to them. Consciously or unconsciously, their parents and guardians knew that they wielded a weapon that would sooner or later strike to their advantage.

CHAPTER NINE

"As Breath into the Wind"

(*Macbeth*, ACT 1 SCENE 3)

WITH Tituba's confession, the terror that had spread through the village intensified. That evening Samuel Sibley, husband of Mary, who had suggested the witch cake, was at Dr. Griggs's house, where lived one of the oldest of the afflicted girls, seventeen-year-old Elizabeth Hubbard. Suddenly Elizabeth cried out. She screamed that Sarah Good stood on the table naked-breasted and bare-legged and that if she had something to do it with she would kill her. Sibley struck with his staff where she pointed.

The next morning, March 2, the constable claimed that Sarah Good's arm was bloody from just below the elbow to the wrist. This was taken as firm evidence that Sarah Good's specter had visited the Griggses', even though Elizabeth Hubbard had claimed that Sibley's blow was to the back. She had said nothing at all of the arm. In a manner that was to become all too familiar as the examinations went on, nobody noticed a small though vital discrepancy.

Also on the evening of March 1, William Allen, a young, unmarried man who worked as a cooper, heard strange sounds and, on approaching them, saw "a strange and unusual beast lying on the ground." This vanished and in its place appeared two or three women who "flew from me, not after the manner of other women, but swiftly vanished away out of our sight, which women we took to be Sarah Good Sarah Osborne and Tituba." A companion, John Hughes, claimed to have seen and heard the same things. Along other dark paths and in other candlelit homes, more villagers glimpsed similar sights.

By this time the notion of witches sending out their "specters" or "shapes," incorporeal beings indistinguishable to those who could see them from the witches themselves, was becoming a familiar one. The specters had human powers of sight, hearing, speech, and touch and superhuman ones of locomotion. They could transport themselves out of prison cells and across distances by flying or just by mysterious instant transmission. Their relationship to their originals was separate yet unified: if the specter was hit, the human being showed the wound.

For most ordinary people, the distinction between original and shape was so blurred as often to disappear altogether. It is as though the notion of witchcraft inspired such terror that clear thought about the beings who practiced it was well nigh impossible. The authorities did nothing to dispel the confusion. Thomas Brattle, a Salem merchant and enlightened thinker, observed that "when the afflicted do mean and intend only the appearance and shape of such an one, say J. Proctor, yet they positively swear that J. Proctor did afflict them; and they were allowed to do so; as though there was no real difference between J. Proctor and the shape of J. Proctor."

Eventually Increase and Cotton Mather and other ministers would apply their minds to the nature and power of specters. In due time they dealt with the crucially significant issue of whether the devil can send out a shape in the likeness of an innocent being without that innocent's knowledge. But they did so too late to save many blameless people whom the specters sent to their deaths.

Meanwhile, the examinations of Tituba, Sarah Good, and Sarah Osborne went on for five days. The three women were kept in jail at night and brought by day to the meetinghouse, together or separately. The proceedings were conducted with considerable fanfare, the magistrates riding from the town in a formal procession accompanied by marshals armed with spears. The number of officials involved is indicated by the expenses at Ingersoll's inn for the first day, March 1. The two magistrates, dining grandly as befitted their station, spent the considerable sum of eight shillings on dinner and drink. The marshals, constables, and their assistants laid out three shillings on victuals and two more on cider. Of these men the two constables, perhaps needing to be especially well fortified against the onerous task of escorting their recalcitrant prisoners to and from jail, spent another ninepence on cider and sixpence on rum.

The next day they may have spent more. The turbulence of soul that made Sarah Good seem a particularly powerful devil's accomplice was given dramatic expression when, on their way to jail in Ipswich, she leaped off her horse, not just once but three times. She also railed against the magistrates, shouted that there was no evidence against her except that of an Indian and therefore she had nothing to fear, but nevertheless "endeavoured to kill herself." The record does not tell us how she did this. It may be simply that the leaps off her horse seemed suicidal.

On that evening of March 2, William Allen saw Sarah Good in his chamber, carrying a strange light. He kicked at her and she vanished. John Hughes saw a great white dog that followed him for a while and then vanished. Later a light appeared in his locked bedroom and, sitting up in bed, he saw a gray cat. However modest, even comic, these hallucinations may seem to us now, to those young men they must have been awesome.

Each day brought new dramas. Also on March 2, Tituba repeated and embellished her previous confession, adding details such as that the devil gave her a pin tied in a stick to let blood so she could sign her name in his book. The next day Ann Putnam saw the apparition of a matron named Elizabeth Proctor in the company of the phantoms of the other three witches. Goody Proctor bit, pinched, and almost choked her, Ann claimed. This sighting may have been a later invention since it was not put in writing till several weeks after the trial. However, Ann claimed that she had not known the woman to be Goody Proctor until Sunday, March 6, when she viewed her in the flesh in the meetinghouse. She had then told "them that held" her that this was her latest tormentor.

Goodwife Proctor was the wife of John Proctor, a successful farmer, entrepreneur, and tavern keeper who lived far from Salem Village center, on the edge of Salem Town. He had never been directly involved in Salem Village politics or litigation with the Putnams, but his interests were diametrically opposed to those of the old, established village elite. He had emigrated from England to Ipswich, Massachusetts, with his parents, moving to Salem Village in 1666. There he had risen to considerable wealth and prestige. Strange as it may seem to us now, in Puritan society to be granted a license as a tavern keeper showed that a man had arrived. But to the Putnams, with their defensive, inflexible outlook, Proctor and his wife remained hated outsiders. What was more, John Proctor was later to voice thoroughgoing skepticism about the girls' fits and the validity of the witchcraft proceedings. Perhaps he had done so already. His wife may have been known to agree with him.

Ann may have seen the apparition of Elizabeth Proctor so early in the course of events because of the view of Proctor that she absorbed from her elders; or her father or mother may, directly or otherwise, have suggested that she name her. It could even be that Ann's claim that she did not know who Elizabeth was till three days after she saw her spectral appearance was a bid to suggest that she had no ulterior motive in making the accusation against her.

From the reference to "them that held" her, we know that on Sunday, March 6, Ann must have been disrupting the service with fits. No doubt the other afflicted girls were doing so too.

On March 5 the examinations of Sarah Good, Sarah Osborne, and Tituba came to an end and on March 7 the three women were sent to Boston jail to await trial. When the jailer submitted an account of his expenses two days later, he included fourteen pounds for chains for Osborne and Good. Presumably Tituba, since she had confessed to witchcraft, was allowed to remain free of manacles.

The village now waited to see if, since the accused were locked up, the girls' fits would cease. They did not. On March 11 Parris invited a group of ministers from neighboring towns to the parsonage for a day of fasting and prayer. That ploy had failed before, but what else could he do? Of course he, and everyone else, could have stopped giving credence to the girls' continuing claims of being tortured by witches. But that course would have had its own dangers. Besides, Tituba's elaborate confession, repeated yet again on a further examination in jail, and her apparently heartfelt repentance encouraged magistrates, clergy, and villagers to believe that witchcraft was truly abroad and that other women, to all outward appearances innocent, had banded with her, Sarah Good, and Sarah Osborne to make pacts with the devil.

It was about now that nine-year-old Betty Parris was sent to stay with Stephen Sewall and his family in Salem Town, presumably because her parents felt that, because of her young age or especially vulnerable character, she was in particular danger of mental or physical harm from continuing fits. They must have guessed that these would cease when she was away from the other girls. They guessed correctly. Although the fits did not finish at once, they gradually lessened and finally ended when Betty confessed to John Hale the illicit fortunetelling that had started them. It seems that by at last easing her conscience she cured the physical symptoms of the emotional disturbance begun in the parsonage in January.

If the other parents and guardians—Thomas Putnam and William Griggs and their wives—had cared only for their children's welfare and had had no hidden agenda, conscious or unconscious, they might well have wondered if all the girls might be cured in time if they were kept apart from each other. If the Parrises had loved Abigail as they did their own daughter, they might have sent her away too. But the girls continued to gather together, at one another's homes, in the meetinghouse, and at Ingersoll's tavern.

They were present at the prayers in the parsonage on the eleventh. During the exercises they were mostly silent but "after one prayer was ended, they would act and speak strangely and ridiculously . . . a girl of eleven or twelve years old, would sometimes seem to be in a convulsion fit, her limbs being twisted several ways, and very stiff, but presently her fit would be over." That girl was either Abigail Williams or Ann Putnam. The ministers, as well as everyone else, took her and the others and their fits as seriously as on their previous visit. Needless to say, the fasting and prayers had no effect whatsoever. Within a few days the girls were seeing visions of two more respectable matrons as well as Elizabeth Proctor. It is worth noting that the first sightings were always by Ann Putnam.

Parris's next move was to invite his ill-fated predecessor, the Reverend Deodat Lawson, to the village from Boston. Lawson had of course been the third of Salem Village's ministers, leaving after Thomas Putnam and his friends failed to have him ordained. Such an apparently independent witness may have come to seem very necessary. By the time the invitation was issued, a fourth "witch" had been accused and arrested, one of the two matrons spectrally seen by Ann Putnam, a woman of rather different character and standing from the despised Osborne and Good, a woman almost as unimpeachably respectable as Elizabeth Proctor.

Martha Cory was the sixty-five-year-old wife of a prosperous though contentious farmer and landowner, Giles Cory, and a member of the Salem Village church. With her arrest the transition was made from accusations of outcasts to those of women fully integrated in the Salem Village community. Martha was the perfect transitional figure since, though her present state was completely respectable, her past carried a taint. She had once given birth to an illegitimate son, a mulatto.

On Saturday, March 12, Edward Putnam, brother of Thomas and uncle of Ann, as well as Ezekiel Cheever, the far from impartial reporter of the accused witches' examinations, called on Martha at her home just over the line from Salem Village in Salem Town. They had come directly from Thomas Putnam's, where twelve-year-old Ann had been complaining that Goody Cory often appeared to her and tortured her. Before they left, they asked her what Cory was wearing. This was ostensibly so they could check that Ann had made no mistake in her identification. However, Ann claimed that, on hearing the two men were intending to visit, Martha Cory had blinded her. No one seemed to be struck by the strangeness of Martha's blinding Ann to the sight of her specter while telling her it was she who was doing so.

The two men found Martha alone in the house. She greeted them with a smile, saying she knew what they had come for, they had come to talk with her about being a witch, "but she was none." She said she could not help it if people were discussing her. Edward Putnam answered that it was an afflicted person's complaining of her that had caused them to come. She asked, "Does she tell you what clothes I have on?" Martha well knew that the girls often described what their supposed tormentors were wearing. Putnam and Cheever told Martha what Ann had told them about being blinded. Martha "made but little answer to this but seemed to smile at it as if she had showed us a pretty trick." They chose to interpret her smile as pleasure in her own cunning instead of grim amusement at Ann's.

Everything in the men's testimony indicates that they saw and heard only what they expected, given their prior conviction that Martha was guilty of witchcraft. They proceeded to lecture her on how greatly the name of God and religion and the church were dishonored by a church member being accused as a witch, "but she seemed to be no way concerned for any thing about it but only to stop the mouths of people that they might not say thus of her." This hardly seems surprising, if she were the innocent victim of false accusations. Martha then said she did not think there were any witches. She meant that she did not think there were any witches in Salem Village, not that witches do not exist. When Putnam and Cheever said they believed there *were* witches, because three had been arrested, she replied that if there were, it was not surprising that those three people should be such, since they were "idle slothful persons" and "minded nothing that was good." But she was a church member; she rejoiced to hear God's word: she was no witch. The men's answer to this was that no outward profession of Christianity could clear her of witchcraft since it was known that witches had often "crept into the churches." She said that "the devil was come down amongst us in great rage," presumably meaning he had inspired the mayhem in the village. This came dangerously close to saying that the afflicted girls were possessed by Satan rather than afflicted by witches.

After further theological discourse, in which Martha seems to have held her own very well, the two men returned to Thomas Putnam's. They found that Ann had been spared persecution during the time they were with her supposed tormentor, though she was to suffer again later that day.

Martha's skepticism may well have been the chief reason for her being accused. She had taken her husband's saddle off his horse to prevent his going to the examinations of Tituba and the rest. She had not seen that his going would be of "any benefit," she said later, at her examination on March 21. The girls themselves, as well as their parents, may have felt both arrogant fury and considerable fear at her questioning their powers of witch detection.

On March 14, when Martha paid a return visit to the Putnams to confront Ann about her accusations, not only Ann but also the seventeen-year-old servant girl Mercy Lewis went into terrifying fits. Ann claimed she saw a yellow bird sucking between Martha Cory's fingers. Four days later Ann Putnam's mother experienced terrifying pains, being "almost pressed and choked to death," on lying down for a rest after tending her "poor afflicted child and maid." She also saw

Martha's specter, which "did torture so as I cannot express, ready to tear me all to pieces." A short time later Martha brought a little red book with a black pen and urged Ann to write. The tortures went on not only for the rest of that day but the whole of the next.

On Saturday, March 19, a warrant was issued for Martha's arrest on the complaint of Edward Putnam and his friend Henry Kenny. It said that she had "done much hurt and injury" to Ann Putnam, wife of Thomas Putnam; Ann Putnam, daughter of Thomas Putnam; Mercy Lewis; Abigail Williams; and Elizabeth Hubbard. It appears that the girls had instinctively, violently turned on someone they saw as an immediate threat to their credibility, position, and power.

Boyer and Nissenbaum have a more elaborate theory as to the cause of the Putnams' accusation of Martha. It is that their fury against Thomas Junior's stepmother, mother of the Joseph who inherited Thomas Senior's wealth, was so overwhelming as to demand murderous revenge, though not on Mary Veren herself but on substitutes. The Putnams suspected Mary of poisoning Thomas Senior's mind against his children and causing him to disinherit them. She thus seemed the source of all their troubles. But they could not cry out against the woman herself, since she was too well connected and powerful, so they pointed the finger at women who, through their links with Salem Town as well as their status, prosperity, and age, represented her in their minds. They started low, with Martha, and gradually moved higher. The process was not one they were aware of themselves; they truly feared witchcraft and thought they were genuinely finding out witches.

This is the one argument in *Salem Possessed* that seems less than persuasive. Certainly the Putnams' tendency to fury and vengefulness toward those they perceived as their enemies is beyond doubt. So is their position as part of an embattled local elite, full of anger and envy at the prosperous merchants of Salem and their friends and connections in the village. But the authors' lateral jump to viewing the Putnams' victims as psychological projections of the woman who had helped cheat them out of their inheritance seems more imaginative than convincing. Many accused witches do not fit the Mary Veren mold, including several men. And there appears to be adequate cause of each "crying out" without the need for such an intricate theory.

Whatever the precise cause of the choice of Martha as the next accused witch, when Deodat Lawson arrived in the village on March 19, he found it in uproar. The numbers of the afflicted were growing by the day, there were three accused witches already in prison, and one church member was under arrest. More names of respectable women were being banded about as in league with the devil. The terror in the air was of a kind afflicting a populace invaded by enemy forces ruled by an unimaginably evil and cunning dictator.

CHAPTER TEN

The Yellow Bird

THE first person Deodat Lawson saw after his arrival at Nathaniel Ingersoll's inn, apart from the innkeeper himself and his servants, was Mary Walcott.

Soon after Lawson had gone into his room, Mary came to speak to him. Perhaps she carried a message from her father, Jonathan Walcott, or from her uncle by marriage Thomas Putnam, or from her close neighbor Samuel Parris. Or perhaps, at least on the face of it, she was simply greeting a man she remembered with respect and affection from four years before, when she was thirteen. Either way, when Lawson and she finished talking she was standing by the door, about to leave, when she suddenly screamed. It was her wrist, she cried. Her wrist hurt. Lawson inspected it by the light of a candle and saw teeth marks, "both upper and lower set, on each side." What happened next we have no way of knowing, but it is clear that Lawson did not interrogate Mary suspiciously. He took her word for what had happened: She had been bitten by a specter.

For the reader today it is difficult to believe that the event was not carefully staged. Mary Walcott's coming to talk to the man invited to witness what was happening, and being bitten while with him, seems extremely convenient, even if we suppose that the teeth marks could be caused by hysteria. But it seems rather more likely that the teeth making the marks were not phantom but physical. Mary probably bit herself hard just before knocking on the door. She knew that Lawson would need a candle to see her wrist clearly since in winter the room would be dark even by day. She knew they need not talk long. Teeth marks do not fade much straightaway.

It may seem strange that a seventeen-year-old girl could bear to cause herself the pain of a bite on the wrist. But self-mutilation is a common phenomenon among the emotionally disturbed. The pain is disregarded or relished. Besides, Mary was highly motivated. She needed to impress Lawson with the genuineness of affliction by witches. He was to witness their apparent biting, strangling, and pinching of her and her friends at Cory's examination two days later. Because he was an independent witness his lack of skepticism was essential for the girls' credibility.

That it was Mary Walcott, instead of Ann Putnam or Elizabeth Hubbard or Mercy Lewis, who played this role in this scene might be due entirely to the closeness of her father's house to the tavern. Or it might be that she was the least innocent of the girls at this early stage of the witch-hunt. Or she may have been the most beguiling, the one likeliest to arouse sympathetic feelings in a middle-aged reverend gentleman's heart. Or she might just have been the best at biting herself.

For the first time in the course of the witch-hunt we see the likelihood of deliberate fraud. All the evidence points to Thomas Putnam, with or without Jonathan Walcott's and Samuel Parris's connivance, lending a hand to hysteria. It is possible the girls themselves, without adult assistance, planned Lawson's gulling. But the adult Putnams' active part in the witchcraft proceedings—in making many of the official complaints against the accused that led to their arrests, and filing many of the depositions detailing their crimes—makes it seem highly likely that they gave Mary Walcott instructions.

Besides, they had reported to Lawson, even before he arrived in the village, that it had been said at an examination of a suspected witch that his wife and daughter, who had both died three years before, had been murdered by "infernal powers." There is no mention of such allegations in the records so far of the examinations of Sarah Good, Sarah Osborne, or Tituba. We cannot know whether the records are incomplete or whether the afflicted girls made these claims in some other place or whether adults invented them. But the report to Lawson cannot but have given him a strong personal interest in the witch-hunt and a bias against the accused, as it was probably intended to do.

That evening Lawson paid a visit to the parsonage. While he was there Abigail had a "grievous fit," running to and fro despite Mrs. Ingersoll's attempts to hold her, stretching her arms up as though trying to fly, crying "Whish! Whish! Whish!" After a while she cried out that she saw Goodwife Nurse. This woman was an unsurpassably respectable seventy-one-year-old church member. Abigail shouted, "Do you not see her? Why there she stands!" and averred that Goody Nurse offered her "the book." She cried several times, "I won't, I won't, I won't, take it, I do not know what book it is: I am sure it is none of God's book, it is the devil's book, for aught I know."

After that, Lawson says, "she run to the fire, and begun to throw fire brands, about the house; and run against the back, as if she would run up chimney."

Those present told Lawson that Abigail had often, during other fits, gone in the fire. The sight of her running between smoldering logs to the back of the fire, where the blackened stone curved to the chimney above, must have been terrifying. So must the throwing of firebrands all around the room. It is interesting that it was Mrs. Ingersoll who tried to restrain her, not her aunt, Mrs. Parris. If Mrs. Parris had been in poor health before, she must have been prostrate by now.

The next day Deodat Lawson did his best to conduct the services in the meetinghouse. It was not easy since not only Ann Putnam but also Abigail Williams, Mary Walcott, Mercy Lewis, Elizabeth Hubbard, and two newcomers to the circle of the afflicted—Mrs. Pope and Goodwife Bibber—had "several sore fits." The chief ostensible cause of these was the presence of Martha Cory. Though the warrant for her arrest had already been issued, it could not be served on the Sabbath so, this last day, she was free. With the courage and independence of mind that seem her chief characteristics, she chose to come to the meetinghouse to meet her accusers instead of staying at home.

The fits "did something interrupt me in my first prayer, being so unusual," Lawson says, his understatement reminding us of the Puritans' emotional control, which was the context and part of the cause of the children's hysteria. He goes on: "After psalm was sung, Abigail Williams said to me, 'Now stand up, and name your text.' And after it was read, she said, 'It is a long text.'"

These outbursts, unlike earlier and later ones, sound less like mental illness than impudence. But, though in that time and place such impudence was so outrageous as to be almost unthinkable, it continued unchecked.

"In the beginning of [the] sermon, Mrs. Pope, a woman afflicted, said to me, 'Now there is enough of that,'" recalls Lawson. "And in the afternoon, Abigail Williams upon my referring to my doctrine said to me, 'I know no doctrine you had. If you did name one, I have forgot it.'"

The girls had achieved a license that was exhilarating but no doubt also disturbing, helping to continue and promote the hysteria. During the sermon the girls' bad behavior escalated again to something more deranged. Abigail Williams called out, "Look where Goodwife Cory sits on the beam suckling her yellow bird betwixt her fingers." The yellow bird, it seems, was by this time firmly established as Martha's spectral familiar.

Lawson continues, "Ann Putnam, another girl afflicted, said there was a yellow-bird sat on my hat as it hung on the pin in the pulpit: but those that were by, restrained her from speaking loud about it." Perhaps even Ann's mother and other well-wishers had the sense that enough was enough. Some of the congregation may have by this stage been showing restiveness at this wild behavior, whatever its supposed cause. Lawson mentions no more disruptions. What Martha thought and felt about the sightings of the yellow bird one can but guess. It shows some courage on her part, and determination not to be bested, that she stayed where she was.

The next day she needed all that courage and more. At twelve o'clock the magistrates arrived at a meetinghouse "thronged with spectators." Parris was seated at a table, set out with paper and pens, ready to write down questions and answers. Perhaps the coming interchange was thought too important to be left to the editorializing, ungrammatical Ezekiel Cheever. Hathorne would be interrogating not a slave, beggar, or half-wit but an intelligent church member.

Maybe because Parris was saving his strength for the task ahead of him, Nicholas Noyes, the Salem Town minister who had taken part in events in the village from the start, ascended the pulpit and said the introductory prayer. It was "very pertinent and pathetic," Lawson tells us. No doubt Noyes, a corpulent forty-five-year-old bachelor who was second to none in his enthusiasm for the witch-hunt, beseeched God in such a manner as to ask His help in finding out the devil's accomplices who were causing His innocent young servants such torture.

As soon as Martha Cory was brought forward and asked by Hathorne why—as always, not *if*, but *why*—she hurt these persons, she requested that she be allowed to say a prayer herself. She must have felt that Noyes's moving plea needed a counter. No doubt she wanted to pray, also pertinently and pathetically, that God would establish her innocence. The girls had already gone into fits. Their power having been proven time and again, there must have seemed little point in delaying them.

"We do not send for you to go to prayer," Hathorne said to Martha, after she had repeated her request several times. "But tell me why you hurt these?"

She must even this early on have felt the prison walls closing in. But what could she do but keep protesting that she was falsely accused?

"I am an innocent person: I never had to do with witchcraft since I was born. I am a gospel woman."

The afflicted girls shouted, "Ah! You are a gospel witch!"

Hathorne asked, "Do not you see these complain of you?" indicating the girls in their fits. And then Martha said a prayer anyway, despite Hathorne's refusal. It was "The Lord open the eyes of the magistrates and ministers: the Lord show his power to discover the guilty."

It did her no good. Sounding like the automaton he was, in his loss of all power to see or act outside the limits already established in his mind, Hathorne said, "Tell us who hurts these children."

"I do not know."

"If you be guilty of this fact do you think you can hide it?"

"The Lord knows . . ."

"Well, tell us what you know of this matter."

"Why, I am a gospel-woman, and do you think I can have to do with witchcraft too?"

Then Hathorne played his trump card. He asked how she had been able to tell that Ann Putnam was asked what clothes she, Martha, was wearing by Edward Putnam and Ezekiel Cheever when they came to visit her. Before she could draw breath to answer, Ezekiel Cheever interrupted and "bid her not begin with a lie." She had still had no chance to utter when Hathorne asked, "Who told you that?"

When she at last was let speak, Martha said that her husband had told her. That is, her husband had told her that the children had described what "others" wore, meaning other accused witches. Hathorne turned to eighty-year-old Giles Cory, seated nearby, and asked if this were true. He said it was not. It soon becomes clear from the record that for Giles Cory this scene was merely the latest of many in a long-running drama of marital conflict. Three days later he filed a deposition complaining, among other things, of being unable to think or speak clearly while trying to pray when Martha was near. He mentions a few incidents of extreme triviality involving an ox and a cat. In each case the animal sickened, then recovered. The court was meant to infer that Martha was responsible for the sickening but not the recovery. Giles also says he has seen his wife kneeling at the hearth after bedtime, as if at prayer, but inaudibly. The fact that he remarks on not being able to hear her makes one wonder if the Puritans always addressed God out loud, even when alone. Since religious observance constituted the only licensed drama they knew, this may have been so. Though Cory never explicitly says that his wife is a witch, all this trivia cast suspicion of witchery.

Perhaps Martha expected her husband's denial. Nevertheless, it must have contributed to the increasingly helpless desperation that can be heard in her answers. Hathorne pressed her again to say who told her the children had been asked what clothes she was wearing. She said, helplessly, "Nobody." Hathorne taxed her with self-contradiction, pointing out that earlier she had said her husband had told her. Martha shifted her ground, saying that what her husband had said was that the children had complained she afflicted them. Hathorne asked, "How do you know what they came for?" meaning Edward Putnam and Ezekiel Cheever. She said at first she had heard it reported that the children said she troubled them, but when Hathorne asked, "But how did you know it?" she was forced to say, lamely, "I thought they did." This line of questioning was repeated and ended with her saying, "I did think so" and his declaiming, "But you said you knew so."

All this time, as the background to Hathorne's hostile questioning, the girls had been screaming that Martha was biting, pinching, and strangling them. Now Mary Walcott and Abigail Williams claimed they saw a man whispering in her ear, taking as their cue the questions about how Martha knew the reason for Putnam and Cheever's visit and the query about Martha's clothes. Emboldened by Hathorne's hostility, Martha's confusion, their previous successes, and the excitement in the meetinghouse of a crowd scenting blood, they brought into the room, right up to Martha's side, Satan himself.

They were emboldened too by sheer numbers. There were nine of them now. As well as Mary Walcott, Mercy Lewis, Elizabeth Hubbard, Abigail Williams, and Ann Putnam, there were four newcomers, all older and married: Ann Putnam Senior, Mrs. Pope, Goodwife Bibber, and "an ancient woman named Goodall." It seems wishful thinking amounting to extraordinary perversity that Parris, in the record, persists in referring to this growing band of increasingly elderly hysterics as "children." What is known of the additional members suggests that they were emotionally disturbed, drawn into the hysteria as a means of venting their rage, perhaps afraid in some cases of being branded as witches themselves if they did not join with the witch finders. Several witnesses were later to testify that Goodwife Bibber was a woman of "an unruly turbulent spirit" who often quarreled with her husband and called him "very bad names" and was "very much given to tattling and tale bearing" and "making mischief among her neighbours." She "would have strange fits when she was crossed." One neighbor went so far as to claim she "could fall into fits as often as she pleased."

Again the question arises as to how far the group were suffering hysterical symptoms and how far practicing fraud. The answer becomes clearer later. Martha Cory herself was unusual, though not wholly alone, in believing them mad.

"What did he say to you?" Hathorne asked her, of the man who had supposedly whispered. She replied, "We must not believe all these distracted children say."

Hathorne asked, "Cannot you tell what that man whispered?" and she said, "I saw no body."

He asked, "But did not you hear?"

She replied, "No."

At this the afflicted began suffering "extreme agony." It may well have been now that Lawson, seated at the front of the meetinghouse, saw "their tongues drawn out of the mouths to a fearful length, their heads turned very much over their shoulders . . . their arms and legs, etc, wrested as if they were quite dislocated," and blood gushing "plentifully out of their mouths."

Hathorne abandoned his questions and urged Martha to confess. She refused to do so. He pressed, "Do not you see how these afflicted do charge you," and she replied, "We must not believe distracted persons." When he asked whom she employed to hurt them and she said "None," he flung her prayer back at her, saying, "Did not you say our eyes were blinded you would open them?" Bravely, she replied, "Yes, to accuse the innocent."

At this point a man named Henry Crossly, the husband of Giles Cory's daughter by a previous wife, gave evidence. Its terms are not included in Parris's record, but they seem to have been to the effect that one or more of the afflicted girls fell down in Martha's presence and she said they could not stand before her and that the devil could not stand before her. She denied having said this. The record states, "Three or four sober witnesses confirmed it." Martha cried, "What can I do? Many rise up against me." Hathorne said, "Why, confess."

"So I would if I were guilty."

What has by now become clear beyond question is that Hathorne and everyone else in the meetinghouse regarded the girls' fits as absolute proof that Martha was a witch. Utterly forgotten were such legal niceties as that this is not a trial but a mere examination; that the competence and truthfulness of witnesses cannot be taken for granted; that the defendant should be defended by counsel; that the magistrate should be impartial; and, most important, that a defendant is innocent until by due process proved guilty.

Such abandonment of the axioms of English justice was less outrageous in Salem than it would have been in the mother country. The Massachusetts Bay Colony legal system was self-invented under the charter. It followed the English system in many of its principles and procedures, as well as much of its content, but in some ways diverged. One marked difference was that the Puritans' assumption of religious and moral infallibility prompted an inquisitorial attitude in their examinations and trials. In some places magistrates had taken to examining suspects, without lawyers present, in their own homes. Their model was the saint or minister beseeching the sinner to repent and confess rather than the secular wise man searching out justice. They were not seeking the truth but assuming that they knew it. By their lights, as upholders of divine revelation about which there could be no debate, they were just. But the notion that the defendant before them was not guilty until he or she was proved so was, from their viewpoint, virtually meaningless.

And, after all, they were all of them amateurs. It was not only John Hathorne who was without legal training. So were all the colonies' magistrates. Neither were the marshals or constables in any sense professionals. They were merely ordinary citizens taking turns at civic duties. Much of England's good legal practice had, in New England, been forgotten or ignored long before 1692 and the examinations for witchcraft.

But what was abandoned in Salem Village as nowhere else in Massachusetts was proper courtroom procedure. The scene in the meetinghouse resembled the trial scene in *Alice in Wonderland* more than it did any normal scene in any normal courtroom. Besides the constant screaming, writhing, twisting, and bleeding of the afflicted girls, there were disruptions caused by people leaping up to attend to them and by others to make comments, as when the "three or four sober witnesses" confirmed Henry Crossly's testimony. Hathorne seems to have made no attempt to keep order. If anything, he encouraged the chaos.

Worse was to come.

Abigail cried out to Martha, "Next Sabbath is sacrament day, but she shall not come there." Hathorne, showing his exasperation as well as unshakable prejudice, ranted, "You charge these children with distraction: it is a note of distraction when persons vary in a minute, but these fix upon you, this is not the manner of distraction." Martha cried out despairingly that all were against her. Hathorne brought up the subject of her prayer again, about the magistrates' and ministers' eyes being blinded, which seemed to rile him more each time he thought about it. Martha laughed, a characteristic response of hers to dangerous absurdity. Hathorne said, "Now tell us how we shall know who doth hurt these if you do not." She cried, "Can an innocent person be guilty?" Then he asked with what she struck the maid at Thomas Putnam's claiming, "Here are two that see you strike her with an iron rod." (Apparently two of the afflicted girls were claiming they would see Martha's specter striking Mercy Lewis with a rod.) She said, "I had no hand in it." He asked if she believed the children were bewitched. She said, "They may be for aught I know, I have no hand in it." Grasping at straws, he cried, "You say you are no witch, maybe you mean you never covenanted with the devil. Did you never deal with any familiar?" She denied that she did. He questioned her about her unwillingness to have her husband come for the "former session." He asked yet again, "Did you not say you would open our eyes?" and she laughed again. Perhaps by this time she was herself near-hysterical.

He said, "Is it a laughing matter to see these afflicted persons?"

She denied that she had laughed. Several of the congregation shouted that she had. She cried out again, "Ye are all against me and I cannot help it." Hathorne's next move was to attack her lack of belief in the existence of witches, at least in the neighborhood. It is remarkable that, beset as she was, she did not contradict herself. When he asked, "Do you not believe there are any witches in the country?" she answered, "I do not know that there is any." And when he then asked, "Do you know that Tituba confessed it?" she prevaricated only so far as to say, "I did not hear her speak."

By this time the mood of the crowd was that of a mob bent on lynching. All eyes were directed at Martha with the loathing that turns the flesh and blood of humanity into the substance of evil. The girls' growing power synchronized rhythms of madness. If Martha leaned her breast against the chair used as a bar, they all screamed of pains in their bowels. When Martha bit her lip, they cried out together that they were bitten. If she pinched her fingers or grasped one hand hard in the other, they all screamed that they were pinched.

They must have been biting and pinching themselves. The fascinating question is whether they did so deliberately or, in their frenzy, unawares. We know that Mary Walcott was able and willing to cause herself injury. It may be that one or more ringleaders knew, or half-knew, what they were doing. Even within the behavior of any one girl, as in the practice of clairvoyants and mediums all through the ages, genuine delusion and trickery can exist side by side.

Some of the girls ran to show their bite marks to the magistrates, ministers, and spectators. Robert Calef, a Boston merchant, writes in his 1697 book *More Wonders of the Invisible World,* that sometimes the bites were compared with the teeth that supposedly caused them. Bites and teeth seemed, to what he drily calls "bewitched eyes," to match. He observes that occasionally an accused witch bit the accusers when he or she "had not one [tooth] in his head." Given the absence of dental care and the fact that before long some very old accused witches were examined, it is completely believable that some of the prisoners were toothless.

But if the girls were biting themselves, why did nobody notice them doing so? The answer must be that no one expected to. Any magician or conjurer will attest to the power of prior assumptions. His success largely depends on them. A well-known British magician has described his ability to cause a wound by touching the flesh with a finger. What no one sees, because no one expects to, is a tiny piece of razor blade under his fingernail. The same magician has spoken of making a cigarette roll slowly over a table, without touching it, apparently by using the power of thought. He is in fact blowing. But it occurs to no one to look at his lips.

No doubt a few in the meetinghouse saw what was happening but kept quiet. If they spoke, no one believed them. Except Robert Calef. He says, "Such as had not bewitched eyes have seen the accusers bite themselves." The afflicted girls were not professional magicians, but they had on their side utter credulity, indeed, more than utter credulity, a *wish* to believe that the teeth marks were put there by witches.

The bullying Nicholas Noyes called out, of Martha, "I believe it is apparent she practiseth witchcraft in the congregation."

Mrs. Pope broke the afflicted girls' rhythm. Shouting that her bowels were being torn out of her, she threw her muff at Martha. This was by its nature the closest projectile to hand, but a most ineffective one. It fell short of its target. Mrs. Pope then took off her shoe and threw that, with greater success. The shoe hit Martha on the head. Hathorne seems to have made no objection. All resemblance to an ordinary law court by this time had vanished.

The coordinated rhythms can be heard again when we read that whenever Martha stirred her feet, the afflicted stamped theirs. They asked her why she did not join the meeting of witches in front of the meetinghouse. Did she not hear the drumbeat? They said again they had seen the shape of a black man whispering in her ear and a yellow bird suck between her fingers. Hathorne ordered her to be searched for a sign of this, but the "girl that saw it, said, it was too late now; she [Martha] had removed a pin, and put it on her head; which they found there sticking upright." The pin would have supposedly drawn blood for the yellow bird to suck on. No doubt its true purpose was to keep Martha's hair in place.

So emboldened now as to feel free to make the gravest as well as most far-fetched accusations without fear of reproof, the girls told Martha that she had covenanted with the devil for ten years, six of them gone, four to come. Hathorne asked her to answer the question in the catechism "How many persons be there in the God-Head?" She "answered it but oddly, yet there was no great thing to be gathered from it," Lawson says.

She denied everything she was charged with and, brave and still confident of justice, said they could not prove her a witch. She was sent to Salem prison.

CHAPTER ELEVEN

Secret Enemies

As soon as Martha was led out of the meetinghouse, the whole of Salem Village must have been wondering who would be next. Those on the fringe of events would have assumed that any name at all might be shrieked in the parsonage and then whispered from one farm to another. Neighbor looked at neighbor, wondering if an apparently God-fearing woman, whom she had known all her life, was in league with the devil. Now that a respectable church member had been found guilty, in the villagers' minds though not yet in law, no one was safe from the Evil One's wiles.

No danger is as menacing as the enemy within. The fear of smiling faces masking murderous hearts is colder and deeper than any. It draws its power from the knowledge of our own evil longings.

Samuel Parris was as frightened of falseness as anyone. The danger of treachery is a constant theme of the sermons he preached from the time he arrived in the village. He emphasized that no one can ever fully be trusted; the most apparently innocent may be the very ones plotting evil. One of the most mentioned biblical characters in his sermons is Judas Iscariot.

Parris was paranoid by nature; but, as the joke has it, even paranoids have enemies. Parris certainly did. Many of his references to traitors clearly have a specific local application. His special interest in Judas becomes all the more understandable when he draws implied parallels between Christ and himself as wronged, misunderstood men beset by secret foes. In February 1691, when some villagers were beginning to withhold payment of the ministry tax, he wrote in a sermon, "They gave thirty pieces of silver to be rid of Christ. They would not give half so much for his gracious presence and holy sermons. For idolatry, men will lavish gold out of the bag. They will not do so very rarely for the maintenance of the pure religion."

It is fascinating that the word "omitted" in brackets under this passage shows he never actually delivered it. Confronted by rows of upturned faces, including those of the men he was about to indict, his nerve must have failed him. He resumed reading aloud farther down the page. What he thought he dared say, as he brooded and seethed in his study, proved a delusion in the presence of others.

A further dimension to Parris's constant theme of evil masquerading as good is crucially important to unfolding events. In December 1689, he claimed that the wrongdoings of King Saul sprang from his being "haunted with an evil and wicked spirit" and having gone for advice "to the Devil, to a witch." In January 1690, he said there exists "a lamentable harmony between wicked men and devils, in their opposition of God's kingdom and interests." In Parris's mind, all human evil arises from conscious collaboration with the forces of darkness. The false friends all around us, even if they have not seen him in person or written their names in his book, are servants of Satan. The villagers had been listening to such messages as they sat for long hours in the meetinghouse through the intense heat and cold of three summers and winters.

For Parris, only in the church in the Puritan sense was there any security to be found from the dangers of treachery. Unlike other ministers, who saw the church as a brotherhood of saints living and working within the wider community for the good of all, Parris viewed it as a sort of Noah's Ark of the blessed in a deluge of evil.

"The Church may meet with storms, but it shall never sink. For Christ sits not idle in the heavens, but takes most faithful care of his little ship (the church) bound for the port of heaven, laden with many precious gems and jewels, a treasure purchased by his own inestimable blood," he preached on February 14, 1692. It is characteristic of Parris that his little ship bound for the next world was filled with items highly prized in this. Only five weeks later, a serpent had entered the Ark. Parris's congregation, taught to expect hidden devilry everywhere but here, had no refuge left.

The resulting paranoia is brilliantly captured in Nathaniel Hawthorne's tale *Young Goodman Brown*. As the great-great-grandson of the magistrate, of whom he was so ashamed he changed the name handed down from him by adding a *w*, Hawthorne had a deep understanding of the Puritan mind and what had happened at Salem. He describes Goodman Brown walking through the forest on his way to an infernal assignment:

"He had taken a dreary road, darkened by all the gloomiest trees of the forest, which barely stood aside to let the narrow path creep through, and closed immediately behind. It was all as lonely as could be; and there is this peculiarity in such a solitude, that the traveller knows not who may be concealed by the innumerable trunks and the thick boughs overhead; so that with lonely footsteps he may yet be passing through an unseen multitude."

Young Goodman Brown meets a fellow traveler whose serpentlike staff reveals his identity. On Brown's saying he fears to meet the eye of the Salem Village minister after this escapade, his companion bursts out laughing. He knows the minister much better than Brown does. At the sight of the pious old dame who taught him his catechism, Brown moves away from the path, only to hear her greet his companion and then say, ". . . my broomstick hath strangely disappeared."

Revelation follows revelation. Goodman Brown finally discovers there is no refuge anywhere from evil. The crude simplicity of the manner in which sin is unmasked in the story reflects the historical Salem Villagers' crude, simple outlook. The disingenuousness, low humor, and crude irony that are employed as narrative devices in the gradual revelation that Goodman Brown's companion is the devil and that the most pious in the land are his servants are tones constantly sounded by the afflicted in the examinations of accused witches and in Deodat Lawson's narrative.

"I won't, I won't, I won't take it, I do not know what book it is: I am sure it is none of God's book, it is the Devil's book, for aught I know," shouted Abigail, ostensibly to the shape of Rebecca Nurse, but with a theatricality that shows she instinctively had a corporeal audience in mind. The afflicted sneered at Martha's examination: "Why did Martha Cory not join the company of Witches massing before the Meeting house? Did she not know the Drum beat?" Examples of such rhetoric, full of sarcasm and scorn, multiplied as the examinations continued.

Hawthorne does not *describe* the simple Puritan's mind but lays it open to view. He shows us the buried anger and fear which give rise to theatrical falsity. He shows too the Puritans' apprehension of evil as something unalterable. It does not inhere in mere wicked actions but in an allegiance in the depths of one's soul.

Hawthorne's tale ends on a note of unrelieved darkness. Goodman Brown's life is blighted by his knowledge of evil; his neighbors "carved no hopeful verse upon his tombstone, for his dying hour was gloom." The Puritans lived in the shade of constant awareness of the depths of human wickedness unrelieved by compassion or tolerance.

The Salem villagers near the center of events knew full well which names would be shrieked next at the Putnams' farm or the parsonage. They had already heard two names whispered. Now they waited in terror to see if these two irreproachable women would be hauled before the magistrates.

Four villagers, however, were not content merely to wait, but took

action. They were kinsmen and friends of the seventy-one-year-old Rebecca Nurse. It was she whose name Abigail Williams had called
between running in the fire and throwing firebrands when the unfortunate Deodat Lawson visited the parsonage on the day of his arrival.
The wife of a respectable farmer, Francis Nurse, and by this time a
great-grandmother, she was famed for her piety. No one came closer in
character to the ideal of a Puritan saint.

Rebecca and her husband had risen considerably in the social scale
since his youth in Salem, when he was a mere artisan, and hers in
Topsfield, a township north of Salem Village, as one of eight children.
In 1678 Francis began renting a fine three-hundred-acre village property and a sturdy, good-sized farmhouse. He was lucky: He struck a
deal with the owner whereby he obtained title to the land over time if
he kept up regular payments. It was in effect a mortgage arrangement,
common enough now but uncommon then. Francis and Rebecca and
their many children and grandchildren were hardworking and responsible as well as fortunate: The property became theirs.

Both land and house today appear amazingly unchanged from how
they were in the late 1600s. Sloping fields and meadows offer beautiful
views over a landscape still rural. The house at the top of the highest
hill for miles, with its fair-sized main room with low ceiling, vast fireplace, wooden floors, and stairs to two bedrooms above, is redolent of
peace and plain comfort. The whole estate stands as a testament to the
industry and care that brought the Nurses prosperity.

Some historians have assumed it was that very prosperity, gained
with unusual speed by newcomers of humble origin and connections,
that angered the Putnams and other Salem Villagers and led to Rebecca's being named as a witch. This is part, and a crucially important
part, of the truth. But there were also other sources of enmity.

It is no coincidence that two of the friends of Rebecca who could
not sit idly by, as the rumors about her spread, were leading members
of the Salem Village faction opposed to the Putnams: Israel Porter
(Joseph's brother) and Daniel Andrew. One of the other two was
Israel's wife, Elizabeth. Strangely, she was the sister of John Hathorne,
the magistrate. But it seems her loyalties were not divided on this issue.
She had been married to Israel for twenty years and stood firmly with
him and Rebecca. The fourth visitor was Peter Cloyce, husband of
Rebecca Nurse's sister Sarah.

Francis Nurse, though not a leader of the anti-Putnam faction, was
associated with it. What was more, he had been involved in bitter
boundary disputes with Nathaniel Putnam. And Rebecca's father, Jacob Towne, had been embroiled in similar disputes with earlier
Putnams. Another count against Rebecca was that, years before, her

mother had been named as a witch though never arrested. Witchcraft was thought of as something passed on from mother to child.

One day between March 13, when Ann Putnam claimed to see Rebecca Nurse's specter sitting in her grandmother's chair, and March 23, when the time for warnings was past, the four friends of the old lady ascended the long, curving path through the Nurse property to the fine wooden farmhouse. By now the snow and ice that had covered the landscape would have at least partly melted, showing brown earth and rough grass. The three men and one woman entered through the heavy front door of dark wood, with the odd feature above it of an oblong sundial set in the wall.

Rebecca was upstairs in bed, having been ill for almost a week. But though in a "weak and low condition," she was pleased to see her visitors and managed to sit up and talk to them, according to the report they wrote later, for the court. They asked her how she was, apart from her weakness, and she said she blessed God that she was more aware of His presence in this sickness than she had been in some others. She quoted that she "would with the apostle press forward to the mark" and other lines of scripture. And then, of her own accord, she began to speak on the subject about which they had come. She talked of the "affliction that was amongst them" and in particular of Mr. Parris's family and of her grief for them though she had not been to see them. The reason she gave for not having done so is revealing: it was "by reason for fits that she formerly use to have." Rebecca had the wisdom to know that "fits" can be catching and that, having had them before, she could have them again. She went on, "for people said it was awful to behold." More than most people, she could imagine those fits.

All this suggests a vulnerable personality who has gained stability and control through self-knowledge. Her own childhood may have had its disturbances: Her mother, after all, attracted to herself accusations of witchcraft. Rebecca was not always tranquil. A neighbor, Sarah Holton, claimed that, three years before, Rebecca had shouted furiously at her husband, Benjamin, because his pigs had invaded her field.

"All we could say to her could no way pacify her," said Sarah. "But she continued railing and scolding a great while together, calling to her son Benjamin Nurse to go and get a gun and kill our pigs and let none of them go out of the field." This sounds like a normally well governed character who snapped. Frustrations suppressed over weeks or months erupted in fury at Holton and his pigs. Sarah Holton went on to claim that her husband's death soon afterward was due to Rebecca Nurse's bewitching him.

But when her friends visited her that March day, Rebecca was all peacefulness. She said that she pitied the afflicted with all her heart and "went to God for them." But she had heard there were persons spoken of as witches whom she believed were as innocent as she was.

If she had said this before, and the girls had heard about it, no wonder they turned on her. Her lack of criticism of their slander of the innocent, and her compassion for their suffering, would not lessen their ire and fear, nor those of their parents and guardians. Though a wholly different personality from Martha Cory, with a skepticism wondering and anxious instead of aggressive, she would have appeared no less threatening. In a way, she would have seemed more so, because her standing in the village was higher.

She talked at some length about the innocence of some of those spoken of. Eventually her friends told her she was spoken of too.

"She sat still awhile, being as it were amazed," her friends recounted. "And then she said, 'Well, as to this thing, I am as innocent as the child unborn. But surely, what sin hath God found out in me unrepented of that he should lay such an affliction upon me in my old age.'"

The four friends' narrative was written to be presented in court on Rebecca's behalf. It was composed with the object of impressing its readers with her innocence and piety. Nevertheless it is unlikely seriously to misrepresent Rebecca's words and behavior.

As was intended, but without straining or falseness, it achieves an effect of great poignancy. Everything Rebecca is reported as saying gives evidence of her goodness. She is suffused with the Puritan religious spirit in a gentler form than is usually met with. Especially touching is her willingness to assume that, though "innocent as the child unborn," she herself is responsible for any afflictions in store for her.

Poignant too, in a different way, is the narrative's conclusion. The writers say, "And according to our best observation we could not discern that she knew what we came for before we told her." They have not forgotten the claim by Martha Cory's visitors, less friendly to Martha than Rebecca's to her, that she knew what they came for. And they have not forgotten the use made of this claim by the court. Israel Porter and the others are anxious to point out that Rebecca, unlike Martha, guessed nothing of their purpose. The poignancy lies in their belief that such a point—or any point that anyone could make on a defendant's behalf—might weigh with the court.

Soon after this visit, another visit was paid, also to a sickbed, but the sickness was of a quite different kind. On Wednesday, March 23, Deodat Lawson called at Thomas Putnam's to see his wife. Ann Putnam had been having fits for days, tormented by the biting, pricking, and pinching of witches. She was assailed first by Martha Cory and then, after that torturer was jailed, by Rebecca. Only the day before, "the apparition of Rebecca Nurse did again set upon me in a most dreadful manner very early in the morning as soon as it was well light. And now she appeared to me only in her shift and night cap and brought a little red book in her hand, urging me vehemently to write in her book. And because I would not yield to her hellish temptations she threatened to tear my soul out of my body."

There is something especially bizarre in the notion of the ailing great-grandmother sending out her specter clad, like the flesh-and-blood original lying in her bed, in nightcap and shift. But specters were their originals' doubles even as to clothes.

The torture of Ann Putnam went on all day. It was no doubt because of it that Lawson paid his visit. Ann told him she had had "a sore fit a little before"; was glad to see him; and asked him to pray with her, "while she was sensible," that is, not having fits. He *did* pray, "though the apparition said, I should not." One assumes that Ann reported the apparition's saying this.

Lawson continues, "At the first beginning she attended; but after a little time, was taken with a fit: yet continued silent, and seemed to be asleep: when prayer was done, her husband going to her, found her in a fit: he took her off the bed, to set her on his knees; but at first she was so stiff, she could not be bended; but she afterwards set down; but quickly began to strive violently with her arms and legs; she then began to complain of, and as it were to converse personally with, Goodwife Nurse, saying, 'Goodwife Nurse be gone! Be gone! Be gone! Are you not ashamed, a woman of your profession, to afflict a poor creature so? what hurt did I ever do you in my life! you have but two years to live, and then the devil will torment your soul, for this your name is blotted out of God's book, and shall never be put in God's book again, be gone for shame, are you not afraid of that which is coming upon you? I know, I know, what will make you afraid; the wrath of an angry God, I am sure that will make you afraid; be gone, do not torment me, I know what you would have (we judged she meant, her soul) but it is out of your reach; it is clothed with the white robes of Christ's righteousness.' "

Despite its theatricality, Ann Putnam's speech has a tone of true desperation. Rebecca Nurse filled her with loathing and terror. Boyer and Nissenbaum argue that in Ann's mind Goodwife Nurse represented Mary Veren, the wicked stepmother who had disinherited her husband. But it seems more likely that a combination of simpler causes —Rebecca's ascent in the world, compared with the Putnams' disappointments and diminishment in riches and power, Rebecca's reputation as Puritan perfection, her link by marriage and kinship with those opposed to the Putnams, her mother's reputation for witchcraft —had aroused the disturbed Ann's envy and hatred. However, she could not fully admit such emotions even to herself. They were sinful. So she projected them onto Rebecca, making her as a result a terrifyingly powerful and malevolent witch figure.

A later deposition intriguingly suggests the process by which Goodwife Nurse evolved into Ann Putnam Senior's ghostly torturer. On March 28 John Tarbell, a son-in-law of Rebecca, was at the Putnams' and asked a most pertinent question: whether the twelve-year-old Ann had claimed that Rebecca Nurse afflicted her before other people suggested the name.

Mercy Lewis and Ann Putnam Senior told him that Ann said she saw the apparition of a pale woman sitting in her grandmother's seat. But she did not know who she was. John Tarbell then asked them who first said to Ann that this was Goody Nurse. He writes, "Mercy Lewis said it was Goody Putnam that said it was Goody Nurse; Goody Putnam said it was Mercy Lewis that told her: thus they turned it upon one and other, saying it was you and it was you that told her: this was before any was afflicted at Thomas Putnam's beside his daughter."

The hysterical child saw a vision of a "witch," associated in her mind with her grandmother since she sat in her chair, but as yet without identity. The girl described the figure to her mother and servant and one or both of them said it sounded like Rebecca Nurse. And so it became Rebecca Nurse, in her mind and theirs. Neither Mercy Lewis nor Ann Putnam Senior wanted to take the responsibility for the identification. Mercy may very well have been telling the truth while Ann Putnam was lying. But we can never know for certain.

Once any afflicted girl saw visions of any particular woman, the others saw them too. In the cases of Martha Cory and Rebecca Nurse, Ann Putnam's mother also became haunted. This is less surprising when one realizes it was probably she who first identified the two women's specters. No doubt Ann Putnam Senior had no strong feelings about Tituba, Sarah Good, and Sarah Osborne, did not suggest their names, and did not see visions of them. But she had very strong feelings about the next two accused witches.

As Lawson listened to her outpourings, he saw her mouth drawn on one side and her body strained: She was trying to name a scriptural text; Rebecca was preventing her. At last, after three or four tries, she got the words out: the third chapter of Revelation. Lawson, despite qualms about whether this was the right thing to do in the circumstances, read the text, and as a result Ann Putnam soon recovered. The biblical chapter is a prolonged reproach and warning to various unworthy churches. One verse is especially notable: "Behold, I will make them of the synagogue of Satan, which say they are Jews, and are not, but do lie."

With the moral support of a man of God, reading on her behalf a scriptural indictment of hypocritical enemies, Ann Putnam was for a while at ease. However, the respite did not last. Later that day the magistrates issued a summons for Rebecca Nurse's arrest on the complaint of Edward Putnam and Jonathan Putnam. Next morning the old lady, still weak from her illness, was roused before daybreak by the marshal and brought to Ingersoll's tavern by eight. At ten she was led before the magistrates.

Mrs. Ann Putnam was seated in her pew. The Reverend John Hale said a prayer. Rebecca was brought forward to be questioned and, together with the rest of the afflicted, Ann Putnam Senior began writhing, choking, and screaming. Soon Rebecca's examination became even more frenzied than Martha Cory's had been. Hathorne asked his usual questions to the customary background of screeching and bodily contortions, often in response to Rebecca's movements of body or hands, which the girls claimed caused them to be pinched or otherwise tortured. Parris added at the end of his record that because of the great noise of the afflicted and other speakers, much that was said and done had to be omitted.

Rebecca insisted, over and over, that she was innocent. At one point she mentioned that she had not been able to get out of doors "these eight or nine days." She had not yet gathered that her specter might be out and about doing harm while she was at home. When asked if the girls suffered voluntarily or involuntarily, she said she could not tell. Hathorne made the point that if they were shamming, she must look on them as murderers, for witchcraft carried the death penalty.

This remark gives us an interesting insight into his reasoning, which carries considerable force. The girls, if they were consciously play-acting, were utterly ruthless. It was impossible for Hathorne to believe that these children, born into Puritan families, were not purely good but, literally, devilish. That their consciences and humanity could have been eroded by the conditions they lived in, to collapse in group madness, was not something he knew.

But Rebecca, conscious of her own innocence and having herself experienced fits, had more insight, though she could not put it clearly into words. She said, at first, "I cannot tell what to think of it." When pressed, she said, "I do not think these suffer against their wills." But, later, she agreed that they were bewitched. She apprehended, however uncertainly, that the girls were colluding with whatever it was that possessed them, that they were suffering involuntarily and yet, in a sense, *not* against their wills.

Meanwhile, Mary Walcott, so experienced at biting, had produced "the marks of teeth on her wrist." Others, too, were bitten, pinched, and bruised. When Rebecca leaned forward against the chair that served as a bar, the girls' breasts hurt. When she leaned back, the girls too leaned back, but so far that it seemed as though their backs had been broken. When Rebecca held her neck to one side, Elizabeth Hubbard had her neck stuck in the same position and Abigail Williams cried out in terror, "Set up Goody Nurse's head, the maid's neck will be broke." Rough hands jerked Rebecca's head upright and Elizabeth's head at once went upright too.

The girls said the black man was whispering in Rebecca's ear, which was why she could not hear the magistrates, and then they said they saw Rebecca's shape riding past the meetinghouse behind that same black man. Ann Putnam Senior cried out—for once to the corporeal Rebecca and not just her shape—"Did you not bring the black man with you, did you not bid me tempt God and die—how oft have you ate and drunk your own damnation." She had so grievous a fit, "to the very great impairing of her strength, and wasting of her spirits, insomuch as she could hardly move hand, or foot," that the magistrates gave her husband permission to carry her out of the meetinghouse.

It was then that Deodat Lawson, having sat in on the examination for a while and then left to attend to other matters—perhaps the sermon he was to deliver later that day—was walking, at a distance from the building, when he heard a screech and noise that amazed him. The proceedings had reached a pitch at which "the whole assembly were struck with consternation and were afraid that those who sat next to them were under the influence of witchcraft." People glanced in terror from side to side, at the neighbors they had known all their lives, wondering who else was possessed. The devil was everywhere: in outcasts and church members, poor and prosperous, old and young.

The last they knew for certain. Rebecca was not examined alone. In the meetinghouse with her, having been arrested that morning on suspicion of witchcraft, was Sarah Good's daughter Dorcas. She was questioned either just before or just after Rebecca. When she cast her eye on the afflicted, they were tormented. Her shape bit them; they showed the magistrates the bite marks.

Two days later, in her cell, Dorcas told Hathorne and Jonathan Corwin and John Higginson, the Salem minister, that she had "a little snake that sucked on the lowest joint of her forefinger." She pointed to the place, where there was a deep red spot about the size of a flea bite. They asked who gave her that snake. Was it the black man? She said, no, it was her mother.

It is not surprising that her mother should still be her mentor. Dorcas was four and a half.

At the end of the examination Hathorne asked Parris to read aloud his report of Ann Putnam's accusations of Rebecca.

"What do you think of this?" Hathorne asked.

Rebecca replied, "The devil may appear in my shape." It was a pertinent remark, for the first time raising the notion that the specters seen by the girls, and tormenting them, might be sent by the devil without the originals' knowledge. Hathorne's response was to send Rebecca, and Dorcas, to Salem prison.

CHAPTER TWELVE

Diabolical Malice

THE jails in Ipswich, Salem, and Boston, among which the accused witches were dispersed, were places not just of privation but of horror. They must have seemed to their prisoners indistinguishable from the last destination of sinners. As the most dangerous inmates, the witches were kept in the dungeons. These were perpetually dark, bitterly cold, and so damp that water ran down the walls. They reeked of unwashed human bodies and excrement. They enclosed as much agony as anywhere human beings have lived.

The stone dungeons of the Salem Town prison were discovered in the 1950s in St. Peter Street when the site was excavated to build a New England Telephone Company building. In 1692 they stood under a wooden structure, twenty feet square, known as the "witch jail." Since they were so close to the banks of a tidal river, they were probably infested with water rats. Certainly they were a breeding ground for disease.

All prisoners endured huge physical suffering. They were kept hungry and thirsty and in winter desperately cold. But accused witches were worse off than the other unfortunates. Their limbs were weighed down and their movements restricted by manacles chained to the walls, so that their specters could less easily escape to wreak havoc. They were treated by wardens and visitors with deliberate cruelty, fair game for sadism since they were enemies of God and mankind. Body searches for "witches' teats" afforded ample opportunities for rough treatment. Such teats, supposedly nipples for familiars to suck on, consisted of any mole, wart, pimple, or growth that could be considered unnatural. Much of the searching was in and around the accused witch's genitals. Eventually many of the accused were tortured, by an assortment of methods, to elicit confessions.

These wretches' only comfort, if comfort it was, was each other's company. Normally several prisoners would be locked up together, though on occasion someone was confined alone to a cell so tiny as to allow inadequate space to lie or even sit down. Of course, company was sometimes not comfort but additional torture. This must have been so in the jail in Boston: Tituba, Sarah Osborne, and Sarah Good could scarcely have afforded each other much solace. Sarah Osborne, bedridden before she was jailed, must have suffered past imagining. She died, still in jail, two months later.

As unimaginable as Sarah Osborne's anguish are Dorcas Good's terror and bewilderment when she was taken from Salem to join the other three. Deodat Lawson said that when he saw her at Ingersoll's tavern, before her examination, she looked as "hale and well as other children." Two weeks later she was removed from Salem jail, no doubt already thinner, larger-eyed, more frightened, and altogether less hale and well, to travel all day by horseback, behind the constable on a pillion, and be sent underground once again into darkness and cold. In this new hell was a new horror that surpassed every other. She was loaded with irons and chained to a wall. Though it is impossible to imagine her feelings, it is all too easy to imagine her screams.

No doubt, even in her first agony she was, at best, largely ignored by the adults around her. Distraught prisoners and cruel wardens lack the motive or impulse to care for a child. It is unlikely that even her mother had much love left to give her. A new baby she had brought into prison had already died or was dying.

Dorcas was to spend many months without seeing the light of the sun, unable to run or walk and with nothing to play with but the rags she was wearing. The little fingers that picked at and twisted and folded the torn, filthy cloth were the only part of her being she could move without hindrance or pain. At first she may have shouted and wept. Perhaps she banged her head on the wall she was chained to. But, like all small children without care, stimulation, or love, in the end she went silent, rocking to and fro, as far as her chains would allow, or lying still, staring blankly.

Eighteen years later her father, William Good, was to write that "she was in prison seven or eight months and being chained in the dungeon was so hardly used and terrified that she hath ever since been very chargeable, having little or no reason to govern herself. By "very chargeable" he meant a financial burden: When she came out and for the rest of her days, he had to pay a keeper to care for her.

How could it happen? How could God-fearing, law-abiding citizens send a four-year-old into hell? Charles Upham argues that "the managers" of the witch-hunt, by whom he means Samuel Parris, Thomas Putnam, and perhaps Edward Putnam, Jonathan Putnam, and Dr. Griggs, wanted to "utterly overwhelm the influence of all natural sentiment in the community" by proceeding against a little child as well as a "venerable and infirm great-grandmother." This theory has the

merit of providing a rational, if evil, motive for Dorcas Good's imprisonment. But it strains our credulity. The evidence is lacking. It appears
far more probable that the girls called Dorcas's name without prompt-
ing. Dorcas, as the child of a witch, was automatically under suspicion
herself, despite her young age. She must have accompanied her
mother on her begging expeditions; she may have copied her irascible
words and behavior. She was very likely transformed in the girls' minds
to a little creature of pure malevolence. They may have seen in her
sharp, hungry looks and heard in her muttering a frightening mirror
of their own angry need. They would have longed to smash such a
mirror. But they may also have seen in her running and skipping, her
clinging to her mother's long skirts, her weeping and laughing, the
enviable freedom of behavior accorded, even by the Puritans, to very
early childhood. Dorcas was at the age of some of their siblings who
were still allowed to play, to display hurt and fear and warm love.
Murderous feelings toward those brothers and sisters may have focused
on this little outcast.

In certain social and psychological conditions all empathy is destroyed and there is only a furious desire to hurt, even kill. In naming
Dorcas, and the other accused witches, the afflicted girls indulged to
the full those impulses that are more often overt in the furious young
—children and adolescents who have been overcontrolled or unloved
or otherwise made to feel worthless—than in their more socialized
elders. Adults find excuses for cruelty. When they kill there is almost
always a motive. Committers of sex crimes find rationalizations. Even
madmen hear voices telling them that their victims are evil. When
children kill, as in the recent case in Liverpool, England, in which two
ten-year-olds murdered the toddler James Bulger, there is often no
motive, just unrationalized fury and pain.

We cannot know whether the furious children of Salem believed the
available excuse for sending people to their deaths. Without question
the adults did. As a pretext for cruelty, witchcraft is perfect. The witch
is the embodiment of evil and her destruction is not just laudable
but necessary. For the destroyer, terrified of his own evil impulses, the
satisfaction is twofold. The impulse to hurt and destroy is assuaged.
At the same time the wickedness inside himself is projected onto
the witch and eliminated. Through the mouths of their wild, merciless
children the people of Salem guiltlessly condemned those they wished
to see dead.

No doubt the adult Putnams and others had no special desire that
Dorcas should suffer. They did not rejoice in her agony as they almost
certainly did rejoice, however secretly, in that of Martha Cory and
Rebecca Nurse. But their satisfaction in the witch-hunt made them

indifferent to Dorcas's pain. The same seems to have been true of the rest of the populace; no protests were made on the child's behalf. Of course, Dorcas was the daughter of an outcast. Had she been the child of a respectable family, she might have had relations to speak for her.

The Salem witch-hunt, like all witch-hunts, was conducted not by an individual acting alone but by a group. All types of groups are capable of behaving in ways that would shock the consciences of their individual members. But those that espouse a morality of censure and blame rather than compassion and empathy are utterly merciless toward objects of hatred. The more a group idealizes itself, its own values, and its God, the more it persecutes both other groups and the dissenters in its midst. In doing so it protects those it prizes from any aggression they arouse by deflecting it.

The "afflicted girls" and Puritan society were both groups espousing a morality of censure and blame to as great a degree as any fanatical nation or sect in world history. In their witch-hunt, as in all witch-hunts, the destructive rage of certain individuals was complemented by the compliance of the rest of the community. Thus cruelty was countenanced that seems beyond what should be humanly possible.

It must have been in a mood of somber relief, close to restrained exhilaration, that the congregation trooped out of the meetinghouse after Rebecca and Dorcas were led to the dungeons. Over cider and cakes at Ingersoll's tavern, each individual's conviction that the great-grandmother and the child were servants of Satan merged in consensus. Men and women swapped memories of Benjamin Holton's demise after Rebecca chastised him for losing control of his pigs and of Dorcas's wicked looks and strange ways.

After two hours everyone moved back down the road and reentered the meetinghouse. As they settled into their pews, the atmosphere was calmer than it had been in that place for some time, though full of expectancy. Deodat Lawson mounted the pulpit, said a prayer, and read out his text. It began: "And the Lord said unto Satan, the Lord rebuke thee, O Satan. . . ." The congregation were about to enjoy the stimulating yet soothing activity of listening to a sermon that would clarify their thoughts while confirming their opinions.

Lawson began by reminding them of Satan's history as a mutinous angel and his aim of destroying mankind. Summarizing part of Zechariah, he said that Christ fought Satan on behalf of Joshua, whom Satan despised "by reason of his filthy garments." Christ rebuked Satan but took his censure to heart, giving Joshua a "change of raiment."

It is hard to imagine the youthful members of a present-day congregation keeping a straight face at this tale of Satan's snobbish contempt for Joshua's wardrobe and Christ's acting as a valet. However, there is no evidence of the existence of humor in Salem. Besides, the merging of the concrete, everyday world and the supernatural, found in this passage, was commonplace, not bizarre, to the Puritans. Satan and Christ were for them visible persons as well as mystical entities. The natural and supernatural in their eyes were essentially one. Presumably nobody smiled.

Lawson went on to give numerous other, more drastic examples of Satan's malignity. He stressed that the Evil One attacks people's souls *and* their bodies. Revealing his hidden agenda, he slipped a crucial message into his catalogue of Satan's evil ways, claiming that local examples of devilish attacks were clearly the "effects of diabolical malice and operations and . . . cannot rationally be imagined to proceed from any other cause whatsoever." He talked of the deep humiliation of "visible members of this church [being] under the awful accusations, and imputations, of being the instruments of Satan."

He also warned against giving way to envy, malice, and hatred of neighbors and of the danger of rashly censuring others or making false accusations. However, he went on to advise of the wrongfulness of bearing a grudge against those who unwittingly made such false accusations. He spoke against superstitious means of finding out witches or guarding against their activities. But he exhorted the congregation to "arm, arm, arm" against Satan, that by "the shield of faith, ye and we all may resist the fiery darts of the wicked."

Later Lawson was to dedicate the printed version of his sermon to the magistrates Bartholomew Gedney, John Hathorne, and Jonathan Corwin and the Salem ministers John Higginson and Nicholas Noyes. But it seems from the text as a whole that, though Lawson was following the Parris/Putnam line, he was not merely performing to order. No doubt he sincerely believed all or most of what he was saying and felt he was doing his duty in saying it. As a minister, he instinctively favored a view that ascribed fits and visions, instead of to mere human delinquency, to the supernatural forces he was paid to explain to the populace.

He may have hoped to promote his career, gaining greater fame and respect, by associating himself with the witch finders. This proved a wrong judgment. Eventually he went back to England, his career not aided but blighted. He ended as an ignominious failure, reduced to sending letters to friends begging for food, clothes, and fuel for his destitute family. He is referred to in passing by an associate, without amplification, as "the unhappy Deodat Lawson." This unfortunate, if well-meaning, dupe of Parris and the Putnams lacked even the consolation of knowing that his "brief and true narrative" would make his name live in history.

It is observable in the modern-day witch-hunt that therapists often argue that child sex abuse actually happened when there seems ample cause to suspect it the product of fantasy. Those therapists, as they promote prosecutions, do not seem to have any particular animus toward the accused but, directly and indirectly, merely to be furthering their professional interests.

Lawson was well aware, when giving his sermon, that not everyone in Salem Village found it as impossible as he did to imagine that the torments of the afflicted proceeded from "any other cause" but the devil. Otherwise he would not have made his claims with such stridency. The undercurrent of skepticism that had been there from the start in Salem Village was growing stronger. It had swelled with the accusations against the two respected church members Martha Cory and Rebecca Nurse. Joseph Putnam had told his estranged half-brothers that he had a gun loaded and a horse saddled in case the marshal came to arrest him. He had no doubt of the political direction the witch-hunt was taking and assumed himself a prime target. As it happens, he was never named. This may have been because he, together with his friend and father-in-law Israel Porter, was too respected and powerful a local figure.

Rebecca Nurse's friends and relations, including Israel, were soon to mount a petition in her favor. It was to be signed by thirty-nine people, including the Sarah Holton who had accused her of bewitching her husband. Knowing Rebecca was in jail and might hang must have made her think twice.

The day after Lawson's sermon, equally serious doubts were far more violently expressed by someone who should have known better, from the point of view of his personal safety. John Proctor, the successful farmer, entrepreneur, and tavern keeper, meeting Samuel Sibley on the road to Salem Village from his house on the edge of the town, said he had allowed his "jade," that is, servant, Mary Warren, to go to the village the day before to attend Rebecca Nurse's examination as one of the afflicted girls. Now he very much wished he had not. He continued by saying that if the girls were left to their own devices, "we should all be devils and witches quickly" and suggested they ought to be whipped. He was going to bring his maid home to "thrash the devil out of her." He had threatened to thrash her when she had first been taken with fits and had kept her "close to her spinning wheel." As a result she had had no more fits till the next day when he was away, "and then she must have her fits again forsooth." He cried, of the afflicted girls, "Hang them! Hang them!"

John Proctor was to rue his rash words. The witch-hunt, whatever else it was, was becoming, ever more inexorably, a battle of wills.

CHAPTER THIRTEEN

One of You Is a Devil

MERCY Lewis, the Putnams' servant, was tortured by Elizabeth Proctor the very next day. That is, Elizabeth's specter supposedly bit and pinched her and urged her to write in her book. But it was not till ten days later that a complaint was filed against Elizabeth, coupled with another complaint against another skeptic about witches, Sarah Cloyce, Rebecca Nurse's sister.

The Sunday after Nurse's examination and Lawson's sermon, Parris delivered his own sermon on the topic on everyone's mind. Its menacing title was "Christ Knows How Many Devils There Are in His Churches, and Who They Are." The text, John 6:70, was "Have I not chosen you twelve, and one of you is a devil."

As soon as Parris declaimed these words from the pulpit, Sarah Cloyce marched out of the meetinghouse, slamming the door. Her reason was obvious to everyone. Her sister, a church member, was in prison, accused of worshiping the devil. Samuel Parris intended to preach a sermon warning that there were church members who, though they seemed irreproachable, were devil worshipers.

The sermon was fully as incendiary as Sarah Cloyce anticipated. There is nothing worse than a church member who is a devil, Parris keeps saying in several different ways. They are "sons and heirs of the devil, the free-holders of hell; whereas other sinners are but tenants." He also declares that Satan would represent the best saints as devils if he could, but it is not easy to imagine that his power is of such an extent. If it were, it would jeopardize the church. Parris in effect rules out any possibility that Martha Cory and Rebecca Nurse might be innocent.

"Oh it is a dreadful thing to be a devil, and yet to sit down at the Lord's table," he declaims. In his paranoia, he makes no distinction between devils in the correct sense of supernatural beings and in the incorrect one of people who are evil. At the beginning of his sermon, he justifies the lax usage by claiming that Christ called Judas a devil. But his obsessive use of the word from then on to mean sinful human beings displays deep personal terror. It comes as no surprise to discover that one of Parris's sons by his second wife went mad. Parris also makes no distinction between those wrongdoers who merely sin and those who are allies of Satan, having put their names in his book. In Parris's mind the line between the two was invisible.

The afflicted girls lost no time in pointing the finger at the mutinous Sarah. While having fits a day or two later in the parsonage, they saw her standing in the field in front of the house in a company of witches who ate bread and drank blood in a parody of the sacrament. Carrying the notion of a devil's church even further, they claimed that Cloyce and Good acted as deacons.

"Oh Goodwife Cloyce, I did not think to see you here!" shouted one of them, in that tone of histrionic derision that was becoming so gratingly familiar. "Is this a time to receive the sacrament? You ran away on the Lord's day, and scorned to receive it in the meetinghouse, and is this a time to receive it? I wonder at you!"

How often must the girls themselves have been chastised in such tones. "I wonder at you!" was no doubt continually on the lips of their mothers, aunts, and stepmothers.

It seems surprising that the marshal was not on Goody Cloyce's doorstep as fast as he could get there. The delay appears to have been due to the swelling wave of skepticism and the Putnams' consequent need to take care. On Monday, March 28, John Tarbell was at the Putnam farm, suspiciously questioning Ann Senior and Mercy Lewis as to which of them first made the identification of a specter, seen by Ann Junior, as that of Rebecca Nurse. The next day it was the turn of another villager, Samuel Barton, to visit the family and as a result find himself harboring doubts about the afflicted girls' integrity. He was "helping to tend the afflicted folks" when he "heard them tell Mercy Lewis that she cried out of Goody Proctor." By "them" he means the Putnams and by "cried out of" he means "named." Mercy Lewis denied she had done any such thing. But Thomas Putnam, his wife, and others kept insisting that Mercy had called Proctor's name; eventually she said "if she did, it was when she was out [of] her head for she saw nobody." Mercy was supposed to have seen Elizabeth bite and pinch her three days earlier. Presumably she had to be made to believe this before it was safe to proceed with Proctor's arrest.

But something else happened that was even more chilling than this. Chilling, that is, from the point of view of what went on in the minds of the girls. Heartening, in terms of hope for the eventual end of the delusion.

This incident also took place on Monday, March 28. Two young men, William Rayment and Daniel Elliot, were at Ingersoll's tavern at the same time as several of the afflicted girls. Rayment, finding himself in this company and hoping for firsthand information, said he had heard that Goody Proctor was to be examined the next day. It was Goody Ingersoll, the tavern keeper's wife, who replied. She was the motherly woman who had tried to restrain Abigail from throwing herself in the fire during Deodat Lawson's visit to the parsonage. She said she did not believe that Goody Proctor was to be examined on the morrow since she had heard nothing of it. At this one of the girls cried out, "There is Goody Proctor, there is Goody Proctor, old witch, I'll have her hang." The others joined in. But it seems that the girl neglected to work herself into a fit to give the words authority. William Rayment said he did not believe her; he could see nothing. Goody Ingersoll sharply reproved the girl. There was nothing there, she said; the girl was lying. In this calm atmosphere, instead of the usual fevered one of the meetinghouse or parsonage, all three observers for once believed the evidence of their eyes instead of the girls' bizarre claims.

Unable to keep up their pretense in the face of such skepticism, the girls made jest of it. One of them said that she did it "for sport, they must have some sport."

No wonder, instead of pressing for arrests and examinations, Parris declared a day of public fasting for the following Thursday. This indicated to those doubting his motives that he was willing to try other means of dealing with the crisis than accusations and imprisonment. It also gave the accusers a chance to regain credibility. The girls, joined by Tituba's husband, John Indian, who felt it was preferable to become one of the afflicted than to suffer the fate of his wife, saw visions of Proctor and Cloyce all through the first part of April, until the eleventh, when the two women were examined.

One of the men who filed the complaint against Elizabeth and Sarah was Nathaniel Ingersoll. The other was his nephew, Thomas Putnam's brother-in-law Jonathan Walcott. Either Ingersoll's wife told her husband nothing of what had happened in the tavern or, more probably, they both believed that the girls were for the most part sincere, shamming only that once. Of course, Nathaniel Ingersoll may have been cynically uncaring as to whether the girls were shamming or not, whatever his wife might think.

Ingersoll was a boyhood friend of John Putnam Senior, the uncle of Jonathan Walcott, a lieutenant in the local militia, and a deacon in the church. His name was on three of the witchcraft complaints. He was a key member of the village elite, led by the Putnams, and a supporter of Parris. That does not necessarily mean he was unscrupulous. He was so highly respected in the community as often to be called on to settle disputes. But he had every motive not to concern himself too closely with the girls' integrity or lack of it.

However, whatever he or anyone else in Salem Village might believe, no doubt there was in fact a distinction between the visions the girls thought they saw, when they worked themselves up to perform, and a barefaced lie told when they had nothing better to do with their time and felt "they must have some sport."

They did not fail to work themselves up for the examination of the eleventh. Indeed, they treated their audience to frenzies as spectacular as anything yet. On this occasion they were not giving just a local performance; Cloyce and Proctor's examination was held in Salem Town. The witch-hunt was no longer a mere Salem Village matter; it was beginning to terrify the whole of New England.

Presiding at the meetinghouse situated in the center of town on the corner of Main and Washington Streets, opposite John Hathorne's large residence, was no less powerful a figure than Thomas Danforth, the deputy governor. Also present were several members of the colony's government, including the minister Samuel Sewall of Boston, later famed as a diarist. He is thought of as a humane, reasonable man, and so he was, by Puritan standards. But he regularly reduced his small children to tears by reminding them of death and eternity. And he writes in his diary constantly, with horror, of "periwigs," regarding them as an abhorrent invention worn only by scoundrels and fools. This preoccupation suggests serious intellectual limits. What is certain is that he possessed insufficient humanity and reason to question the proceedings of the examinations or to prevent him from acting as a judge at the trials.

John Hathorne and Jonathan Corwin were naturally present in the meetinghouse. Many Salem Villagers traveled to the examination along with the accused and the afflicted, including Samuel Parris, again the official recorder. Salem Town emptied itself into the remaining galleries and pews.

If the governor, Simon Bradstreet, had been less old and infirm, events might not have taken the course they did. Bradstreet was of a moderate, equable temperament, less fanatical than many younger Puritans. He had been born in England and was the husband of the poet Anne Bradstreet, who paid the most moving tributes in her verses to his kindness, gentleness, and love. But he was now eighty-seven and Danforth, a very different personality, was effectively in charge of the colony. Danforth's turning the mere pretrial examination into a major Massachusetts event fatally upgraded the witch-hunt. It gave the girls and their allies even greater authority and the process of arrests and examinations a new, unstoppable impetus.

It was Danforth himself who asked the questions. Since he was as firm a believer in the guilt of the accused as John Hathorne, his line of inquiry differed from the magistrate's only in that it was directed as much at the afflicted girls as at the accused witches. But this was merely to establish the dreadful things done to them, and by whom, not to probe their mental competence or integrity. Those were never in question. He asked John Indian, Mary Walcott, and Abigail Williams, in turn, who had hurt them. Some of the questions make clear he already knew the answers.

"Abigail Williams! did you see a company at Mr. Parris' house eat and drink?"

"Yes, sir, that was their sacrament."

"How many were there?"

"About forty, and Goody Cloyce and Goody Good were our deacons."

Danforth asked Mary Walcott if she had seen a "white man." She replied that she had, and he was "a fine grave man, and when he came, he made all the witches to tremble." Presumably the "white man" was meant to be Christ.

Mary Walcott was not the only girl to have seen him. Deodat Lawson wrote that on the first of April Mercy Lewis saw "a white man and was with him in a glorious place, which had no candles nor sun, yet was full of light and brightness; where there was a great multitude in white glittering robes." She was reluctant to leave this "glorious place." Some of the other girls had seen the white man too, he said. These sights suggest longings in the girls' psyches that were the other side of the coin from the desire to torture and kill. They reveal yearnings for ecstasy and peace.

All the girls were on the verge of or well into adolescence. There were, in that time and place, no opportunities for sexual exploration outside marriage without whipping in this world and hellfire in the next. Even sexual yearnings were sinful, to be repressed or converted to something more acceptable, such as visions of angels.

But the girls' secret longings may not have been only sexual. In their fantasies of being pinched, pricked, and choked, they displayed the rage of a baby in pain. In their visions of heaven they glimpsed the loved baby's bliss when held close at the breast in the arms of her mother. Puritan mothers breastfed their babies for up to two years. When the next infant arrived, the suckling was set on its feet to take its first steps on the arduous road to self-discipline. The transition was sudden and brutal; the children who had suffered it must surely have retained secret rages and longings. Of course, such psychological speculation can only ever remain speculation. But attempts to understand emotional disturbance must embrace early as well as later experiences. Among multiple causes of hidden fury and longing, profound loss in the earliest years may be among the most fundamental.

Danforth did not pursue the subject of the "white man." If he had, the course of events might have changed. Boyer and Nissenbaum point out that, if the adults around the afflicted girls had shown more interest in their visions of Christ and his angels and less in their sightings of witches and devils, they might have caused them to instigate not a witch-hunt but a religious revival. Only forty years later, in Northampton, Massachusetts, a group of young people suffered torments similar to those of the afflicted in Salem. But the minister and townspeople chose to regard these as a "remarkable pouring out of the spirit of God" and the result was the "Little Awakening," the precursor of the "Great Awakening," the evangelical movement that swept the North American colonies from the late 1730s to the 1760s.

However, Danforth's main interest, like Cotton Mather's and Parris's and the elder Putnams', was not the glorious light of the world beyond but its darkness. He next asked who was present at a gathering of witches described by Abigail Williams at Nathaniel Ingersoll's. Abigail replied, "Goody Cloyce, Goody Nurse, Goody Cory and Goody Good," which not surprisingly caused Cloyce to ask for water and faint. This sent the girls into fits. With the ingenuity of turning any event to their purposes, which they displayed ever more frequently as the examinations went on, they called out that Goody Cloyce's spirit had joined Sarah Good in prison.

Danforth asked all the girls in turn if Elizabeth Proctor hurt them, but none of them at that moment was able to speak. Abigail had her hand thrust in her mouth. As Elizabeth looked at them, they went into fits. But when they regained the use of their vocal chords, they accused her of all the usual witches' activities. It appears that Goody Proctor was of as truly saintly a nature as Arthur Miller portrays her in *The Crucible*. As those who have seen or read the play will remember, the Proctors and Abigail are the main characters—John the tragic hero, Elizabeth his long-suffering wife, and Abigail, six years older in the play than in reality, John's ex-mistress. She wants to see Elizabeth hanged so John can be hers. There is no historical evidence that Proctor even knew eleven-year-old Abigail. Miller has invented a love triangle with no basis in fact. But the characters of John as well as Elizabeth Proctor in the play are firmly based on those of the people whose words we read in the records. When (in history, not *The Crucible*) Abigail accused Elizabeth of trying to make her sign the devil's book and of telling her that her maid, Mary Warren, had already signed it. Elizabeth said, "Dear child, it is not so. There is another judgement, dear child." She was gently reminding Abigail of the eventual judgment of heaven. Perhaps she saw that, with whatever willful self-delusion and even wickedness Abigail behaved, she was a young child, led horribly astray and to be pitied, not blamed.

Abigail's response to this kindness was to cry out that Goody Proctor (that is, her shape) was sitting on a beam. A moment later she and the rest accused John Proctor, too, of afflicting them and of being a wizard. Proctor, who had come to the meetinghouse to be with his wife in her ordeal, may well at this accusation have lost his last shred of self-control, perhaps shouting again that the girls should be hanged.

From this point the examination went wild. Mrs. Pope, previously given to throwing things, now fell over backward, since her feet were "taken up" by John Proctor, or rather his phantom. Abigail Williams several times cried out that John Proctor was about to afflict someone. In turn, Mrs. Pope, Goodwife Bibber, Mary Walcott, then "divers others" at the sound of their names went into fits. Abigail touched Proctor's head and then screamed that her fingers were burning. The only quiet one of the afflicted girls was Elizabeth Hubbard, who lay, throughout the proceedings, in a trance.

There was a further examination the next day during which Mary Walcott sat quietly knitting, occasionally confirming statements such as that Goodman Proctor was sitting in the magistrate's lap. That afternoon both Proctors and Sarah Cloyce were sent to Boston jail. Rebecca Nurse and Dorcas Good were brought to join them from the prison in Salem.

CHAPTER FOURTEEN

Apparitions of a Hundred Persons

A$_T$ this point in the story the records yield a fascinating new clue as to the afflicted girls' states of mind. So far they have suggested a mixture of hysteria, vengeful fury, evil mischief, and longing. They have revealed variations of character. Abigail Williams and Ann Putnam Junior, though capable of intentional lying, seem the most frenzied, the most consistently hysterical. But Ann Putnam also appears the most quick-witted and resourceful. Both girls, of course, lived in the families most closely involved in the witch-hunt. Ann's mother had, for the time being, ceased having fits, playing no part in pointing the finger at Sarah Cloyce or the Proctors. But her tendency to paranoia and delusion had in no way abated. She was to claim, later that spring, that Rebecca Nurse had murdered several children. The extent of her husband's enthusiasm for the witch-hunt is shown by the fact that he made more complaints against possible witches than any other person: ten in all. Thomas may well have been pressuring his daughter to make accusations and see them through to conviction. Twelve-year-old Ann may have been afraid for her own welfare if any of the accused witches were freed. Abigail, of course, was under the care of the fanatical Parris and a weak, ailing aunt. One slave in the household had been taken to prison; the other had become one of the afflicted and was often in fits. In both families normal activities, including regular meals, must have been sadly neglected.

Mary Walcott appears to have been the calmest of the girls, but her calm seems that of a psychopath. She quietly got on with her knitting throughout the second examination of the Proctors despite seeing their shapes. The record comments several times on her composure. Her proficiency at biting herself when required also argues deep mental disturbance. She saw visions, including that of the "white man." But she was also capable of committing cold-blooded fraud. During one of the examinations a "young woman" was afflicted by a specter wrapped in a white sheet. Her father "being by her" tried to take hold of it and, as the specter passed away, violently twitched his

hand. In its grasp was displayed the sheet's torn-off corner. Deodat
Lawson, who gives us this account, does not name the young woman or
the father, but they seem likely to have been Mary and Jonathan
Walcott. The only other possible father-daughter conjuring team in the
witch-hunt were Thomas and Ann Putnam, and twelve-year-old Ann is
unlikely to have been referred to as "a young woman." Jonathan
Walcott was Thomas Putnam's brother-in-law and was assiduous
enough in the prosecution of witches to make three complaints. That
no one in the meetinghouse openly wondered whether the man had
brought the piece of sheet in with him shows the hold the girls and
their allies had on the crowd.

Mercy Lewis was full of unsatisfied longings. They may have been
the cause of her going astray: Some years later she gave birth to an
illegitimate baby. Any happiness she had known had been destroyed
three years before the witchcraft hysteria began, when she was fourteen and her parents were murdered by Indians. She was rescued by
George Burroughs and his family in Casco, placed in a household in
Salem, and finally taken as a servant by the Putnams. Since her own
family was socially inferior to her new employers, in a highly class-
conscious society, she may have felt not only unloved but despised. It
seems scarcely a surprise that she "grieved that she could tarry no
longer" in the "glorious place . . . full of light and brightness" that
she saw in a vision. In the examinations and when having fits at the
Putnams', she appears mainly to have been led by the others.

Elizabeth Hubbard was less badly off than Mercy Lewis. Though a
servant, she at least served members of her own family, her uncle and
aunt. And as a doctor her uncle was a man of considerable standing.
But she too was without parents and must have felt very alone in the
world. A deposition shows that she was either deeply deluded or full of
black mischief. She was riding home from the meetinghouse on the
pillion of a man named Clement Coldum when she urged him to ride
faster. He asked why. She said "because the woods were full of devils."
Further on she said he could slow down now since they had outridden
them. He asked if she was not afraid of the devil and she said no, she
could speak with the devil "as well as with him." She is also notable for
remaining in a trance for an unusually long time: the whole of the
Proctors' examination.

One of the witch-hunt's severest contemporary critics, the Boston
merchant Robert Calef, wrote in 1697 that the afflicted girls were "vile
varlets" guilty of whoredom and incest before the witch-hunt as well as
after. He was scarcely an impartial observer, but his remark is intriguing. Since he says elsewhere that Abigail and Betty and the "one or two
more of the neighbourhood" who first had fits "had been well edu-

Cotton Mather

Samuel Parris

Samuel Sewall

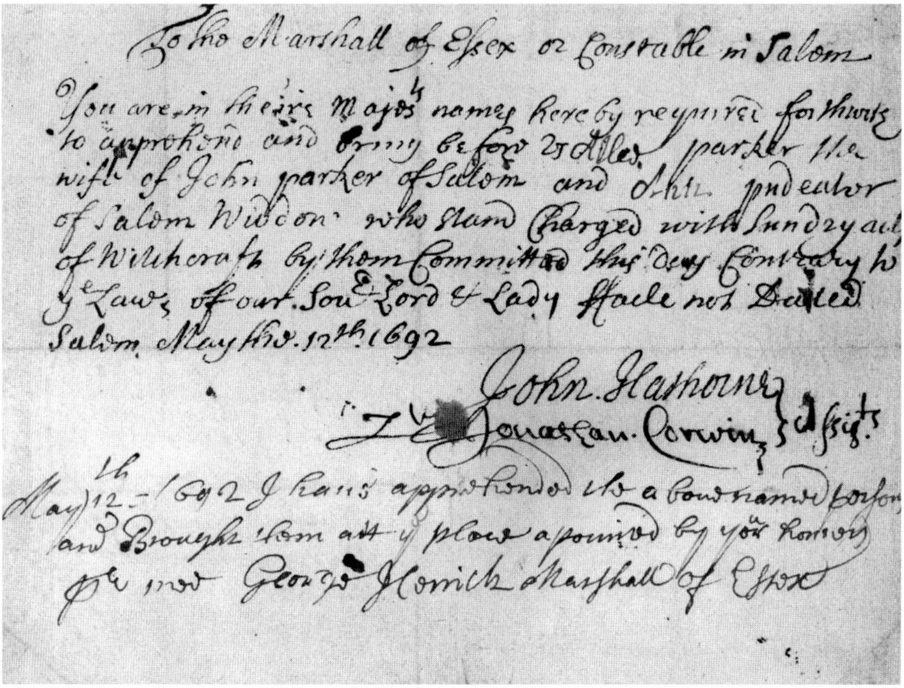

To the Marshall of Essex or Constable in Salem

You are in theire Majests names hereby required forthwith to apprehend and bring before us Alles parker the wife of John parker of Salem and Ann pudeator of Salem Widdow who stand charged with sundry acts of Witchcraft by them Committed this day Contrary to ye Laws of our Sovereign Lord & Lady Faile not Dated Salem May the 12th 1692

John Hathorne
Jonathan Corwin } Assists

May 12th 1692 I have apprehended ye above named persons and Brought them att ye place apointed by your honors
p me George Herrick Marshall of Essex

Warrant for the arrest of Ann Pudeator

21 March 1691/2

Mr Hathorne: You are now in the hands of Authority tell me now why you hurt these persons

Martha Kory: I do not.

Who doth?

Pray give me leave to goe to prayer
    This request was made sundry times

We do not send for you to goe to prayer

But tell me why you hurt these?

I am an innocent person: I never had to do with witchcraft since I was born. I am a Gospell woman

Do not you see these complain of you
    The Lord open the eyes of the Magistrates & Ministers: the Lord show his power to discover the guilty.

Tell us who hurts these children.

I do not know.

If you be guilty of this fact do you think you can hide it.

The Lord knows _____

Well tell us what you know of this matter

Why I am a Gospell-woman, & do you think I can have to do with witchcraft too?

How could you tell then that the child was bid to observe what clothes you wore when some came to speak with you

Cheever interrupted her & bid her not begin with a lye & so Edw: Putnam declared the matter

Mr Hall: Who told you that

He said the child said

Cheever: you speak falsly

Then Edw: Putnam read again

Mr H: Why did you ask if the child told what clothes you wore

My husband told me the others told

Who told you about the cloathes? why did you ask that question

Because I heard the children told what cloathes the others wore

Goodman Kory did you tell her

The old man denyed that he told her.

Did you not say your husband told you so

H: Who hurts these children now look upon them.

I cannot help it

Did you not say you would tell the truth why you asked if question how came you to the knowledge —

I did but ask

You dare thus to lye in all this assembly

You are now before Authority, I expect the truth, you promised it, speak now & tell what clothes who told you what clothes

No body

How came you to know that the children would be examined what cloth I wore

Because I thought the child was wiser than any body if she knew

Give an answer you said your husband told you

He told me the children said I afflicted them

How do you know that they came for, answer me this truly, will you say how you came to know what they came for

I had heard speech that the children said I afflicted them & I thought that they might come to examine

But how did you know it

I thought they did

Did not you say you would tell the truth, who told you what they came for

No body

How did you know

I did think so

But you said you knew so

Child: There is a man whispering in her ear.

H: What did he say to you

We must not beleive all that these distracted children say

Cannot you tell what that man whispered

I saw no body

But did not you hear

No, here was extream agony of all the afflicted

If you expect mercy of God you must look for it in Gods way by confession

Do you think to find mercy by aggravating your sins

A true thing

Look for it then in Gods way

So I do

Give glory to God & confess then

But I cannot confess

Do not you see how these afflicted do charge you

We must not beleive distracted persons

Who do you improve to hurt them

I improve none

First page of the examination of Martha Cory,
March 21, 1692

The humbl petition of mary Estik unto the honoured Judge and Bench now Sitting In Judicature in Salem and the Reuerend ministers humbly sheweth

That whereas your poor and humble Petition being condemned to die Doe humbly begg of you to take it into your Judicious and pious considerations that your poor and humble petitioner knowing my own Innocencye Blised be the lord for it and seeing plainly the wiles and subtility of my accusers by my selfe can not but Judg charitably of others that are going the same way of my selfe if the Lord steps not mightily in I was confined a whole month upon the same account that I am condemned now for and then cleared by the afflicted persons as some of your honours know and in two dayes time I was cryed out upon by them and have been confined and now am condemned to die the lord aboue knows my Innocencye then and likewise does know at the great day will be knowen to men and Angells I Petition to your honours not for my own life for I know I must die and my appointed time is sett but the Lord he knowes it is that if it be possible no more Innocent blood may be shed which undoubtidly cannot be Avoyded In the way and course you goe in I Question not but your honours does to the uttmost of your powers in the discovery and deteering of witchcraft and witches and would not be gulty of Innocent blood for the world but by my own Innocencye I know you are in the wrong way the lord in his infinite mercy direct you in this great work if it be his blessed will that no Innocent blood be shed I would humbly begg of you that your honours would be plesed to examine theis Afflicted persons strictly and keepe them apart some time and likewise to try some of these confesing witches I being confident there is seuerall of them has belyed themselues and others as will appeare if not in this world I am sure in the world to come wither I am now going and I question not but youle see an alteration of thes things they say my selfe and others hauing made league with the Diuel we cannot confesse I know and the Lord knowes as will shortly appeare they belye me and so I Question not but they doe others the Lord aboue who is the searsher of all hearts knowes that as I shall answer it att the

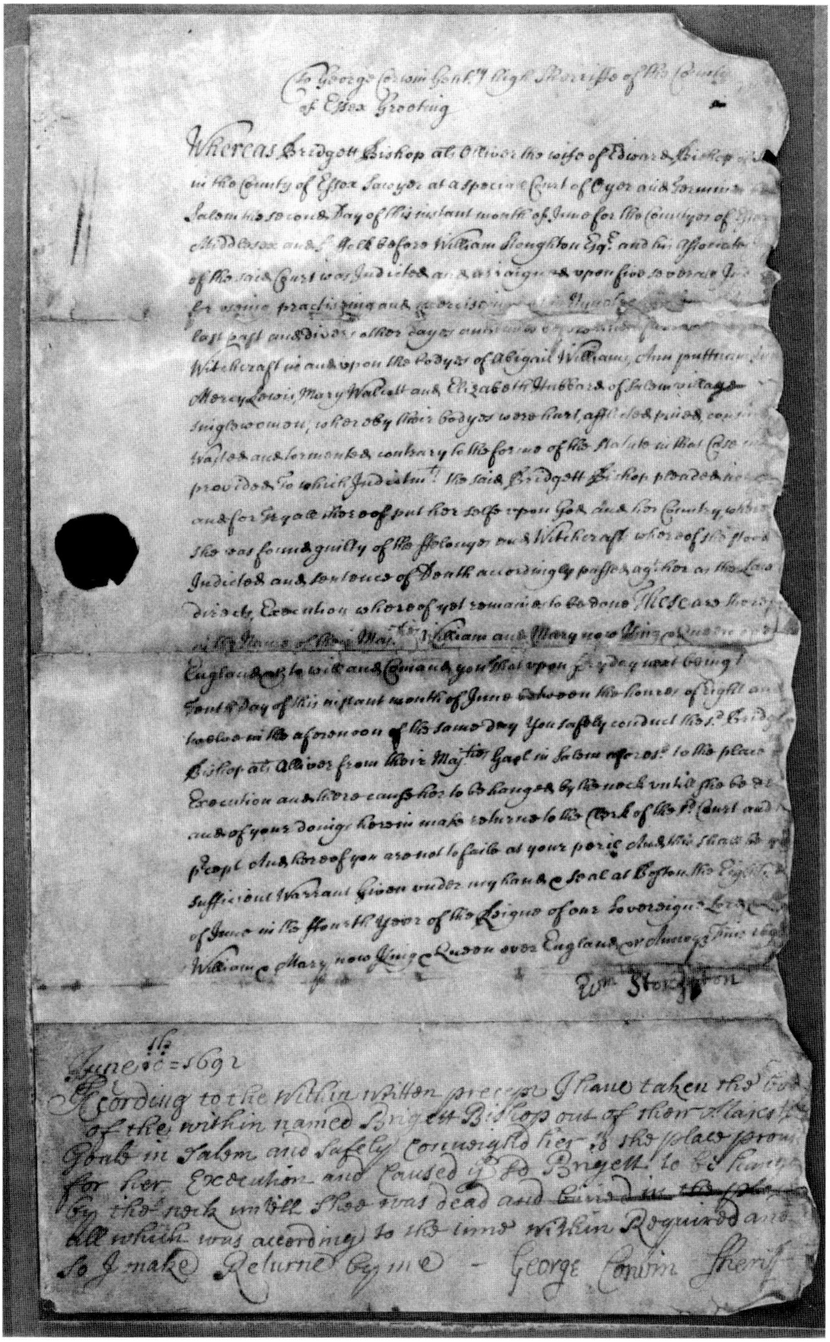

To George Corwin Gent.n High Sherriffe of the County of Essex Greeting

Whereas Bridgett Bishop al[ia]s Oliver the wife of Edward Bishop of … in the County of Essex Sawyer at a speciall Court of Oyer and Terminer … Salem the second Day of this instant month of June for the Countyes of Essex Middlesex and Suffolk before William Stoughton Esq.r and his Associate[s] of the said Court was Indicted and arraigned upon five severall Ind… for using practising and exercising … last past and divers other dayes and times … Witchcraft in and upon the bodyes of Abigail Williams, Ann puttnam … Mercy Lewis, Mary Walcott and Elizabeth Hubbard of Salem village singlewomen, whereby their bodyes were hurt, afflicted pined, con… wasted and tormented contrary to the forme of the Statute in that Case … provided To which Indictm.ts the said Bridgett Bishop pleaded not … and for Tryall thereof put her selfe upon God and her Country, where… she was found guilty of the ffelonyes and Witchcraft whereof she stood Indicted and sentence of Death accordingly passed ag.t her as the Law directs, Execution whereof yet remaines to be done These are therefore in the Name of their Maj.ties William and Mary now King & Queen over England &c. to will and Comand you that upon ffryday next being the Tenth day of this instant month of June between the houres of Eight and twelve in the aforenoon of the same day You safely conduct the s.d Bridgett Bishop al[ia]s Olliver from their Maj.ties Goal in Salem aforesd to the place of Execution and there cause her to be hanged by the neck untill she be dead and of your doings herein make returne to the Clerk of the s.d Court and … and hereof you are not to faile at your perill and this shall be … sufficient Warrant Given under my hand & seal at Boston the Eighth of June in the ffourth Year of the Reigne of our Soveraigne Lord … William & Mary now King & Queen over England &c. Anno …

Wm Stoughton

June 10 = 1692

According to the within written precept I have taken the bod… of the within named Brigett Bishop out of their Majest… Goale in Salem and Safely Conveighd her to the place provi… for her Execution and Caused ye sd Brigett to be hang… by the neck untill Shee was dead and ~~buried in the place~~ all which was according to the time within Required and so I make Returne by me — George Corwin Sherif…

Bridget Bishop's death warrant,
June 10, 1692

The reconstructed meetinghouse

The Rebecca Nurse homestead
in Salem Village (Danvers, Massachusetts)

The Phillip English house,
built in 1685, taken down in 1833

The tombstone of George Jacobs

The Rebecca Nurse Monument

The Danvers Memorial
in memory of all those who died during the "Salem Witchcraft Hysteria."
Located opposite the site of the meetinghouse in Danvers, Massachusetts.

cated and of good behaviour," he presumably does not include either of Parris's charges, Ann Putnam, or Elizabeth Hubbard. In any case, all the young girls among the afflicted so far, except Mercy Lewis, were the daughters of "good," if disturbed, Puritan families. Even in the deep darkness of 1692 it seems improbable that a substantial farmer, respected doctor, or dedicated pastor would have molested a young daughter or niece. And since Mercy Lewis did not live with her family, incest for her was not a possibility. She was to give birth to her illegitimate baby, though afterward she married the father. However, Calef may have been thinking of some of the later additions to the ranks of the afflicted, yet to appear.

The Proctors' maid, Mary Warren, had by the beginning of April appeared as an accuser just once. John Proctor told Samuel Sibley that she was one of the afflicted girls at Rebecca Nurse's examination. The second mention of her name in the records is by Abigail when she says, during the Proctors' examination, that Elizabeth Proctor told her that Mary Warren had signed the devil's book.

After the Proctors' imprisonment, Mary may have wandered the house from which her master and mistress had been taken, at a loss to comfort or help the Proctors' five abandoned children, of whom the youngest was only three. She may have witnessed the sheriff's arrival to seize all the Proctors' worldly goods. An accused witch's estate became forfeit, in theory to the Crown but probably in practice to the sheriff and his men to dispose of more or less as they liked, when the witch was convicted. In the Proctors' case, George Corwin, the twenty-six-year-old nephew of the magistrate Jonathan Corwin, appointed high sheriff of Essex County when the court was set up, anticipated the guilty verdict. Perhaps because John Proctor was especially loathed for his outspoken contempt for the witch-hunt, the seizure was unusually ruthless and vindictive.

"John Proctor and his wife being in prison, the sheriff came to his house and seized all the goods, provisions and cattle that he could come at, and sold some of the cattle at half price, and killed others, and put them up for the West Indies; threw out the beer out of a barrel, and carried away the barrel; emptied a pot of broth, and took away the pot, and left nothing in the house for the support of the children," Calef writes.

The next mention of Mary in the records is eight days after Elizabeth Proctor and Sarah Cloyce's examination. The tables had turned: She was now being examined herself. John Hathorne was back in the questioner's chair, and back in Salem Village. Mary Warren stood at the bar, her erstwhile friends and allies in front of her, already in fits.

These had begun as Mary walked through the crowd to where she now stood.

"You were a little while ago an afflicted person, now you are an afflicter: how comes this to pass?" John Hathorne asked her. His question for once was a good one. How indeed? Mary could not enlighten him. She cried, "I look up to God, and take it to be a great mercy of God." Naturally Hathorne wondered how it could be that to afflict others was a great mercy of God. But then Elizabeth Hubbard, on this occasion not in a trance, gave him his answer. Elizabeth averred that a little while after Mary stopped having fits, she, Mary, claimed that "the afflicted persons did but dissemble."

John Proctor, it seems, had done as he promised Samuel Sibley. After taking Mary home from Rebecca Nurse's examination, he "thrashed the devil out of her." Under the sway of his aggressive but protective personality, she was freed of delusion. She saw the truth and spoke it. The girls "did but dissemble." What precisely she meant by "dissemble" becomes clearer later.

Her betrayal provided further cause for the girls to accuse the Proctors of witchcraft. At their examination, from which Mary had been absent, Abigail had prepared the ground for her arrest by saying that Elizabeth had told her that her maid, Mary, had signed the devil's book. Mary had duly been arrested.

After Elizabeth Hubbard spoke at Mary's examination in the Salem Village meetinghouse, Mrs. Pope, uncharacteristically quiet till now, fell into a fit. Suddenly all the afflicted except John Indian were screaming, writhing, and choking. A few moments later, John Indian was doing so too.

Mary Warren was in the novel position of watching, rather than taking part in, the hysteria. She had turned from a mouthpiece of furious hostility to its target. Hathorne, Corwin, Parris, and the entire congregation eyed her with loathing. No one defended her. The man who had made her see reason was locked up in jail. She was faced with a choice between remaining faithful to what she knew to be true and as a result being thrown in a dungeon and tried as a witch, or letting herself slide back into frenzy. The choice she made seems inevitable. After all, it involved no difficult conscious decision. She merely let well-known feelings take over.

But, on doing so, she stopped short of making accusations. She came close, shouting, "I will speak . . . Oh, I am sorry for it, I am sorry for it," and, later, "I will tell, I will tell, they brought me to it." But she did not name names. She was given every encouragement; her friends screamed that she was about to confess, but Goody Cory and

John Proctor and his wife appeared, struck her down, and silenced her.

She was deeply divided. She wanted safety, but not to send her master to the gallows. Her fits continued so unflaggingly that she was taken out for a time while another accused witch was examined. But when she came back, the fits started again. Later she was examined privately by the magistrates and ministers but still would not name names. She was sent off to prison.

When first examined in jail, she accused her mistress of witchcraft. But she still did not implicate her master. By May 12, after three weeks in chains in the dungeons, she confessed to anything and everything the magistrates wished her to.

"I have considered of it . . . and it was the devil's book that my Master Proctor brought to me."

She was being examined in the meetinghouse. These words were the first part of what seems, from its unprompted length, a prepared statement. There followed a flood of accusations, chiefly of John Proctor, whose shape, she poignantly claimed, she "caught hold of . . . and pulled down into my lap." The fantasy suggests feelings for her master hidden even from herself. Poor Mary Warren was being forced to condemn the only person who cared anything for her, a stern but just father figure who, though sixty years old, was still sexually powerful. He had had three wives and eleven children, with a twelfth on the way. His forceful, emotional character made him highly effective in his ordinary dealings with the world but hugely vulnerable when circumspection or guile were needed. It is hard to believe that Mary did not long to "pull down" John Proctor himself, not just his shape, into her lap. Her accusations were also of most of the witches so far examined. By this time, they came to a considerable number.

The allegations were undoubtedly fed to her. They are too full of precise names and places to be Mary's invention. Particularly detailed are her indictments of the two women who were examined with her that day, Alice Parker, the wife of a Salem mariner, and Ann Pudeator, a well-to-do seventy-year-old widow. Mary said that Goody Parker confessed to her that she had lately killed a man on board a ship by striking him in the side, had sunk a second ship, had drowned a boy in the harbor, and had bewitched another boy to death "as his master was carrying him out to sea." Names and locations were given. A like inventory of misdeeds was produced for Goody Pudeator, though hers were all land-based.

Mary was earning her freedom and forgiveness by returning, to extremely useful effect for the complainants and magistrates, to the ranks of the witch finders.

But when first in prison, before her mental freedom was destroyed, she had said in the hearing of four witnesses that the magistrates "might as well examine Keysar's daughter, that has been distracted many years, and take notice of what she said, as . . . any of the afflicted persons." Keysar was Elizer Keysar, a tanner and cousin of Thomas Putnam living in Salem, whose daughter was mad. Mary Warren went on to say that "when I was afflicted I thought I saw the apparitions of a hundred persons," but that was because her head "was distempered" and she "did not know what she said." When "she was well again she could not say that she saw any of [the] apparitions."

No doubt the experiences of all the girls in their fits were similar to this. However, Mary was never again to accuse them, or herself, of dissembling.

CHAPTER FIFTEEN

A Black Man with an Hat

By the time Mary Warren poured out her accusations, in mid-May, thirty-six accused witches were in jail. After the examination of Elizabeth Proctor and Sarah Cloyce in Salem Town, the warrants began flying from the magistrates not one at a time but in clusters. Since the witch-hunt had been given the seal of approval by the highest authorities, the Putnams felt free to complain of almost whomever they pleased. The few exceptions were certain powerful enemies in Salem Village itself. The girls also grew bolder, calling the names of any who doubted or displeased them, with the same few exceptions. Men and girls worked together, though which were instigators, which followers, in any given instance, can only be guessed at. However, sometimes the guessing is not all that difficult.

One man and two women were examined with Mary Warren on April 19. The man was Giles Cory, who had helped send his wife to prison only one month before. He was eighty years old and well known in the village as a cantankerous, obstinate character. It may be that his testifying against his wife had backfired: Relatives of witches were automatically suspected of witchcraft. He had no specific quarrel with the Putnams. But, born in England, a fairly recent arrival in Salem Village, successful and prosperous, he was exactly the kind of outsider they loathed.

The two women examined with Warren were Abigail Hobbs and Bridget Bishop. Abigail, twenty-two, was a strange creature, a rebel of a kind perhaps Ann Putnam or Abigail Williams might have been had they come from homes of lower standing governed by less powerful fathers. Neither of Abigail Hobbs's parents were church members and her father had not even been to a service in the meetinghouse for a very long time. His occupation is not recorded, which suggests he was a laborer, finding work where he could. The family had lived a few years earlier at Casco, Maine, in the remote region to the northeast of Salem that was repeatedly devastated by Indian raids. The Hobbs family now resided on the edge of Salem Village in an area that was to become part of Topsfield.

Abigail was as wild as the forests she resided so close to. She roamed them at night, sleeping under the stars. Her parents had lost all control of her. When she visited a seventeen-year-old friend with her mother, she was so rude and unseemly that the friend gave her a lecture, saying she ought to be ashamed. In response Abigail told her to hold her tongue or she would make such a racket as would raise the whole neighborhood. Then she said that "Old Nick sat over the bedstead." All her helpless mother could do was sigh that she "little thought to be the mother of such a daughter." Eighteen months earlier the same friend, Lydia Nichols, had asked Abigail how she dared lie out at night in the woods all alone. "She told me," Lydia said, "she had sold herself body and soul to the old boy."

Such dissidence in those times seems amazing. It helps confirm the impression of a changing society and the gradual erosion of previously ironclad Puritan control, so frightening a prospect to those who clung to old ways, including Cotton Mather, Samuel Parris, and Thomas Putnam.

When questioned by Hathorne, Abigail confessed to anything and everything. Her reputation had preceded her: She must have realized that denials would never be credited. She may even have believed much of what she was saying. An aquaintance claimed, when she was "discoursing with" Abigail about her disobedience to her father and mother, that "she told me she did not care what anybody said to her for she had seen the devil and had made a covenant or bargain with him." In any case, this was the kind of attention she had been seeking for years. No doubt the seriousness with which the magistrate was treating her claims to talks with the devil was exceedingly gratifying.

After an initial statement to the effect that she had been very wicked but hoped, with God's help, to be better, she spoke with surprising assurance. She said the devil had promised her fine things if she did what he said. Hathorne asked, "What would he have you do?" She replied, "Why, he would have me be a witch." That "Why" carries the same attitude of defiant independence as sent her roaming the woods in the night.

Hathorne asked, of her time in the Eastward, "What other creatures did you see?"

"I saw things like men."

"What did they say to you?"

"Why, they said I had better put my hand to the book."

She agreed with Hathorne that she had allowed the devil, in her shape, to hurt Mercy Lewis and Ann Putnam. The devil appeared as "a black man with an hat." Supernatural creatures had never sucked at her body but had spoken to her. Hathorne continued to ask questions about these creatures, but Abigail could no longer hear him. She had gone deaf. The girls said they had seen Sarah Good and Sarah Osborne run their fingers in her ears. A little later Abigail cried out that Sarah Good said she should not speak. After that she was dumb. This seems a convenient way of ending questions she had begun to find tiresome.

The court ordered her to be taken away.

During the whole of Abigail Hobbs's examination, the afflicted girls refrained from having fits since she was confessing, not practicing, witchcraft. Afterward they "said openly in Court, they were sorry for the condition this poor Abigail Hobbs was in, which compassion they expressed over and over again."

Such so-called compassion is chilling. It did not extend to their asking the magistrates if Abigail Hobbs might be kept out of jail. No doubt they gloried in the admiration it produced in the court. There is a self-indulgence and melodrama in their expressing it "over and over again." It is part of the same posturing as their histrionic scorn of less cooperative victims.

That scorn, in the examination of Bridget Bishop, immediately following that of Abigail Hobbs, took the physical form of the mimicking of hand, neck, and head movements. When Bridget bent her neck, the girls followed suit. When she turned up her eyes to the ceiling, they turned up theirs. Poor Bridget was bewildered.

"You are here accused by four or five of hurting them. What do you say to it?" Hathorne asked.

"I never saw these persons before, nor I never was in this place before," Bridget wailed. No doubt she spoke the truth. She lived in Salem, the wife of a sawyer. There was no reason she should have ever come to Salem Village. The girls would have known her not by sight, but by reputation.

She had been taken to court on an accusation of witchcraft twelve years before. Though she was found innocent, there remained in circulation any number of stories about her supernatural activities. In 1692 these were gathered as evidence, though all bear reliable witness to only one thing, the witnesses' and judges' credulity.

A sum that Bridget paid a man, of threepence, unaccountably vanished from his pocket. In English folklore it was a standard witch's trick to pay with disappearing money. The same man was driving his cart, a little way from where Bridget was standing, when its wheels stuck in a hole. He extricated the cart, but when he went back later to look for the hole, he could not find it.

All this had happened many years before. From such simple begin-
nings Bridget's reputation grew to embrace the bewitching to death of
several small children. She was also accused of spectral nighttime visits
to men. She lay on the "breast or body" of one Richard Coman so that
he could not speak or stir or wake his wife; she sat on thirty-two-year-
old John Louder's stomach, took hold of his throat, and almost choked
him.

In the accounts of these deeds by the sufferers is heard real anguish
and dread. This is especially true of a long narrative by a couple called
the Shattucks, who describe the loss of wits, physical agonies, and eventual death of their eldest child from no natural cause that they knew
of. They linked the onset of his illness to a visit from Bridget. Its increasing severity seemed caused by her continuing calls at the house
on what seemed to them pretexts.

The horror they felt as they watched their beloved son deteriorate
became attached to the woman they believed was responsible. Others
who assumed she had brought about their own equally dire misfortunes had similar feelings. For some young men, horror seems to have
merged with sexual yearning. Two of them, in their accounts of
Bridget's nighttime visits, described her clothes, which they recognized
as her daytime apparel, including a flamboyant "red paragon bodice."
Though the notion that the Puritans always wore black is mistaken,
such a bodice sounds unusual. But in any case the very fact that the
men had noticed her raiment suggests a striking appearance. Perhaps
Bridget had unusual allure. She visited the Shattucks with "a smooth
flattering manner." But, as a traditional witch suspect, she chiefly represented not sexual longings but the desire to humble and destroy and
the terrifying power to do so through the force of that desire itself.
Fundamentally, the fear of the witch was the terror of a pitiless Fate
whose blows may magically be caused by one's own hidden wickedness.

Another rumor about Bridget was that she had bewitched her first
husband to death. Hathorne taxed her with this.

"If it please your worship, I know nothing of it," Bridget said. She
showed no defiance or skepticism in any of her answers, only puzzle-
ment and a hint, in her deference, of the "smooth flattering manner."

Yet Hathorne did not spare her his clever legal questioning. Halfway
through the examination she said, "I am innocent to a witch. I know
not what a witch is."

"How do you know then that you are not a witch?"

"I do not know what you say."

"How can you know you are no witch and yet not know what a witch
is?"

"I am clear: if I were any such person you should know it." By "clear," she meant innocent.

Magistrate and defendant were talking two different languages, one that of legal debate, the other of honest common sense. Never were any defendants so in need of defense lawyers as these in Salem Village. But legal representation in examinations in Puritan New England was considered unnecessary. If a defendant was innocent, God would reveal it.

Bridget was given the full accusers' treatment. She was tricked into the appearance of a lie by being asked if she knew that other accused witches had that day confessed. When she said she did not, she was informed that two of those present had told her about it. Her simple "I did not hear them" was ignored.

That gifted family of conjurers, the Walcotts, gave a similar display to the torn sheet routine as described by Deodat Lawson. However, this time Mary was assisted by her brother Jonathan, not her father. Mary cried out that he had struck Bridget's "appearance" with his sword and torn her coat. She had heard it tear. When Bridget's coat was examined it was found to be torn "two ways." But it did not look as though the tear was caused by a sword. The cut was not clean enough. However, "Jonathan Walcott saith that the sword that he struck at Goody Bishop with was not naked, but was within the scabbard, so that the rent may very probably be the very same that Mary Walcott did tell that she had in her coat."

That such transparent fast thinking and trickery went unchallenged shows yet again what a hold the girls had established. It was self-perpetuating. Those who openly doubted would soon find themselves at the bar, with the next step the dungeons. That was Bridget Bishop's destination, in the company of Giles Cory, Abigail Hobbs, and Mary Warren.

CHAPTER SIXTEEN

Into the Unknown

OVER the next few weeks they were joined by thirty other accused witches. All had one thing in common: They were people whom the complainants and accusers wished to destroy. Ironically, the accusers of witches had acquired the mythical power of witches. Merely by turning their anger and scorn on their victims they could injure and kill them.

But those victims were no longer necessarily personally disliked by or even known to the girls who called out their names. The first witches, from the point of view of the Putnams, had been outsiders socially or spiritually, but not geographically. They either were misfits, such as Sarah Good or Sarah Osborne, or represented different interests and values, as did Rebecca Nurse, Martha Cory, and the Proctors. They lacked deference and respect for the elite of which the Putnams were leaders. But now the girls had begun to name people who were literally outsiders.

The first had been Bridget Bishop, who lived in Salem Town. The girls had never laid eyes on her until she stood in front of them while they went into fits in the courtroom. They had probably never seen Abigail Hobbs either, since she lived on the border of Topsfield. The magistrates may have asked Ezekiel Cheever and John Putnam Junior, when they complained of Bridget's and Abigail's witchcraft "on the bodies" of Ann Putnam and the rest, how the girls knew it was they who were pinching and choking them. The men would have said that Bridget's and Abigail's specters themselves told the girls their names. Later, in depositions concerning another witch they had never met, Sarah Averill Wildes, Mary Walcott and Ann Putnam said that even while she was afflicting them Sarah had said who she was. Why Sarah should incriminate herself in this way is a mystery. The magistrates were uneasy over this matter of identification, as later comes clear, but their commitment to the witch-hunt made them want to believe the accusers' explanations.

Bridget and Abigail were just the first of a great many accused witches whose shapes the girls recognized though they had never seen the originals.

On April 21 six more women and three more men were examined. Three of them had family ties with people already in prison: William and Deliverance Hobbs, Abigail Hobbs's unfortunate parents, and Mary Easty, a sister of Rebecca Nurse and Sarah Cloyce. A fourth accused witch was the Sarah Wildes who had introduced herself to Mary Walcott while pinching and pricking her. She had a long-standing reputation for witchcraft and had been named by Abigail Hobbs, at her examination, as torturing her mother, Deliverance.

All these four were from the border area between Salem Village and the township of Topsfield to the north. The girls had seen none of them before. But, unlike some of the accused witches to come, they were at least personally known to the girls' adult relatives.

For years there had been enormous tension between the Putnams, together with some other Salem Villagers, and certain Topsfield inhabitants. The foundations of the conflict had been laid by the Massachusetts General Court when, in 1639, it gave Salem permission to expand in the direction of the Ipswich River and then, four years later, authorized some inhabitants of Ipswich to found a village in just the same area. That village later became Topsfield. As a result of these competing claims, quarrels about boundaries went on for a century.

One of the early Salem settlers of this outlying area was John Putnam, the founding father of the clan, who was soon involved in bitter warfare over the ownership of woodland with three families: the Townes, Howes, and Eastys. Jacob Towne was the father of Rebecca Nurse and her sisters. Early on, he and John Howe cut down a tree that Putnam regarded as his, in front of his eyes. Soon afterward Putnam traveled forth with a band of nephews and sons to fell all the trees in the area. Two Towne men and two Easty men arrived to protest but were outnumbered. Putnam won that battle, but the war did not stop. It went on from one generation to another, in the style of a Sicilian blood feud, except that the blood was not shed over time but conserved for the climax.

There was particular bitterness over land boundaries between Nathaniel Putnam and Francis Nurse. It is no coincidence that the three sisters who were accused witches were not only all daughters of a Topsfield man but all married to Topsfield men: Nurse, Towne, and Easty.

Another accused was Mary Black, a negro slave. Two more were Edward and Sarah Bishop, an unlicensed tavern owner and his wife.

This couple lived far from the center of Salem Village, on the Ipswich Road, near the border of Beverly. Though Sarah was a member of the Beverly church, she took a relaxed view of what pleasures were permissible for Puritans. The Bishops' tavern offered not only alcohol but shuffleboard, a game in which small disks of wood are propelled across the floor or a table with the hand or a stick toward areas marked by lines. Points were scored according to where the disks landed. The drinking and playing went on late, causing discord in neighborhood families. Though alcohol was not frowned on, drunkenness was, and so were game playing and keeping late hours.

The revelry so incensed one local matron that she went to the tavern, snatched up the shuffleboard pieces, and threw them in the fire. The woman later went mad and was eventually found dead. Her windpipe had been cut out. She also had a wound through the gullet and another through the jugular. The Reverend John Hale, pastor of Beverly, to whom she had turned for advice, held the view that she could not have so "mangled herself" with the short pair of scissors she had used in what was surely a suicide "without some extraordinary work of the devil or witchcraft." He suspected Sarah Bishop.

Any husband of a witch suspect automatically came under suspicion himself. But there was a separate cause for Edward Bishop's arrest. After the Proctors' examination in Salem, when the Salem Villagers went to an inn for refreshments, the slave John Indian became unruly; Edward Bishop took charge of him and made him behave himself. But as they all rode home, John Indian had another fit, keeping himself on his horse only by holding on with his teeth to the back of the man riding in front of him. Bishop hit him with his stick and John Indian recovered and promised he would "do so no more." Bishop replied that he could cure all the afflicted persons with similar treatment.

As soon as Bishop and the girls parted company, at the junction where the girls turned left for the center of Salem Village and Bishop headed up the Ipswich Road toward his home, the girls began crying out that he tortured them. No doubt John Indian joined in. Edward Bishop was duly arrested, with his wife, ten days later.

The eighth of this group of accused witches was a new phenomenon among the girls' victims: the wife of a leading Salem merchant.

Even after the upgrading of the witch-hunt, the girls did not dare name such powerful Salem Village enemies as Israel Porter and Joseph Putnam since habits of deference to important local figures, whom they had known all their lives, went too deep. What was more, such figures might have proved all too effective as opponents. But the girls could easily imagine, or pretend, they were tortured by prominent people they had never encountered, without fear of the consequences.

The girls would have heard Mary English talked about ever since they could remember. She was born in 1652, the only child of William Hollingsworth, a Salem merchant, and Eleanor Hollingsworth, an unusually independent woman who, in 1675, was granted a license as a tavern owner. She continued to run the Blue Anchor, on the shore road in Salem, after her husband died two years later. It was rumored, a century and a half later, that she was the model for Nathaniel Hawthorne's Hester Prynne in *The Scarlet Letter*. In the summer of 1692 the girls were to name her too as afflicting them, unaware that she was dead.

But Mary was famous less for her parentage than for her marriage to the wealthiest merchant in Salem. Phillip English, more than anyone else, represented the new colonial spirit of cosmopolitan commercialism that seemed so threatening to the struggling Salem Village farmers. He was of exotic ancestry, coming from the Channel Island of Jersey where the influence of France was as strong as that of England. His original name was l'Anglois but he had anglicized it on coming to America.

Among the various reasons for his enormous commercial success were his international contacts. He was the first seventeenth-century New England merchant to trade with France, Spain, and Portugal as well as with England and the West Indies. By 1692 he owned fourteen town lots, a wharf, more than twenty sailing ships, and a house of extraordinary splendor. It was enormous, beautifully proportioned, and stood in imposing isolation with spectacular views over the harbor. There were many grand houses in Salem that impressed even visitors from London, but this was the grandest. No wonder the Salem farmers, for whom the four-room parsonage seemed impressive, felt a wicked urge to pull it down, with its inhabitants in it.

Their feelings toward Salem Town and its merchants were similar to those traditionally harbored by the northern English toward London. As well as resentment of the greater wealth and sophistication of the metropolis is the grievance that the morally worthier northerners who, as they think, are more honest and hardworking than southerners, do not benefit from such virtue but suffer because of it. Their scorn and contempt mask their envy. Of course, not all northern English people have this attitude, as not all Salem Villagers felt hostile toward Salem, but it is hard to travel for long in the north without coming across it. There is no comparable attitude in America today. Life in U.S. cities does not create envy. The particular loathing of New York by the rest of the country is based mainly on racial and ethnic fear and a dislike of liberal politics. It is hard to detect any sense of inferiority underlying the complacency. There was such a sense once, and it has been converted to triumph at New York's slide into chaos and squalor.

In its patterns of class and regional suspicion and envy, Puritan New England was more like present-day England than like America. However, in its widespread distrust of worldly and sensual pleasures, and also the arts, and its intolerance of those who did not conform, it laid cultural foundations that still underlie American society and create an ethos more similar to that of its colonial predecessor than that of the present-day Old Country.

There was additional cause of animosity toward Phillip English. In April 1692 he and Daniel Andrew, a prosperous recent arrival in Salem Village, had been elected as Salem Town selectmen. Their success followed a failed attempt by the Putnams to make a comeback in town politics. It cannot be a coincidence that warrants for the arrest of both men for witchcraft were issued a few weeks after they assumed office. They both escaped arrest, but English and his wife were seized later and kept prisoner for several weeks, till escaping again.

Eight of the nine accused witches were given the usual hysterical display by the girls and the usual short shrift by the magistrates. But Hathorne showed sensitivity to the possible charge that the afflicted were naming people they had never seen by ordering Deliverance Hobbs to be brought into the meetinghouse, where the girls were assembled, without her name being mentioned. He asked Mercy Lewis and another girl if they knew her. Both were "struck dumb." However, after a while Ann Putnam Junior, no doubt fed the name by a relative, said this was Goody Hobbs.

Deliverance began by denying she was a witch. But she said she had seen "sundry sights" of animals and shapes and agreed she had been afflicted by witches. Gradually she was led on by Hathorne to say she had signed the devil's book. Goody Wildes had brought it to her. After that she confessed to sticking pins in images and seeing "a tall black man with an high-crowned hat." She had the same mental image of the devil as her daughter had described. In the end Hathorne's leading questions and the girls' fits induced Deliverance to say everything they wanted.

Strong personalities could withstand the sight and sound of the girls' agonies, which everyone in the court believed they were causing, but weaker ones found them unbearable. When Deliverance began to confess, the girls' fits ceased, offering a powerful incentive for her to continue confessing.

Deliverance was to prove to the magistrates one of the most useful of all the accused witches. Once in prison, she was prevailed on to make a detailed statement. No doubt each item was fed to her and she merely agreed to it, but her confession is written out in the record as though she had volunteered everything. Calef describes the process, saying the examiners asked the accused, " 'Were you at such a witch-meeting?' or 'Have you signed the devil's book?' etc. Upon their reply-ing, 'Yes,' the whole was drawn into form as their confession."

The statement Deliverance made was perfect for silencing doubters and confirming everyone else's worst fears. She claimed there was a witches' church in Salem Village that held meetings that were black parodies of proper church meetings. They took place in the pasture next to Mr. Parris's house. (That pasture can be glimpsed today, through trees. The house is long gone, but its foundations have been excavated and can be visited.) There were deacons, who gave out red bread and red wine, and a preacher who administered the sacrament. That preacher was an especially sinister figure. He was seated at a table next to a man wearing a high-crowned white hat. The hat's unexpected whiteness, like the devil's blackness of complexion, was a negative image, the reverse of what was normal since the traditional Puritan high-crowned hat was of course black.

The minister urged his followers to bewitch everyone in the village, "telling them they should do it gradually, not all at once [and] assur-ing them they should prevail." The deacons were Rebecca Nurse and Sarah Wildes. The minister was George Burroughs.

If the Putnams and others ever laid plans to ensnare any one person in the course of the witch-hunt, that person was Burroughs. Many names were called out on a whim or after some maneuvering, but Burroughs was complained of only after careful preparation. This was necessary to give credibility to an accusation of witchcraft against a respected Harvard graduate and minister. It was also necessary to give a sense of urgency to the arrest of someone who had to be brought, with much labor and expense, all the way to Salem Village from far-away Casco.

None of the other eight accused witches examined on April 21 were of any assistance in the plot against Burroughs. Seven went to prison denying their guilt. One of the most interesting of these was Mary Easty, the sister of Rebecca Nurse and Sarah Cloyce. She made her denials with such cogency and force that Hathorne, most unusually, asked the girls if they were sure "this was the woman." As later events were to show, she was a person of striking intelligence, strength of character, and integrity.

He asked her how far she "complied with Satan."

"Sir, I never complied, but prayed against him all my days. I have no compliance with Satan, in this. What would you have me do?"

"Confess, if you be guilty."

"I will say it, if it was my last time, I am clear of this sin."

"Of what sin?"

"Of witchcraft."

At first, after this, when Hathorne asked if they were sure of Mary's identity, the girls could not speak. But soon Ann Putnam and Elizabeth Hubbard cried out, "Oh, Goody Easty, Goody Easty, you are the woman, you are the woman."

Hathorne's doubts were dissolved.

Mary Black, the negro slave, made her denials far more lamely. When asked how long she had been a witch, she said, "I cannot tell." She was then asked, "But have you been a witch?" and helplessly replied, "I cannot tell you." But she was adamant that she had hurt no one. She was owned by Benjamin Putnam, Nathaniel Putnam's son, and had presumably in some way displeased him or one of his nieces. Sarah Wildes had little chance to say anything beyond "I am not guilty, Sir," and "I never saw the book in my life and I never saw these persons before." The afflicted girls kept shouting that they saw her "upon the beam." Hathorne believed them.

Sarah Averill Wildes' twenty-seven-year-old son, Ephraim Wildes, had his own theory as to why Deliverance Hobbs accused his mother of afflicting her. As constable for Topsfield, he was given the task of arresting William and Deliverance Hobbs. He believed that Deliverance was getting her revenge. The woman "did show a very bad spirit" when he seized her, he said in a deposition, so that "one might almost see revenge in her face." Presumably he was not aware that Abigail Hobbs had already claimed a week earlier that Sarah Wildes had afflicted her mother. He went on bravely and touchingly to defend his mother from the accusation of witchcraft, saying that "she hath always instructed me well in the Christian religion and the ways of God, ever since I was able to take instructions."

The last of this group of witches holds a unique place in the history of the witch-hunt. Nehemiah Abbott was another inhabitant of Topsfield, a twenty-seven-year-old weaver. After being led into the meetinghouse in the usual way, he was asked if he were guilty of witchcraft. He said, "No, Sir, I say before God, before whom I stand, that I know nothing of witchcraft." Hathorne asked, "Who is this man?" and Ann Putnam named him. Abbott continued to maintain his innocence in an articulate, confident fashion. As in the case of Mary Easty, Hathorne's own certainty faltered. He said to the girls, "Charge him not unless it be he." Then came the turning point. Some of the girls said, "This is the man," but others lost their nerve and said, "He is very like him." Hathorne then asked Ann Putnam, "How did you know his name?" and she said, "He did not tell me himself, but other witches told me." Mary Walcott could not say it was the man and Mercy Lewis said he was not the man. At this Abbott was sent out while others were examined.

When he was brought back in, there were so many people in front of the windows blocking the light that the accusers could not get a clear view of him and the magistrates ordered everyone outside. There the girls spoke quietly with him and finally acquitted him, saying he was just like the apparition they had seen except that he did not have a wart on his nose. Once face to face with their victim, in the open air, away from the charged atmosphere inside the meetinghouse, they could not maintain their fantasy, or fiction, that this man had bewitched them. He was the only accused witch ever to be let off.

Abbott benefited from an assured manner combined with the concern in John Hathorne's mind as to how the girls could identify witches they had never before seen. That concern undermined the girls' self-confidence, except for that of Ann Putnam. Hathorne had shown it already in the examinations of Deliverance Hobbs and Mary Easty. It had needed all of Ann's exceptional nerve and quick thinking to prevent it from growing. In the case of Abbott, those talents proved inadequate.

This episode shows that Hathorne was a closed-minded fanatic but was not actually corrupt. It gives support to John Hale's claim in his soul-searching *A Modest Enquiry*, written four years after the witch-hunt, that "there was in the justices, judges and others concerned, a conscientious desire to do the thing that was right."

In Parris's case, there is more room for doubt. As usual he wrote the record of the examination. He felt it necessary defensively to add at the end that Abbott was "a hilly faced man and stood shaded by reason of his own hair, so that for a time he seemed to some by-standers and observers, to be considerably like the person the afflicted did describe."

But Hathorne, Parris, the girls themselves and everyone else rapidly grew accustomed to the notion of people whom the girls had never seen in the flesh appearing as apparitions and explaining who they were. No one else was to be let off as a result of doubts about their identity.

CHAPTER SEVENTEEN

A Wheel within a Wheel

BUT the Putnams had been given a scare. This is perhaps one of the reasons they took as much trouble as they did to prepare the ground for the complaint against George Burroughs. As soon as the examinations of Deliverance Hobbs and the rest were finished, Thomas Putnam wrote a letter, both unctuous and melodramatic, to John Hathorne and Jonathan Corwin to alert them to an extraordinary development.

"Much honoured," it begins. "After most humble and hearty thanks presented to your Honours for the great care and pains you have already taken for us . . . we . . . thought it our duty to inform your Honours of what we conceive you have not heard, which are high and dreadful: of a wheel within a wheel, at which our ears do tingle."

Having aroused their curiosity, this missive left the magistrates hanging. It gave no clue as to the nature of the ear-tingling news but ended with a plea for the magistrates' prayers and help "in this distressed case" and piously "praying almighty God continually to prepare you, that you may be a terror to evil-doers and a praise to them that do well." There is in this veiled exhortation a hint of Putnam's sense of his own power as well as his anxiety.

The letter gives us a unique glimpse of Ann Putnam's formidable father in action. It shows a fawning, manipulative approach toward those above him, apparently humble but in reality arrogant. Putnam assumes the magistrates will be intrigued by, not contemptuous of, the tingling of his ears. His tone is reminiscent of that of the Shakespearean character often considered the embodiment of evil. Iago's wicked plotting, often thought to be motiveless, was in fact based on sexual and political envy and fury at having been passed over as Othello's lieutenant in favor of a rival. It seems a reasonable assumption that Thomas was not unlike Iago in his vengefulness, given the great number of his complaints against accused witches and the even greater number of his depositions testifying to their crimes. If so, he

may well have been like Iago in his venomous loathing of all those who
thwarted him.

No doubt very soon after sending his cliff-hanger of a letter Putnam
set Hathorne's and Corwin's own ears atingle on a personal visit.
There can be little doubt of what he told them. The day before he
wrote to them, Ann Putnam Junior had undergone the most terrifying
visionary experience she had yet known. She had seen the apparition
of a minister of God who tortured her and tried to force her to write in
his book. When she asked him his name he told her that it was George
Burroughs and that he had had three wives and had bewitched the first
two of them to death. He also said he had killed Deodat Lawson's wife
and child and very many soldiers in the Eastward and that he had
made Abigail Hobbs and several other people witches. He claimed he
was "above a witch for he was a conjurer." Burroughs was being set up
by the Putnams as not just a witch but a leader of witches.

Even in her terror and pain Ann Putnam treated Burroughs to one
of those lectures she and Abigail Williams were so prone to, full of
theological statements of the obvious, such as that it was an especially
dreadful thing that a minister, whose task was to teach little children to
fear God, should try to persuade people to give their souls to the devil.
Her tone of artificial shocked piety and the information about Burroughs's wives, as well as his time in Salem Village and Casco Bay, must
have come from adults. But in what manner and with what degree of
cynicism, we can never know for certain. Did Thomas and his wife
speak freely of their enemies in front of their children with no ulterior
motive? Did they talk of Burroughs in terms which they knew would
send young Ann into fits and cause her to imagine she saw him? Or did
they merely cynically write her deposition for her later? Did themselves believe she saw Burroughs's specter? Did *she* believe it? A
mixture of guile and manipulation and self-delusion seems more probable than sheer conscious fraud. It is true that if any one person
involved in the witch-hunt was utterly cynical and unscrupulous, that
person was Putnam. But on the whole it seems likely that Ann genuinely suffered the hallucinations described in the evidence. Two
witnesses, neither of them Putnams, were with her during the experience, as well as her father.

Two weeks later, a few days before his examination, she was to have
an even more terrifying vision of the devilish Burroughs. He told her
that his dead wives would appear to her and tell her many lies. Two
women in winding sheets duly rose up and turned their faces toward
him, looking red and angry, and told him that he had been very cruel
to them and that their blood cried for vengeance. Burroughs vanished
and the two women turned their faces, now "as pale as a white wall,"

toward Ann; they told her that they were Mr. Burroughs's first two wives and that he had murdered them. One said he had stabbed her under the left arm and put a piece of sealing wax on the place. She pulled aside the winding sheet to show Ann the wound. The other said Burroughs had killed her on board ship when she was coming home to her family in Salem.

Their manner of turning first to Burroughs, then to Ann, their faces red and then white, has a dreamlike quality that suggests this was a true hallucination. Only Thomas and Edward Putnam were present this time, although during Ann's former vision two other witnesses, neither of them family, had been present. And Ann Senior's similar experiences had been seen not just by relatives but also by Deodat Lawson. All this strengthens the probability that this hallucination also was not merely invented. In that case, it must have been terrifying indeed. It suggests an extraordinary imagination, fed on tales of horror as terrible as anything seen on television or video by children today. In a way, the horror stories that shaped Ann's soul were worse because they featured real people. She had never met Burroughs but had been hearing about him and his wives all her life. Perhaps Thomas Putnam would have concocted Ann's depositions for her if he had had to. But there was no need.

A question nobody asked was why, since Burroughs had already accused himself of multiple murder, he should defend himself from his dead wives' accusations by telling Ann they would lie about him. No one involved in the witch-hunt was interested in anomalies such as this, casting doubt on the evidence.

It took some time for a marshal to reach Wells, in Maine, apprehend Burroughs, and bring him back to Salem. Meanwhile, Deliverance Hobbs made her confession and several of the afflicted girls besides Ann Putnam were tortured by Burroughs's specter and asked to sign his book. Their accounts of these experiences are unusually long, dramatic, and detailed. Elizabeth Hubbard said that the lines in Burroughs's book were "red as blood"; Mercy Lewis said he carried her up "to an exceeding high mountain and showed [her] all the kingdoms of the earth and told [her] that he would give them all to [her] if she would write in his book." A newcomer, eighteen-year-old Susannah Sheldon, from Maine, who as a baby had narrowly escaped death in an Indian attack and later had seen both her father and brother killed by Indians, said that Burroughs told her he had murdered three of his children as well as two of his wives.

Benjamin Hutchinson, the twenty-four-year-old adopted son of Nathaniel Ingersoll, claimed he saw Abigail Hobbs point to where Burroughs's specter stood in the "great room" of his father's tavern

and struck at the spot with his rapier. This was on April 21, the day
Putnam wrote his letter. At Hutchinson's thrust, Abigail cried out that
Burroughs's phantom had turned into a cat. She then claimed to see
Sarah Good appear from nowhere and snatch it away. Abigail's hallucination or fantasy, recounted by Hutchinson, goes on for a long time
and ends with the vision of a great company of witches outside on the
hill, three lying dead. It is highly reminiscent of those rambling tales
made up by small children when absorbed in imaginative play.

Meanwhile, whatever agonies he had inflicted on others, Burroughs
had been having no easy time of it himself. During the period of his
stay in the Eastward, Indian attacks had devastated several settlements,
leaving Casco, where he was based, as the farthest colonial outpost.
The French joined forces with the Indians, and Burroughs himself was
involved in fierce fighting. By now he was the only preacher left in the
region; all the others had fled. In 1690 he moved south to Wells with
his seven children, his second wife having died, though presumably
not as a result of his witchcraft. Though Wells was not attacked, it was
constantly threatened and life was lived in the garrison as though under siege. Two years later, the nearby town of York was destroyed, its
refugees fleeing to Wells. Four months after that the field marshal of
the province of New Hampshire and Maine arrived with a company of
soldiers, and the townspeople joyfully assumed that these were the
reinforcements they had been requesting for years. But the field marshal had come on quite a different mission: to arrest the town's
minister for witchcraft.

By the time George Burroughs was brought back to Salem, four
more accused witches had been examined and imprisoned. Two of
them, Dorcas Hoar of Beverly and Susannah Martin of Amesbury, were
widows long suspected of witchcraft. Dorcas was believed to have bewitched to death not only her own husband but also the Reverend
John Hale's twelve-year-old daughter. This was because the child had
told her father that Hoar's children, in league with some of his servants, had been "conveying goods" from his house to theirs.
Susannah, like Bridget Bishop, went into men's bedrooms and lay on
them in the night. Both Dorcas and Susannah were skeptical of the
witch-hunt.

When Hathorne asked Martin what she thought ailed the afflicted
girls, she said, "I do not desire to spend my judgement upon it."

"Do not you think they are bewitched?"

"No, I do not think they are."

A little later she remarked that since the devil can appear in the
shape of Samuel, "a glorified saint," he "can appear in anyone's
shape." She referred to the biblical tale of Saul's visit to the Witch of

Endor to consult the ghost of the prophet Samuel. The witch produced what seemed to be the shape of Samuel but was really the devil.

The possibility that every one of the specters could be the devil in
disguise had now been raised for the second time by one of the accused in an examination. And this time it had been raised in a manner
underlining its biblical authority. But Hathorne, instead of responding
to the point, merely resumed his attack. He asked if Susannah believed
that the girls told the truth. She answered, "They may lie for aught I
know."

"May not you lie?" Hathorne asked.

Susannah said, "I dare not tell a lie if it would save my life."

"Then you will speak the truth."

"I have spoke nothing else."

Dorcas accused the afflicted girls of falsehood even more directly
than Susannah had done. When several of the girls said they saw a
black man whispering in her ears, she shouted, "Oh! You are liars!"
She added, "God will stop the mouths of liars."

Hathorne exclaimed, "You are not to speak after this manner in the
court."

"I will speak the truth as long as I live."

This brave claim proved false. Fearing death, with the date set for
her hanging, Dorcas in September would make a confession of witchcraft to John Hale and Nicholas Noyes, who then petitioned the court
for a stay of execution. It was granted, and eventually she was reprieved.

The third of this group of accused, Lydia Dustin, was another widow
with a long-standing reputation for witchcraft. She had been born in
England, was about sixty-five, and lived in Reading, west of Salem Village. Two of her daughters and her granddaughter were also to be
arrested, examined, and imprisoned. All were eventually released except Lydia herself who, though acquitted of witchcraft, was kept in
prison for nonpayment of fees and died there the following spring.

The fourth accused was Sarah Morey, a fourteen-year-old girl living
with her parents in Beverly. She survived the witch-hunt and eventually
married. But years later her mother petitioned for compensation for
prison fees and traveling expenses during her daughter's nine months
of imprisonment. She wrote that the "imprisonment was more to our
damage than I can think of, know, or can speak."

A warrant for the arrest of another accused witch had also been
issued on April 30, along with the warrants for the four women and
Burroughs. But Phillip English must have been forewarned, because
when the marshal came to arrest him he could not be found.

Burroughs arrived from Wells after the four women had been sent to Boston jail, and, since no more arrests had been made, he was examined on his own. Although it was no doubt accidental, solitary questioning seems appropriate for someone "above a witch." The examination was conducted not just by John Hathorne and Jonathan Corwin but also by two figures as elevated in the Puritan hierarchy as was Burroughs in its demonology: William Stoughton and Samuel Sewall. It took place in a tavern in Salem owned by Thomas Beadle.

William Stoughton was a minister turned full-time politician. He had recently regained the favor of the Boston Puritan elite, having lost it through playing a questionable part in the recent troubled events in the colony. He had served on the council of Sir Edmund Andros, the royal governor loathed by the Puritans who was appointed in 1686 and overthrown in 1689. He had emerged from under this cloud, largely through his friendship with Increase and Cotton Mather, to become the new deputy governor. At the beginning of May he had been appointed but not yet taken office, since the new charter had been written and signed but was still on its slow journey by boat to New England. Stoughton, as much as Cotton Mather himself, embodied Puritan rigidity. The Reverend Samuel Sewall, born in England, was, as we have seen, a more benign character. His brief diary entries on the witch-hunt suggest pained regret rather than the fury, fear, and contempt expressed by Cotton Mather and others.

The four magistrates began Burroughs's examination in private, away from the afflicted girls. They wanted to establish some facts, quickly and quietly, before the onset of the screaming and shouting. First, they asked him when he last took communion. He said so long ago he could not remember. He made the damning admission that he had been to church services twice when the sacrament was offered and yet did not partake of it.

Next, the magistrates asked him if his house was haunted. They must have heard rumors. He denied it but "owned there were toads." The absurdity of this admission fades slightly on remembering that a toad in Puritan eyes was a sinister creature, perhaps one of Satan's minions, perhaps Satan himself. Burroughs then denied that he made his wife swear she would not write to her father without his endorsement of the letter.

Burroughs's treatment of his wives is a recurrent theme in the case against him. Perhaps that treatment was in reality harsh. But in the case of the second wife, extended family tensions were also involved. When Burroughs married her, she was the daughter of a well-off Salem merchant. She was also the widow of John Hathorne's brother William. Her ghostly speech to Ann Putnam, saying she was killed on board ship, is so worded as to imply that Burroughs's motive in bewitching her was fear and resentment of her returning to her parents in Salem. William Hathorne had died in mysterious circumstances, and Burroughs had married his widow in Salem Village in 1691. She was a good catch for a mere village minister. The eminent Hathorne family, friends of Sarah's own kin, may have disapproved of the marriage.

That John Hathorne may have disliked and even hated Burroughs is mere speculation. But its possibility reminds us of the existence of countless alliances and animosities, beyond the ones we can trace, that lie behind the witch-hunt. Massachusetts in 1692 was still a small place. Almost everyone was connected, by numerous family, church, commercial, neighborly, and military networks, with almost everyone else. The four men who interrogated George Burroughs on May 9 would have been facing not a stranger, but a man known to them at least by reputation and probably personally.

They next asked whether his children had been baptized. Burroughs had to admit that none of them had, apart from the eldest. That admission must have seemed damning indeed. The minister was then led into the tavern's main room and at once "many if not all of the bewitched were grievously tortured." He now saw and heard for the first time the fits of which news may have reached him in faraway Wells. They would there have seemed strange and intriguing but irrelevant to his immediate concern, fear of the Indians. He now confronted the girls' dementia in all its terrifying power. He was dumbfounded.

But his astonishment increased beyond bounds when Susannah Sheldon cried out that Burroughs's first two wives were present in their winding sheets and that both accused him of killing them. He was told to look at this girl. She was standing apart from the others, on the far side of him. When he looked back again at the other afflicted girls, now behind him, they collapsed as though felled by his gaze. Mercy Lewis was helped to her feet. She was about to read her deposition, but he looked her way and again she "fell into a dreadful and tedious fit." As soon as Mary Walcott and Elizabeth Hubbard began reading their testimonies, the same thing occurred. Next Susannah Sheldon and Ann Putnam both cried that he "brought the book and would have them write."

Burroughs was asked what he thought of these things. He said that "it was an amazing and humbling providence but he understood nothing of it." He added, "When they begin to name my name, they cannot name it," no doubt hoping to suggest they had got the wrong man. But the hope was in vain. Susannah Sheldon, with Ann Putnam, again testified that his two wives and two children accused him. At this point some of the bewitched were "so tortured" that the magistrates ordered them to be taken away.

In the ensuing relative quiet, a stream of witnesses came forward to testify to Burroughs's history of witchcraft. Abigail Hobbs said she had been present at the witches' meeting in the pasture next to Parris's house at which Burroughs administered the sacrament. So did her mother, Deliverance. Elizer Keysar, father of the mad girl referred to by Mary Warren, claimed to have had the evil eye put on him by Burroughs at Beadle's tavern in Salem a few days before. As a result he saw strange lights in his chimney. Several soldiers who had fought with Burroughs in Casco Bay testified to his supernatural strength, saying he had lifted a barrel of molasses with one finger. He had even hoisted a gun six feet long with one finger. Presumably the soldiers were made to believe that it was advisable, for their own welfare, to repeat these tall tales. There is no evidence of personal animosity on their part toward Burroughs.

The minister's physical strength was, literally, a legend. The repetition, with small variations, of the same anecdotes by several men suggests that one or two remarkable incidents had grown to vastly exaggerated proportions in numerous retellings.

Calef points out that Burroughs's "contemporaries in the schools during his minority could have testified, that his strength was then as much superior to theirs as ever . . . it was discovered to be since," so it need hardly be attributed to a recent pact with the devil.

Two women testified to Burroughs's harshness to his second wife. But their testimony was based on the wife's complaints, not the evidence of their eyes. Captain John Putnam recounted his story of the covenant Burroughs had made his first wife sign, in 1680, to agree not to tell any of his secrets. Burroughs was led off to jail.

CHAPTER EIGHTEEN

Such Horrid Lies

WITH Burroughs safely behind bars, Thomas Putnam could turn his attention to other objects of his hatred. During May and June he and his friends made twenty complaints to the magistrates, many of them listing three or more suspected witches. One listed eight, another eleven. Thomas signed six of these documents, and he may have signed more. We cannot know for certain since seven of the complaints have been lost.

The ranks of those thrown into jail during this time were made up partly of people with reputations for witchcraft, partly of people connected by family with men or women already accused, and partly of political enemies of the Putnams or representatives of the prosperous Salem society they loathed. A few individuals cannot be fit into any of these categories since sufficient information about them is lacking.

As the number of prisoners increased, so did the despair throughout eastern Massachusetts. Spring was turning to summer, but the tending of crops and the care of cattle and poultry were widely neglected. Hundreds of people had relatives in jail. They were forced to abandon their daily activities to sell goods to pay jail fees and to travel long distances for examinations and visits with jailed parents, spouses, or children.

One complaint netted a grandfather and granddaughter, George and Margaret Jacobs. George was in his seventies and walked with two sticks; Margaret was sixteen. They were relatives by marriage of Daniel Andrew, a leading opponent of the Putnams. The old man's chief accuser at his examination was a newcomer among the afflicted, his twenty-year-old servant girl Sarah Churchill. Like so many of the girls, she was an orphan; like Mercy Lewis, she had lived in Maine and seen her parents murdered by Indians. George was as forthright in his skepticism of the witch-hunt as Dorcas Hoar or Susannah Martin. "The devil can go in any shape," he declared. As always when confronted with this highly pertinent point, Hathorne did not respond. Later, however, when Jacobs said, "The devil can take any likeness," Hathorne finally made a reply: "Not without their consent."

That was his credo. It was to the misfortune of the accused that all the magistrates and judges in the examinations and trials appear to have shared it. Not all Puritans did. There was no firm authority for it. Hathorne and the other magistrates apparently felt it *ought* to be true. They give no indication of having been convinced by sound arguments.

Perhaps George's great age gave him courage. Whatever might happen to him, he would not live long. When Sarah Churchill said she had been frightened when her master's shape came to her, George declared, "Well, burn me or hang me, I will stand in the truth of Christ, I know nothing of it." It may have been his resolution that made a second examination necessary the next day. This time, all the girls suffered violent fits. Together with his granddaughter, George was remanded to jail.

Sixteen-year-old Margaret, in a separate room from her grandfather in Beadle's tavern, where their examination was held, made a confession. Unlike her grandfather, she had her whole life before her. The magistrates told her that if she did not confess she would be hanged; if she did confess she would live.

This policy of sparing confessors had evolved not only as a means of encouraging confessions but also because confessors were too useful to die. They were needed to testify against others. The justices may have intended that the confessors perish eventually but only after no suspects were still walking free. Margaret not only told the magistrates she was a witch but also accused her grandfather and George Burroughs of witchcraft. In mid-August she recanted: "May it please the honoured court, I was cried out upon by some of the possessed persons, as afflicting them; whereupon I was brought to my examination, which persons at the sight of me fell down, which did very much startle and affright me. The Lord above knows I knew nothing, in the least measure, how or who afflicted them; they told me, without doubt I did, or else they would not fall down at me; they told me, if I would not confess, I should be put down into the dungeon and would be hanged, but if I would confess I should have my life. . . . The very first night after I had made confession, I was in such horror of conscience that I could not sleep for fear the devil should carry me away for telling such horrid lies. The Lord, I hope, in whom I trust, out of the abundance of his mercy, will forgive me my false forswearing myself. What I said, was altogether false against my grandfather, and Mr. Burroughs, which I did to save my life and to have my liberty; but the Lord, charging it to my conscience, made me in so much horror, that I could not contain myself before I had denied my confession, which I did though I saw nothing but death before me, choosing rather death with a quiet conscience, than to live in such horror, which I could not suffer. Where, upon my denying my confession, I was committed to close prison, where I have enjoyed more felicity in spirit, a thousand times, than I did before in my enlargement."

The magistrates did not believe Margaret's recantation. But she stuck to it, though "close confined in a loathsome dungeon" and certain she would die. On August 18 she went to George Burroughs to ask his forgiveness. He not only forgave her but prayed with her. Two days later she wrote a letter to her father, explaining everything that had happened and asking him to pray for her too. She expressed her hope for "a joyful and happy meeting in heaven."

This brave girl was saved from execution by falling ill at the time of her trial. However, she remained in prison a year longer, for some months after all the other suspected witches were freed, since she lacked money to pay her prison fees. Only after a kindly stranger heard of her case and paid the fees for her did she go free.

A second recantation was made as a consequence of the examination of George Jacobs and his granddaughter. On the afternoon of June 1, Sarah Ingersoll, the thirty-year-old daughter of the innkeeper, was sought out by a distraught young woman who had just been examined by the magistrates, probably in the tavern. That young woman was Sarah Churchill, who had earlier made accusations against George Jacobs, her master.

In a deposition, Sarah Ingersoll wrote: "She came to me crying and wringing her hands, seemingly to be much troubled in spirit. I asked her what she ailed. She answered, she had undone herself. She said, in belying herself and others in saying she had set her hand to the devil's book, whereas, she said, she never did. I told her I believed she had set her hand to the book. She answered, crying, and said, 'No, no, no: I never did.' I asked her then what made her say she did. She answered, because they threatened her, and told her they would put her into the dungeon, and put her along with Mr. Burroughs; and thus several times she followed me up and down, telling me that she had undone herself, in belying herself and others. I asked her why she did not deny she wrote it. She told me, because she had stood out so long in it, that now she durst not. She said also, that, if she told Mr. Noyes but once she had set her hand to the book, he would believe her; but, if she told the truth, and said she had not set her hand to the book a hundred times, he would not believe her."

After making her accusations against old George Jacobs, Sarah Churchill had herself been thrown into jail. Like Mary Warren, she had been overheard casting doubt on the afflicted girls' probity. On June 1 she was examined in private by the magistrates and agreed that she had signed the devil's book, that Bridget Bishop had told her she had killed a child, and that her master Jacobs had called her a "bitch witch." It was immediately after this that she had gone in distress to Sarah Ingersoll. But she must have kept her silence thereafter for she remained at liberty and appeared as one of the afflicted at several of the trials. Sarah Ingersoll's deposition about Sarah Churchill lay ignored in the files.

A few days after Jacobs's and his granddaughter's examinations, another of the family, George's daughter-in-law Rebecca, was seized in a roundup that should also have included her brother, the prosperous and powerful Daniel Andrew, and her husband, George Jacobs Junior. But both brother and husband, like Phillip English before them, had fled. Rebecca was at home with four children, one of them a nursling, when the constable arrived. He was Jonathan Putnam, a cousin of Thomas. Maintaining the family's high standards of cunning, he tricked Rebecca into leaving the house and going away with him, saying she would come back home soon. Rebecca had been feeble-minded for more than twelve years, since a child of hers had died. She may have been driven even closer to madness a few days earlier when her eldest daughter, Margaret, was jailed. As Rebecca went down the road with Putnam and his officers, her children ran a great way after her, crying. Rebecca was to languish in prison for ten months. During that time the neighbors, out of pity, took care of the children to "preserve them from perishing."

Before the next roundup, this time of eleven people, a suspect named Elizabeth Cary found herself at the bar prematurely. Her name had been bandied about for some days. On May 24 her husband, a rich merchant living in Charlestown, decided to take matters into his own hands instead of waiting for the constable and his officers to appear at the door. Successful and prosperous, living in a society that was worldly in outlook compared with Salem Village, Nathaniel Cary was used to shaping events in his and his family's interest by use of his reason and influence. He rode with his wife to Salem Village to try to establish that this was a case of mistaken identity. They arrived to find an examination about to begin; once Cary, characteristically, had "taken care to get a convenient place," they seated themselves in the meetinghouse. His eyewitness account of what happened is the most detailed we have of the procedure and the behavior of everyone involved during an examination of accused witches.

"The afflicted were two girls of about ten years old, and about two or three other, of about eighteen," he writes. "One of the girls talked most and could discern more than the rest." This was probably Ann Putnam. "The prisoners were called in one by one, and as they came in were cried out of, etc." In other words, the girls screamed that the accused were afflicting them. "The prisoner was placed about seven or eight foot from the justices, and the accusers between the justices and them. The prisoner was ordered to stand right before the justices, with an officer appointed to hold each hand, lest they should therefore afflict [the girls] and the prisoner's eyes must be constantly on the justices, for if they looked at the afflicted they would either fall into fits or cry out of being hurt by them."

After the prisoners were questioned, they were made to say the Lord's Prayer. It was considered proof of being a witch if they failed to say it perfectly. When the girls recovered from their fits, they stared silently at "some one person" and the magistrates said they were struck dumb. After a while they began to speak again. Then the justices said to the accusers, "Which of you will go and touch the prisoner at the bar?" One of the girls would go forward but before she had made three steps would fall down in a fit. The justices would order her to be picked up and carried to the prisoner, to touch him or her; as soon as she did so, the justices would say she was well.

This part of Cary's account describes the "touch test." The witch's evil was thought to flow back from the afflicted girl to the witch during physical contact, and the girl was made well again. But Cary finishes his description by saying that the justice pronounced the girl well "before he could discern any alteration." It appears from the perfunctory manner in which the test was conducted that an element of ritual had crept into the display.

The wise and distinguished Thomas Brattle had no doubts on that issue. "I know a man that will venture two to one with any Salemite whatever, that let the matter be duly managed, and the afflicted person shall come out of her fit upon the touch of the most religious hand in Salem," he wrote.

So far Cary was only a spectator. His wife was with him, but no notice was taken of her by the afflicted girls except that they came up to her and asked her name. If Cary had been a little less confident of the force of reason and influence and a little more aware of the evil surrounding him, he would at that moment have taken her by the hand, led her out of the meetinghouse, and conveyed her as far from Salem Village as money and influence could take him.

Instead he talked to John Hale, an old acquaintance, about what he should do. Hale promised that he would arrange for him to speak to the girl who had been accusing his wife. Cary "reposed [his] trust in him." This was unwise. When the examination was over, Hale said that it was not possible after all, as promised, for Cary to meet Abigail Williams in private at Mr. Parris's house and instead took Cary and his wife to the tavern.

At first all went well. John Indian, who helped at Ingersoll's when he was not needed at the Parris's or rolling about on the floor having fits, waited on the Carys. In return for some cider, he showed them some scars on his body that he claimed were caused by witchcraft. He also explained that his wife had been imprisoned as a witch. But then all the accusers burst into the room and "began to tumble down like swine." The Carys had still trustingly expected Abigail alone to appear. Everyone stood, agog, waiting to see whose name the afflicted would call. It was Elizabeth Cary's.

"Immediately after, a warrant was sent from the justices to bring my wife before them, who were sitting in a chamber near by, waiting for this," Nathaniel writes. The Reverend Hale had either plotted with the girls and magistrates and Thomas Putnam who, with Benjamin Hutchinson, had signed the complaint requesting the warrant or, at the very least, had not prevented an outcome he must have foreseen.

Cary says that when Elizabeth was brought before the justices, her chief accusers were two girls. "My wife declared to the justices that she never had any knowledge of them before that day. She was forced to stand with her arms stretched out. I did request that I might hold one of her hands, but it was denied me; then she desired me to wipe the tears from her eyes, and the sweat from her face, which I did; then she desired she might lean herself on me, saying she should faint.

"Justice Hathorne replied, she had strength enough to torment those persons, and she should have strength enough to stand." At that Cary protested at their "cruel proceedings." They told him that unless he was silent "he would be turned out of the room."

This was probably the first time in his adult life that Nathaniel Cary had found himself powerless. John Indian was brought in as another accuser. He "fell down and tumbled about like a hog but said nothing." The merchant may have reflected that he had had no trouble staying upright and rational in Elizabeth's presence while quaffing cider and showing his scars.

Cary continues, "The justices asked the girls, who afflicted the Indian? They answered she, meaning my wife. . . . The justices ordered her to touch him . . . but her head must be turned another way, lest instead of curing, she should make him worse, by her looking on him." Elizabeth's hand was guided to take hold of John's, "but the Indian took hold on her hand and pulled her down on the floor in a barbarous manner." But then his hand was removed "and her hand put on his and the cure was quickly wrought." The normally self-controlled Nathaniel was by now provoked beyond bearing. "I being extremely troubled at their inhumane dealings, uttered a hasty speech, that God would take vengeance on them, and desired that God would deliver us out of the hands of unmerciful men."

This outburst did him no good. A warrant was written consigning Elizabeth to jail, where she was to go the next day. With difficulty and at great cost, Nathaniel obtained the use of a room at the inn for the night but without any beds in it. Even if there had been beds, he writes, he and his wife would have gotten little rest. In the morning Elizabeth was taken to Boston prison. But later that day Nathaniel obtained a habeas corpus to remove her to the jail in Cambridge, which was in the Carys' home county of Middlesex, rather than in Essex.

"Having been there one night, next morning the jailer put irons on her legs, having received such a command. The weight of them was about eight pounds. These irons and her other afflictions soon brought her into convulsion fits, so that I thought she would have died that night. I sent to entreat that the irons might be taken off, but all entreaties were in vain . . . so in this condition she must continue."

Cary then tried to save her life by every means within the law. When the trials began in July he rode to Salem to observe for himself the judges' impartiality or lack of it. On seeing that the afflicted girls' visions and idle and malicious gossip were as solemnly received as evidence as they had been at the examinations, he "did easily perceive" how things would go for his wife.

"I acquainted her with the danger, and that if she were carried to Salem to be tried, I feared she would never return." He attempted to arrange for her to be tried in Middlesex County instead of Salem and was "put in hopes of it." But he soon realized the hopes had been raised by men with no real intention of fulfilling them, and he had to abandon them.

He was a law-abiding man. Also, like so many others in Massachusetts, he could not believe in what was happening until it happened to him. But when all legal means failed to lessen the likelihood that his innocent wife would be hanged, he had no other recourse but to turn to illegal ones. He contrived her escape, probably by bribery.

The couple fled first to Rhode Island, then New York, where they were courteously received by the governor, Benjamin Fletcher. Thanks to Nathaniel's tireless efforts, the Carys' ordeal ended not in tragedy but in the eventual return to their normal married life together. Back in Massachusetts, Nathaniel was in time to become a justice himself and a member of the General Court.

The tone of his account, written several years after the event, is of deep pain and sorrow rather than rage. The monstrousness of what was done to his wife caused emotions more profound than mere personal fury. Later he witnessed some of the executions. What he said of them shall be seen in due course.

CHAPTER NINETEEN

A Bold Fellow with His Hat On

ANOTHER eyewitness account has come down to us, of an examination held shortly after Elizabeth Cary's. John Alden, a mariner of Boston, was one of the batch of eleven complained of on May 28. He was not just any mariner. Son of the John Alden who came over on the *Mayflower* and cofounded Plymouth Colony and whose romantic love for his Priscilla entered legend and inspired a Longfellow poem, John was by 1692 seventy years old and a prominent Massachusetts figure. He was a church member and a merchant, owned considerable property, had been a naval commander, and had seen service in the French and Indian War. At the time he was seized he had just spent two months in Canada, redeeming captives taken by the Indians. He was rich, important, and respected. His varied life and breadth of outlook challenged narrow attitudes. No wonder the girls and Thomas Putnam hated him. Or, rather, the idea of him. None had ever met the man.

For *them,* in his turn, Alden felt contempt. This is shown in the first sentence of his account of his ordeal, when he describes the afflicted girls as "a company of poor distracted or possessed creatures or witches." They were so beneath his notice that he did not even bother clearly to identify them. His contempt was not lessened by closer acquaintance.

"Those wenches . . . who played their juggling tricks, falling down, crying out and staring in people's faces, the magistrates demanded of them several times, who it was of all the people in the room that hurt them? One of these accusers pointed several times at one Captain Hill, there present, but spake nothing. The same accuser had a man standing at her back to hold her up. He stooped down to her ear, then she cried out, 'Alden, Alden afflicted her.' One of the magistrates asked her if she had ever seen Alden. She answered no. He asked her how she knew it was Alden. She said, 'the man told her so.' " It is notable that the accuser did not any longer feel it necessary to pretend Alden's specter had told her his name. There seems a fair chance her prompter was either Thomas Putnam or Jonathan Walcott.

However, the magistrates felt concerned enough about appearing to establish the accurate identity of witches to send Alden and the girls out into the street, where they would see him more clearly, as a month earlier they had sent out Nehemiah Abbott. But this time the result was quite different. Far from being abashed by the break in the rhythm of the proceedings and the change from the gloomy interior to the daylight outside, the girls were further inspired. They formed a ring with Alden in the center and the one who had been given his name called out, "There stands Alden, a bold fellow with his hat on before the judges. He sells powder and shot to the Indians and French and lies with the Indian squaws and has Indian papooses."

There is no evidence that these accusations were true. However, only an adventurous, unconventional character would have prompted them. The "bold fellow with his hat on" was insufficiently awed not only by the rules of Puritan society as the Putnams understood them but, what was worse, by the proceedings of the Salem Villagers' beloved, sacrosanct court.

Alden goes on, "Then was Alden committed to the marshal's custody and his sword taken from him, for they said he afflicted them with his sword." (He writes his account almost entirely in the third person.) It seems that the initial questioning had taken place in Ingersoll's tavern for he says, "After some hours Alden was sent for to the meetinghouse in the village before the magistrates, who required Alden to stand upon a chair, to the open view of all the people." He goes on, "The accusers cried out that Alden did pinch them" despite his elevated position, in the sight of all the people, a good distance away from them. One of the magistrates told the marshal to hold Alden's hands open so he could not "pinch those creatures." Alden asked why they should think he would come to "that village" to afflict "those persons" when he had never seen them before. Needless to say, no one answered him. Bartholomew Gedney, a third magistrate who presided on this and subsequent occasions alongside Hathorne and Corwin, told him to confess. He said he had known Alden many years, had been at sea with him, and always looked on him as an honest man, "but now he did see cause to alter his judgement." Alden again proclaimed his innocence. Gedney told him to look at the accusers, which he did, and they fell down. Alden asked Gedney why *he* did not fall down when he looked at him.

"But no reason was given that I heard." The lapse into the first person speaks of Alden's outrage.

The accusers were brought to him and at his touch recovered from their fits. Alden said, no doubt in angry despair, that it must be God's will that these creatures accused innocent persons. Nicholas Noyes, that stout bully, angrily demanded what gave Alden the right to speak of God's will. He continued to lecture him and thus "stopped Alden's mouth." Later Alden seized the chance to tell Mr. Gedney that there was "a lying spirit" in the girls "for I can assure you that there is not a word of truth in all these say of me."

Alden was sent to Boston prison. Like Elizabeth Cary, he made his escape before coming to trial, after getting wind of the way in which the trials were conducted and what evidence was taken. It seems that, for anyone rich enough, escaping was easy. Prison keepers were not so much public servants as entrepreneurs; they were paid a small salary but made much of their living from their charges to prisoners for food, lodging, and chains. Moreover, salary payments were far from reliable. In December 1693 the Salem jail keeper petitioned for nine years' back pay of five pounds a year. No wonder such officials were open to bribery. Alden was eventually caught and brought back to Boston for trial. But by then the witch-hunt was virtually over. No one came forward against him, and he was cleared by proclamation.

Among a long list of humbler witches examined during the following month were Job Tookey of Beverly, Elizabeth Howe of Topsfield, Martha Carrier of the township of Andover and, from Salem Town, a black slave called Candy.

Job Tookey had made rash comments about the witch-hunt. He claimed that he could raise the devil when he pleased and that he would "take Mr. Burroughs's part," that is, that he would place himself on George Burroughs's side at his trial. He is the only one of the accused witches who has left us an account of his life. It makes painful but most interesting reading, both in itself and in the light it casts on some of the factors that created the victims of the witch-hunt. Many of the accused witches had either risen or fallen in social status, causing anger and resentment in both themselves and others. Job Tookey had fallen, from a great height.

His father had been a distinguished preacher in England and had intended that his son should be a scholar. But he had been forced because of financial reversals to withdraw Job from Emmanuel College, Cambridge, and send him to London as an apprentice. But by further bad luck the Great Fire of London bankrupted Job's employer and the boy went to sea. He hurt his hand, became unemployable, and got badly into debt. Further bad luck was compounded by his turbulent nature. He quarreled violently with a Marblehead shipowner who had paid his debts and given him a job as a ship hand. When young Tookey tried to break his contract, the shipowner had him thrown into jail. A tremendous battle of wills then developed. The shipowner tried to shame Tookey into obedience and deference, threatening to send him as a slave to Virginia and casting aspersions on his preacher father, claiming he was an "anabaptistical quaking rogue." But as a result Tookey grew ever more defiant. His fury was fueled by his sense of the degradation of his situation, as is shown by his harping on his origins in his petitions to the court.

"Consider, I beseech you, my education and bringing-up," he wrote, pointing to the contrast between these and his present accommodation, where he was "almost poisoned with the stink of my own dung."

The shipowner withdrew his charges after three months and Job was let free. That was in 1682. Ten years later, a laborer in Beverly, Tookey was declaring that the devil was his servant. The afflicted girls, who by this time included a new recruit of eighteen named Elizabeth Booth, claimed that he had murdered several men, women, and children. Their ghosts appeared to the afflicted during his examination, crying out for vengeance. But for once in his life Tookey was lucky. He was never tried and hanged, though he never made a confession. He was freed in January 1693.

Elizabeth Howe, like the Towne sisters (Rebecca Nurse, Mary Easty, and Sarah Cloyce), accused witches from the same troubled region, was a woman of excellent character and intelligence. She too was accused because she belonged by marriage and birth to families opposed to the Putnams in land disputes. When Mercy Lewis and Mary Walcott fell into fits and Ann Putnam said she had hurt her three times, Elizabeth said, "If it was the last moment I was to live, God knows I am innocent of anything in this nature." She kept her composure even as Ann Putnam showed a pin stuck into her hand and Abigail Williams displayed "great prints" on her arm where she had been pinched and Mary Warren "violently fell down" when Elizabeth looked at her. She pointed out that she had never heard of any of these people before she was arrested. Of course, that availed her nothing.

Once she was in jail, a number of depositions were collected from her neighbors, claiming she had bewitched their cows, mares, and, in the case of a certain Samuel Perley and his wife, their ten-year-old daughter. But several depositions in Elizabeth's favor were also put forward. One of them, from the minister of the township of Rowley, beyond Topsfield, testifies to her having spoken to the Perleys' daughter after she had a fit in her presence. Elizabeth took her by the hand and asked whether she had ever done her any hurt. The girl said, "No, never, and if I did complain of you in my fits I know not that I did so." Even more revealing is the testimony by the same witness that the girl's brother, seeing his sister outdoors, called to her through the window, "Say Goodwife Howe is a witch, say she is a witch." The deponent pertinently adds, "No wonder that the child in her fits did mention Goodwife Howe, when her nearest relations were so frequent in expressing their suspicions in the child's hearing . . . that the said Goodwife Howe, was an instrument of mischief to the child."

If anyone had noted this testimony from the clearheaded minister, they might have realized they had the simple answer to the question of how it could be that so many God-fearing women came to be accused of dealing in witchcraft by a small group of girls afflicted with fits.

The most moving testament to Elizabeth's character came from her ninety-four-year-old father-in-law. Not only was she a wonderful daughter, he said, but also "loving, obedient and kind" to her blind husband, "tenderly leading him about by the hand."

Like so many accused witches who were principled and brave enough to refuse to confess when faced with the gallows, Elizabeth was one of those people most loved and needed by others and most missed when they are gone.

Martha Carrier of Andover, though extremely courageous, does not belong in this category. Her angry answers to the magistrates' questions, while refreshingly forthright and thoroughly justified, suggest an abrasive personality more akin to that of Sarah Good than that of Elizabeth Proctor or Rebecca Nurse or Elizabeth Howe.

"Can you look upon these and not knock them down?" Hathorne asked.

"They will dissemble if I look upon them."

"You see, you look upon them and they fall down."

To this she replied that the devil was a liar.

When the magistrate asked her, "What black man did you see?" she snapped back, "I saw no black man but your own presence." Later she declared, "It is a shameful thing that you should mind these folks that are out of their wits."

Martha's two teenage sons were later to confess to witchcraft and testify against her. They did so, according to a letter written from Salem prison by John Proctor, after being tied neck and heels "till the blood was ready to come out of their noses." The practice of "tying neck and heels" had been used in England in the Middle Ages as the most secure means of manacling prisoners but had later evolved into an unofficial means of torture. In Shakespeare's *Tempest* Prospero threatens Ferdinand by saying, "I'll manacle thy neck and feet together." Accused witches in Salem were kept tied in that way for twenty-four hours or longer. This happened to John Proctor's own son, William. But even though the blood "gushed out at his nose," William would not confess. Large-hearted John bred loyal, honest children.

The Carrier sons never recanted even when their mother faced the gallows.

Two other children of Martha Carrier confessed to witchcraft without being forced to.

"How long hast thou been a witch?" Hathorne asked the girl child.

"Ever since I was six years old."

"How old are you now?"

"Near eight years old. Brother Richard says I shall be eight years old in November next."

She claimed that her mother carried her to people to afflict them and, when her mother was in prison, came to her in the form of a black cat. Her brother Thomas said he had been a witch for a week. Both children were imprisoned though in due course let out on bail.

Their mother was the first of the accused witches from Andover; there were to be very many more, in fact more than from any other region, even Salem Village. We do not know why this should be, but it appears that a semi-independent witch-hunt may have started there, with local people stoking the fires in the manner of the Putnams. But the blaze was first brought there from Salem Village, via another township, Billerica. Martha's arrest followed that of a Billerica resident, her brother-in-law Dr. Roger Toothaker, who made the dangerous claim that his adult daughter had killed a witch. Her method had been to put some of an afflicted person's urine in a pot and place it in an oven overnight. The witch was dead in the morning. The girls may well have regarded this exploit and Toothaker's boasting of it as an offensive or even threatening challenge to their status and power. Once Toothaker was in jail, all his relatives became suspect. Martha Carrier, his wife's sister, had the kind of reputation that in itself might attract the girls' attention. She and her family had been accused of bringing smallpox to Andover in 1689. She had also had many witchcraft accusations leveled against her. Roger's wife, Mary, his young daughter, Margaret, and Martha Carrier were all arrested on May 28.

Two weeks later Toothaker died in Boston prison. The coroner's court went to considerable trouble to establish that he died from natural causes, requiring no less than fifteen jurors to examine his body and obtain "the best information" they could "from the persons near and present at his death." Clearly the death was suspicious. Perhaps the elderly physician knew he might find the rigors of prison unbearable and had smuggled in the means to bring them to an end.

Mary Toothaker was, in late July, to make a rambling confession in which she talked at length of her fear of the Indians. This fear proved well founded. She was murdered by them three years later in a raid on

Billerica. Her daughter Martha, now twelve, was taken captive and never again seen by white people.

The Andover witch-hunt gained tremendous added momentum when a man named Joseph Ballard called on some of the afflicted girls, sometime in May or early June, to discover who was afflicting his wife, ill with a fever. He sent a "horse and man" for each girl as today a television studio might send a car with a chauffeur for a celebrity. Other people of Andover soon did the same. The accusers, appreciating this proper recognition of their status, went into fits wherever they were taken. Before long more than fifty people were accused. And they soon began confessing.

The Andover confessions were among the most colorful of any made anywhere. Ann Foster, who later died in prison, told John Hale that she had ridden from Andover to a Salem Village witch meeting on a stick but that the stick had broken and given her a fall. She was still sore, she claimed. When she later repeated this confession, she added, in response to Hale's query as to what she did for food, that she carried bread and cheese in her pocket. She described all the witches at the meeting enjoying a picnic under a tree before getting down to their devilish business.

Very evident here is the widespread confusion about witches and their specters: Ann Foster never says it was her *specter* that rode to Salem Village. Yet the afflicted girls had claimed to see people at witch meetings whose bodily selves were elsewhere at the time, sometimes manacled in prison, sometimes standing in front of the whole congregation in the meetinghouse. Were witch meetings made up of a bizarre mixture of flesh-and-blood witches and spirits? The question never got asked.

Ann Foster also talked of her fear that George Burroughs and Martha Carrier would kill her. They had come to her in prison with an iron spindle and threatened to stab her for confessing her witchcraft and accusing them of corrupting her. She is clear that in this case she means their specters since the originals were kept in "other rooms" in the prison. She talked of the fear again to John Hale a month later. It was, he says, "much upon her spirits." The premonition of death, if not of its means, proved all too true. She perished soon afterward.

The Andover confessions may have been so numerous and detailed because they were elicited by the relatives of the accused as well as the magistrates. Many Andover men, convinced that their children or wives must be witches if the afflicted girls said so, or else fearing for their lives if they insisted on their innocence, persuaded them to say they were guilty. At a terrifying roundup in the Andover meetinghouse, a number of accused witches were blindfolded and had their hands laid on the afflicted persons, who then came out of their fits. They were at once taken as prisoners to Salem. A petition from six of them, after graphically recounting this episode, describes their being persuaded to confess first by their husbands and then by "some gentlemen," probably Hathorne and Gedney, who told "us that we were witches and they knew it and we knew it and they knew that we knew it, which made us think that it was so; and our understanding, our faculties and our reason almost gone, we were not capable of judging our condition. . . . And most of what we said was in effect but a consenting to what they said." All these women languished in jail for months but none was hanged despite renouncing their confessions. By then events had moved on.

Meanwhile, many young people of Andover joined the afflicted girls from Salem Village in their fits and also boasted spectral sight. Dudley Bradstreet, a justice of the peace in Andover and a son of Governor Bradstreet, sent thirty or forty to prison but then refused to grant any more warrants. Soon afterward he and his wife were themselves accused of being witches but fled before being seized.

What brought Andover's own witch-hunt to an end was the reaction of "a worthy gentleman of Boston" to being named as a witch by accusers there. He issued a writ demanding a thousand pounds for defamation. No more was heard of the accusations against him and thereafter other Andover accusations "generally ceased."

The last witches from Salem to be examined before the focus of the witch-hunt moved beyond the borders of that region to Andover and elsewhere were two women who had come from Barbados, Margaret Hawkes and her negro slave Candy. Candy's examination on July 4 shows no lessening of the accusing girls' energies. They went into violent fits when the slave, who had confessed to witchcraft, produced rags that she said she had used in afflicting people.

"A bit of one of the rags being set on fire, the afflicted all said they were burned, and cried out dreadfully. The rags being put into water, two of the aforenamed persons were in dreadful fits almost choked, and the other was violently running down to the river, but was stopped."

Perhaps the true cause of such violent displays, merely to net a slave and her mistress, was that several or perhaps all of the afflicted in this case were accused-turned-accusers: they included Mary Warren, Deliverance Hobbs, and Abigail Hobbs. Mary Warren may have feared being sent back to prison, and the Hobbses may have hoped to be let out.

Margaret Hawkes was a newcomer to Salem and the widow of a

merchant, thus on two counts disliked and despised. But she was no Phillip English, Daniel Andrew, or Nathaniel Cary. By this time the leading accusers—Ann Putnam, Abigail Williams, Mary Walcott, and Elizabeth Hubbard—had more important tasks to perform than throwing fits at examinations of insignificant Salemites.

CHAPTER TWENTY

Loud Cries and Clamours

In mid-May a truly momentous event had occurred. Increase Mather had returned from England bearing the colony's new charter. It was long overdue. Two years after the old charter was abrogated in 1684 by the English king, the formerly self-governing colony came under the rule of a governor from England. But once he was overthrown in 1689 Massachusetts was without legal government. As a result, the legal system devised by the Puritans had ceased to have validity. It was for this reason that only preliminary examinations, not trials, of accused witches had as yet taken place.

Increase Mather had finished negotiating the new charter the previous October but it had taken all these months for him, and it, to make the long, hazardous voyage from the old country. Massachusetts was now officially not a colony but a province. It had lost many of its privileges. Under the new terms the Puritans could no longer enforce Puritan worship on the populace or outlaw other religions. All male property owners, not just male church members, had the vote. This spelled the beginning of the end for the Puritan theocracy, though its leaders did not yet know it.

The redoubtable Increase, sailing toward Boston, had reason to think himself politically secure. The new governor, traveling with him, had been the minister's own nominee to the king. And, as his son Cotton recorded in his diary, the new governing body, the council, was made up entirely of his allies. Writing in the privacy of his study, for no eyes but his own, Mather *fils* does not hide either his jubilation or his paranoia: "The time for favour has now come! . . . I am now to receive an answer of so many prayers. All the councillors of the province are of my father's nomination and my father-in-law, with several related unto me, and several brethren of my own church, are among them. The governor of the province is not *my enemy*, but one whom I baptized, namely, Sir William Phipps, one of my own flock, and one of my dearest friends."

Sir William Phipps might have seemed an unlikely dear friend of

Cotton Mather. He had been born in Maine but had served the English Crown by taking possession of the treasure of a sunken Spanish galleon. It was for that he was knighted. The king had chosen him as governor over William Stoughton, also a friend and ally of the Mathers and now deputy governor, because of his extensive military experience. The chief difficulty facing the province, as far as anyone in England was aware, was the threat of war with the French aided by Indians. However, though not a minister himself, Sir William was willing to toe the hard Puritan line in matters of religion. It was primarily for that reason that Cotton saw him as an ally.

Increase and Sir William were surprised when they stepped onto the shore to find themselves confronting a quite different, far trickier problem from that of French and Indian enemies. The prisons of Boston, Salem, and Ipswich were full to overflowing with witches. And complaints, arrests, and examinations were still going on.

"When I first arrived I found this province miserably harrassed with a most horrible witchcraft or possession of devils which had broke in upon several towns," Sir William wrote. "Some scores of poor people were taken with preternatural torments, some scalded with brimstone, some had pins stuck in their flesh, others hurried into the fire and water and some [were] dragged out of their houses and carried over the tops of trees and hills for many miles together."

The "scores" of poor people Sir William refers to presumably include many of those confessing to witchcraft. Tituba had talked of being carried great distances through the air on a pole. There was a fine line between confessors and afflicted that was crossed and recrossed by Tituba herself, Mary Warren, Deliverance Hobbs, Sarah Churchill, and others.

A man of military background, Sir William took immediate, though questionable, action. Later when the questions were asked, he tried, in less than military spirit, to shift responsibility. He claimed it was at other people's insistence that he founded, as an emergency measure, a Court of Oyer and Terminer. This was an English ad hoc court set up traditionally to deal with cases of social disorder. It was a measure, in the circumstances, of dubious legality. But Sir William's defensiveness relates not so much to the court's possible illegality as to its consequences. The letters to England in which he excuses his actions were written after nineteen had been hanged and many died in jail. No one was sure any longer if they had been guilty or innocent.

No doubt Sir William spoke the truth when he claimed he was prevailed on to found the court by "the loud cries and clamours of the friends of the afflicted people with the advice of the deputy governor." Thomas Putnam and his allies would have been pressing him hard to bring the accused witches to justice. And William Stoughton, an even dearer friend of the Mathers than his namesake, would have been foremost among those urging this way of doing it. He was appointed the new court's chief judge and performed his office with zeal. A combination of Puritan rigidity and political ambition made him as relentless in his treatment of witch suspects as Hathorne had been, and as blind to chicanery.

Associate judges of the new court were Nathaniel Saltonstall, John Richards, Bartholomew Gedney, Wait Winthrop, Samuel Sewall, and Peter Sargent. They were all members of the new council and all magistrates.

Events moved quickly. Stephen Sewall, Samuel's brother, in whose family Betty Parris was living, was appointed clerk of the court. A jury was impaneled. On May 31 the new attorney general, Thomas Newton, ordered nine accused witches to be transported to Salem from Boston for trial. They were Sarah Good, Rebecca Nurse, John Willard, John and Elizabeth Proctor, Susannah Martin, Bridget Bishop, Alice Parker, and Tituba. Newton specified that the last named be kept separate from the rest since she was coming to give evidence and not to be tried. He made all these demands in a long, breathless letter that conveys the sense of excitement felt throughout the province. As is always the case, urgent action by strong leaders in a time of national emergency thrilled the population.

It must have even seemed exciting when on May 26 a fast was held as a measure against witchcraft throughout Massachusetts. Prayer and fasting were always the Puritans' first line of defense against attacks by the devil, but fasts were usually mere local affairs. There had been several fasts in Salem Village since the start of the witch-hunt. A fast ordered by the General Court itself, covering the whole of the province, was extremely unusual and showed the depths of the alarm.

Newton wrote, "I fear we shall not this week try all that we have sent for, by reason the trials will be tedious, and the afflicted persons cannot readily give their testimonies, being struck . . . senseless . . . at the name of the accused." He knew of the girls' time-consuming fits from firsthand experience since he had spent all day at Salem Village with "the gentlemen of the council" at the examinations, where he "beheld most strange things scarce credible but to the spectators." The people examined had been John Alden, Martha Carrier, Phillip English, Elizabeth Howe, William Proctor, Wilmot Redd, and Sarah Rice. It had been a good show, with John Alden taken outside to be examined in the light, Martha Carrier openly expressing her skepticism, Phillip English at last brought to the bar after previously escaping, and Elizabeth Howe showing extraordinary patience and wisdom.

Newton went on to say that Alden and English had been sent to prison along with the rest, "for the afflicted spare no person of what quality soever, neither conceal their crimes, though never so heinous."

The witch-hunt had been amazing enough even before; now it had entered a phase in which humble Salem Villagers were finding witches among the most powerful men in the province. Moreover, those men and all the other accused would be tried by the highest authorities and, if found guilty, sent to the gallows.

But alongside excitement was direst misery. And alongside the determination to stamp out witchcraft and save New England from Satan was growing revulsion at the sight of so many respectable people languishing and even dying in jail. Those committed to the witch-hunt were reinforced in their fears by the numbers who had confessed. Eventually about fifty were to do so. But even by this stage the confessors made up a sizable proportion of the hundred people in jail. What was more, the confessions all tallied; to most observers this proved they were genuine. But a few people suspected the truth. All the accused witches were being fed the same stories. The other side of the coin from the hardening of belief was the deepening of skepticism.

In early May no less than thirty-nine people signed a petition on behalf of Rebecca Nurse, saying, "We never had any cause or grounds to suspect her of any such thing as she is now accused of." Among the signatories were several important and influential men belonging to the anti-Putnam faction in Salem Village: Israel Porter, Daniel Andrew, and Joseph Putnam. But there were also many lesser folk who must have known they could be putting themselves in grave danger. And there were some whose names on such a list comes as a surprise. Jonathan Putnam, cousin of Thomas, had signed the original complaint against Rebecca. Either he regretted that now or he had bowed to powerful pressure from the Porters and Nurses. Other unexpected petitioners were John Putnam Senior, Thomas's uncle, and Benjamin Putnam, another cousin, together with their wives. They must have held respect for Rebecca and the truth above family loyalties, or else they too had been pressured.

Nathaniel Putnam Senior, another uncle of Thomas, did not sign the petition but filed a deposition, saying, "I have known [Rebecca] differ with her neighbours but I never knew or heard of any that did accuse [her] of what she is now charged with." John Putnam Senior and his wife also testified on Rebecca's behalf.

A considerable number of ordinary people had by this time come forward to testify in favor of various accused witches or to cast doubt on the afflicted girls' credibility. Many more were to do so. John Higginson, the elderly pastor of Salem church, who had long since handed over most of his duties to the corpulent but fanatical Nicholas Noyes, made a deposition in favor of one of his church members, Sarah Buckley, who was complained of by Nathaniel Ingersoll and Thomas Putnam on May 14 and examined four days later. Higginson had kept out of the witch-hunt from the start, giving the "infirmities of a decrepit old age" as the reason. He claimed later that the judges and juries proceeded with integrity, "according to their best light," and said the blame for errors should lie with the English laws and customs used as the models for the examinations and trials. Yet he was moved to support someone he believed to be innocent.

"This is the woman that hath bit me with her scragged teeth a great many times," cried Abigail Williams of his protégé Sarah Buckley at her examination. Sarah was originally from England and, with her husband, William, had come on hard times. The couple, as impoverished newcomers in Salem Village, were obvious targets for the Putnams. So was their widowed daughter, Mary Witheridge, who lived with them and was arrested, examined, and imprisoned with her mother. The consequences of imprisonment to the family were vaster than are easily imagined.

"Old William Buckley died this evening. He died with the cold, I fear, for want of comforts and good tending. Lord forgive! He was about eighty years old," wrote the pastor who replaced Samuel Parris in Salem Village in 1697. By the time he inscribed those words in his diary, ten years after the witch-hunt was over, Sarah was dead. The Buckleys had never recovered from the state of destitution caused by Sarah and Mary's imprisonment and the sheriff's seizure of their goods. As a result, old William died from the want of life's basic necessities.

The kindly pastor may have implicitly been asking the Lord's forgiveness not only for the afflicted girls and the judges and magistrates but also for those who tried to help the Buckleys too late. John Higginson's testimony on Sarah's behalf was not given till January of 1693. It was couched in extremely careful language even though by that time the witch-hunt was virtually over. But the fact that the afflicted girls targeted his daughter, Ann Dolliver, who was duly examined and committed to jail in early June, strongly suggests they were well aware of the old pastor's doubts and saw him as an enemy.

On May 18 Mary Easty was let out of jail. The reason for this is unknown, though she herself says she was "cleared by the afflicted persons." Three days later she was back behind bars again. The girls had had unusually spectacular fits while she was at large; Mercy Lewis nearly died. "Dear Lord receive my soul," she cried out, and "Lord let them not kill me quite." She was at the time being tortured by the shapes of Mary Easty, John Willard, and Mary Witheridge together.

It may have been the opposition to the witch-hunt that caused Mary's release and rejailing. Of the three intelligent and pious Towne sisters, Mary Easty seems to have been the most pious and intelligent. Perhaps in the face of growing restiveness toward the witch-hunt in general and the imprisonment of Rebecca Nurse, Sarah Cloyce, and Mary Easty in particular, it seemed a good plan to release this paragon from prison and demonstrate the dire effects. Sir William Phipps had arrived four days before. Perhaps the "cries and clamours of the friends of the afflicted people" were made louder in his ears by their claims of Mary's torturing. It seems highly likely that Thomas Putnam was capable of this kind of plotting.

Mary Easty may also have been chosen over Rebecca Nurse for such a propaganda exercise because as a Salem Village resident, allied to the Porter faction but with advocates also among Putnams, Rebecca could not be released and rearrested without causing uproar. It may even have been primarily the strong advocacy of Rebecca that brought about Mary's three days of freedom.

As the nine witch suspects rode with the constables from Boston to Salem, their guilt was by no means a foregone conclusion in everyone's minds.

It was probably for this reason that the first accused witch selected for trial was the one with the most evidence against her besides that provided by the band of the afflicted. In a letter of advice to John Richards, on May 31, Cotton Mather warned against relying for evidence on the tortured girls' visions.

"It is very certain that the devils have sometimes represented the shapes of persons not only innocent but also very virtuous," Mather wrote. If anyone had a solid, long-standing reputation for witchcraft, it was Bridget Bishop (previously Oliver) of Salem. She had been brought to court on suspicion of witchcraft twelve years before. The complaint was of bewitching horses and turning into a cat. Nothing came of that action. But the troubles she caused the community were not just those of witchcraft. She had been tried, ten years earlier even than that, for fighting with her second husband, Thomas Oliver. Marital quarreling was a criminal offense among the New England Puritans. Bridget once appeared in public with a bloody face; another time, covered in bruises; and her husband said she had also hit *him*. Later Bridget was brought to court yet again for calling the same husband names such as "old rogue" and "old devil" on the Sabbath. The couple were ordered to stand back to back in the marketplace for an

hour, gagged, with notices describing their offenses tied to their foreheads. It seems that Bridget was a thorn in the flesh despite the
"smooth manner" mentioned by the Shattucks, who accused her of
killing their son. And, what was more, she was without powerful
friends. On June 2 she was brought before William Stoughton and the
other judges in the courthouse in Salem.

There is no extant official record of her trial, as there is no extant
official record of any of the trials. But Cotton Mather's accounts of five
of them, including Bishop's, in his book *The Wonders of the Invisible
World* were based on the records still in existence when he wrote the
book during that summer. And his accounts tally with surviving depositions. Though Cotton makes biased comments, his accounts of the
proceedings seem essentially accurate.

Bridget's ordeal began all too predictably with the afflicted girls
being led in and going into fits. When capable of speaking, they said
the prisoner's shape pinched, choked, and bit them and urged them
to write their names in her book. "There was little occasion to prove
the witchcraft, it being evident and notorious to all beholders," observes Cotton, characteristically. One girl claimed that Bridget's shape
had taken her from her spinning wheel, carried her to the river, and
threatened to drown her if she still did not sign. Another said the
specter had bragged that she "had been the death of sundry persons."
She also claimed that apparitions appeared in the court and cried out
to Bishop, "You murdered us!"

Whenever Bridget looked at her accusers, they fell down. But they
were revived by her touch. When she shook her head or turned her
eyes, they adopted painful variations of those postures. Someone then
testified that a man, striking at the place where Bridget's specter had
stood, tore her coat. This event had occurred at Bridget's examination
and the man had been Jonathan Walcott, brother of Mary. Presumably
the testifier was one of that family of conjurers. It became commonplace for events that took place at the examinations to be brought in as
evidence at the trials.

Deliverance Hobbs, that star among confessors, said that Bishop had
tempted her to sign the book again and to deny her confession. She
had whipped her with iron rods, she averred. This testimony was followed by that of all those neighbors who over the years had suspected
Bishop of witchcraft. One of them, Samuel Gray, claimed that fourteen
years before, Bishop had caused the death of his child by witchcraft.
He was later to confess, on his deathbed, that he had lied. A particularly telling deposition was made by a father and son employed by
Bridget to demolish the cellar wall of a house she had lived in. They

found in holes in this wall several "poppets," small dolls made of rags and hogs' bristles with pins in them with the points sticking outward.

Perhaps Bridget had indeed been attempting to inflict harm on her enemies by the methods of folklore. More likely there was some natural explanation for the presence in the wall of rags, pigs' bristles, and pins. They may have been a few items in the midst of other rubbish. Or perhaps the poppets were planted. But Bridget had no defense lawyer to suggest either of these theories to the court. The rags and the rest were taken as hard evidence of witchcraft.

Equally hard evidence, in the eyes of the magistrates, was the existence on Bridget's body of a "preternatural teat." Nine women jurors strip-searched six of the accused witches before the start of Bishop's trial and found an "excrescence of flesh" between the vagina and anus on three of them. The other two women were Rebecca Nurse and Elizabeth Proctor. The three without blemish were Susannah Martin, Sarah Good, and Alice Parker. The searchers described the "excrescences" as "much like to teats and not usual in women." How did they know? Did they often explore women's bodies in intimate places? Of course nobody asked this. Presumably if the excrescences existed at all outside the imaginations of the searchers, they were pimples or moles. A second search was made at four that afternoon; both Bridget's and Elizabeth's "teats" had disappeared. This was taken as additional proof of witchcraft rather than as evidence of a pimple, or theory, having burst.

Rebecca Nurse's "excrescence" had also subsided by the afternoon and become a flap of dry skin. So the surgeon in charge of the searches reported, with considerable relish. It was with even greater relish that he commented on Susannah Martin's breasts: "In the morning search [they] appeared to us very full, the nipples fresh and starting, now at this searching [they are] all lank and pendant." He is presumably insinuating that Susannah had fed her familiars. The discomfort and indignity of two intimate body searches in one day, conducted by a prurient surgeon and seven ignorant women who could not sign their names to their testimony but merely make their marks, must have been horrible. But for Bridget, after one additional piece of testimony was given, far worse was in store.

That additional testimony was that, as Bridget passed the Salem meetinghouse under guard on her way to the court, a demon invisibly entered the building and pulled part of it down. This was as a result of her turning her eyes on it. Those running in found a board, which had been fastened with nails, some distance from its original location.

This tale was taken as seriously as the afflicted girls' visions, the neighbors' ancient gossip, the poppets in the wall, and the vanishing teat. As a result, Bridget Bishop was pronounced guilty of witchcraft and ordered to be taken the next Friday to the place of execution and hanged by the neck till she was dead.

CHAPTER TWENTY-ONE

Full of Grief

NOT everyone in authority was satisfied with the evidence on which Bridget Bishop was condemned. One of the judges, Nathaniel Saltonstall, resigned. Later he was himself to be named as a witch, though never arrested. But if a witch was ever to be found guilty at all, it had to be on the kind of testimony used in Bridget's trial. By its nature, witchcraft cannot provide the sort of evidence normally admitted as valid in court. Nobody can see a witch doing harm or find her footprints or bloodstained clothing or the murder weapon, since the malicious acts take place in her mind.

Despite this drawback, witchcraft had been a criminal offense in England since 1542. But the statute of that date was supplanted by the act "against conjuration, witchcraft and dealing with evil and wicked spirits" passed in the reign of James I in 1604. It was this measure under which the first Salem prosecutions were brought. The colony's own laws against witchcraft had ceased to have effect with the abrogation of the charter. They were to be reinstated at a session of the General Court in October. But meanwhile, the indictments of accused witches closely echoed the phraseology of the 1604 Act. "Whereby any person shall be [by witchcraft] killed, destroyed, wasted, consumed, pined or lamed," the Act said, "such offender . . . shall suffer pains of death." Bridget Bishop's indictment averred that Mercy Lewis "was and is hurt, tortured, afflicted, pined, consumed, wasted and tormented."

Just as the Salem court relied on English law to prosecute witches, so it relied on English custom and experience in admitting and weighing the evidence against them. Those who later defended the judges and juries of the Salem court made much of this fact. John Hale wrote in 1697 that it was because of "the power of former precedents" as well as "the tortures and lamentations of the afflicted" that "we walked in the clouds and could not see our way." He recognized that he was deeply implicated in the witch-hunt, and his *Modest Enquiry* attempts, half-sincerely, half-defensively, to show what went wrong. He explains that when he was a boy, about fifty years before, a neighbor of his was tried for witchcraft "and the reverence I bore to aged, learned and judicious persons caused me to drink in their principle in these things, with a kind of implicit faith." He would have been no more than twelve at the time. The neighbor, in Charlestown, was Margaret Jones, the first accused witch hanged in Massachusetts. No doubt other ministers and magistrates had been similarly influenced.

Hale lists the English books consulted by the judges and Parris and Hathorne, which describe and approve the types of evidence brought against Bishop. They include Sir Matthew Hale's *Trial of Witches,* Joseph Glanvill's *Collection of Sundry Trials in England and Ireland,* Richard Bernard's *Guide to Jurymen,* and Baxter's *Certainty of the World of Spirits.* Additional proofs of witchcraft endorsed by some of these authorities, and used in later trials, were the failure to recite the Lord's Prayer without making a mistake and the testimony by witnesses of supernatural strength. It was thought that Satan would not allow his followers to say the Lord's Prayer correctly. It was also believed he was the source of unusual physical power, such as was allegedly displayed by George Burroughs.

Great store was set by the discovery of "witches' teats" and poppets because they seemed, on the face of it, like the hard evidence found in ordinary crimes. Of course, there was never any proof that an "excrescence" was actually used for feeding familiars or that poppets were employed in performing dark deeds. But nobody at that time was disturbed by that. The very existence of these things implied their employment. However, two aspects of the evidence brought against Bishop did cause unease. In the cases known to the court from the past, the afflicted had been bewitched by people who had threatened them already. It was unprecedented for a group of afflicted persons to be tortured by strangers with no grievance against them. In the trial of Bridget Bishop, as in all the examinations of accused witches, the afflicted girls' sufferings were of paramount significance. As already noted, the reason Bishop was the first witch to be tried was that a greater array of other evidence could be summoned against her than in any other case. But the afflicted girls' fits remained central. Bridget's death warrant states that she was "found guilty of the felonies and witchcrafts whereof she stood indicted," that is, "witchcraft in and upon the bodies of Abigail Williams, Ann Putnam Junior, Mercy Lewis, Mary Walcott and Elizabeth Hubbard."

Why *should* Bishop afflict Abigail Williams and the rest, when she had nothing against them? Hale argues that some witches tortured the afflicted on behalf of other witches. Moreover, he says, the motive of some "was to destroy the Church of God . . . which is a greater piece of revenge than to be avenged upon one particular person."

However specious such arguments, they satisfied Hale. But he was left with a more intractable difficulty posed by the afflicted girls' tortures. As we have seen, by no means all Puritan authorities believed that what was called "spectral evidence" was valid. An apparition might be the devil disguised as a particular, and innocent, human being. Hale says that "a person eminent for wisdom, piety and learning" wrote that "the devil could not assume the shape of an innocent person in doing mischief unto mankind," but it is not clear who this eminent person actually was. Even Cotton Mather, as shown in his letter to Judge Richards, distrusted spectral evidence. Sir William Phipps was troubled enough about the matter, after the hanging of Bridget Bishop, to write to the ministers of Boston asking their opinion.

On June 10, at eight in the morning, Bishop was carried on a cart from Salem jail near North River, along Prison Lane to Essex Street, along Essex Street out of town to the Boston Road and thence to a tall, rocky hill. She was taken to the summit and hanged from the branch of an oak tree. Her body was buried nearby. Its probable resting place was in a crevice in the sheer drop on one side of the hill.

In the wake of this shocking and sobering event, the Boston ministers sent a reply to the governor, dated June 15, urging caution. But they also urged speed and vigor in continuing the legal action against witches.

It is believed that Cotton Mather penned the text of the *Return of the Several Ministers Consulted.* He speaks for his father and the other leaders of the Puritan theocracy as well as himself when he writes that a demon may appear in the shape of an innocent and even virtuous man and therefore no one should be convicted on spectral evidence alone. He also speaks for his fellows when he suggests that the "touch test" is unreliable since it can be abused by "the Devil's legerdemains." Other words of caution are against the "noise, company and openness" of the examinations and against superstitious tests of witchcraft such as the saying of the Lord's Prayer. The *Return* recommends as guides to proper methods of witchcraft detection William Perkins's *The Damned Art of Witchcraft* and Richard Bernard's *Guide to Jurymen,* the most cautious of the English authorities. And it warns that "exceeding tenderness" should be used toward those complained of, "especially if they have been persons formerly of unblemished reputation." But it closes with words that undermine everything so far written. They are in contradiction to the rest not only in spirit but in all their practical implications:

"Nevertheless, we cannot but humbly recommend unto the Government the speedy and vigorous prosecution of such as have rendered themselves obnoxious, according to the direction given in the laws of God, and the wholesome statutes of the English nation, for the detection of witchcrafts."

Whether the other ministers saw and approved this last paragraph or left Cotton to write out their conclusions and never knew the slant he was putting on them, we cannot know. But the effect was to give Stoughton and his court the ministers' seal of approval. The judges could not prosecute speedily and vigorously except by employing the methods they had already been using, including spectral evidence. Unless the ministers followed up their strictures about the need for caution and set aside their recommendations for vigor and speed, it was inevitable that juries would continue to convict accused witches and that judges would continue to sentence them to death. They would do so on the evidence that had damned the accused at their examinations, that is, the afflicted girls' tortures. The *Return* would not impede the course of events but encourage it.

The ministers wanted to voice their misgivings without opposing the judges. If they had been wholehearted about the unreliability of spectral evidence, they would have suggested barring the girls from the courtroom. Then the cases against most of the accused witches would have collapsed and the trials would have ceased. But the ministers chose to be swept along by a dangerous tide instead of trying to stem it. The Mathers and Stoughton were particular friends; and all the judges and ministers were to some extent allies. Together they formed the Puritan elite. It was in their interests to promote superstition. What was more, there was vociferous demand among many people, despite the growing opposition, for convictions. None of the ministers, however great their unease, wanted to step out of line. As a result, Stoughton reconvened the court on June 29. The next witches to be tried were Sarah Good, Rebecca Nurse, Susannah Martin, Elizabeth Howe and Sarah Wildes.

At these five trials the accusations of the afflicted girls were of even more obviously central significance than at the trial of Bridget Bishop. Not only did they go into fits as the accused were brought in, but their previous tortures at the examinations were brought forward as evidence. The "touch test," so decried by the ministers, was made use of as a matter of course. Cotton Mather, in his account of the trial of Elizabeth Howe in *The Wonders of the Invisible World,* forgets his warnings about the devil's skills as a conjurer and refers to the use of the test with unqualified approval. Fifteen deponents besides the girls testified against Howe. Almost as many testified against Susannah Martin, and several, though fewer, against the other accused. But the role of the girls was of paramount importance. They performed in exactly the same manner as at the examinations, using all the same tricks.

During Sarah Good's trial one of them cried out that the prisoner had stabbed her in the breast with a knife. She produced part of a blade. Then a young man came forward to say that the day before, when the afflicted girl was nearby, he happened to break his knife and threw the upper part away. He showed the court a knife handle with a section of blade still attached. The two pieces fit; they were two parts of one knife. Was the afflicted girl thrown out of court? On the contrary. After being told not to tell lies, she was allowed to continue to give evidence.

At one of the trials an accuser named the Reverend Samuel Willard, one of Boston's leading ministers, as afflicting her. She *was* sent out of court, but only temporarily. The magistrates told those in attendance that this was a case of mistaken identity. At Rebecca Nurse's trial Sarah, Rebecca's adult daughter, saw Goodwife Bibber pull pins out of her clothes, stick them in her knees, and cry out that Goody Nurse pinched her.

All appeals to the court for greater fairness in taking and assessing the evidence were useless. Rebecca Nurse made a plea for a second search of her body by a different set of women from the first. "The most skilful, prudent person" of those who had searched her before had disagreed with the others, she said. She had seen nothing on Rebecca but "what might arise from a natural cause." Rebecca's own explanation of her excrescence was exceeding weakness and the hardships of traveling from one prison to another. This suggests that her protuberance, if not those of others, might have been a dropped womb. Her plea was ignored. There was no second body search.

But justice and decency were not extinguished completely in that court. The jury found Rebecca not guilty.

The jurors must have been more impressed by the prisoner's obvious goodness and dignified manner than by the girls' screaming and writhing. They knew Rebecca's reputation for saintliness. They had heard of the petition in her favor signed by a great number of highly respectable people. If any accused person was innocent of witchcraft, it was she.

The jurors trooped back into the court and the foreman, Thomas Fisk, spoke the verdict. There was a momentary hush. Then the accusers went wild. Spectators and judges alike were astonished at their "hideous outcry." Given the impact of even their workaday fits, this exhibition must have been amazing indeed. It may have been planned.

Whether planned or spontaneous, it suggests utter terror at the prospect of Rebecca's acquittal.

Very soon others, standing outside the court, also began clamoring. It seems that at the trials, unlike the examinations, not all those who were afflicted by witches were allowed in the courtroom. There were even more of them by now, names unknown to us. Gathered outside, hearing the screaming and shouting and getting news of the verdict, they went as wild as the girls in the building.

One of the judges stated that he was not satisfied with the verdict; another, walking off the bench, threatened to have Rebecca retried. Stoughton declared that he had no wish to impose on the jury but wondered if they had sufficiently considered the remark Rebecca had made when Deliverance Hobbs and her daughter Abigail had been brought in to give evidence. Rebecca had turned her head and exclaimed, "What, do you bring her? She is one of us." What Rebecca meant, Stoughton suggested, was "one of us witches."

As a result of this pressure, the jury went out again. This time they could not agree. They returned not with a new verdict, but to question the prisoner. Thomas Fisk walked up to Rebecca where she stood at the bar and asked her what she had meant by her words. She did not reply. He assumed that she was silently assenting to the judge's interpretation, and the jury changed its verdict. She was sentenced to hang. Later she wrote a declaration to the court explaining what had happened.

"I intended no otherways, than as they were prisoners with us," she said, explaining that she therefore believed them not qualified to give evidence. "And I being something hard of hearing, and full of grief," she continued, had not realized how the court had interpreted her words and had had no opportunity to explain what she meant.

It is clear that when Fisk had asked her his question she had been so overwhelmed by anxiety and distress that she neither saw nor heard him. But her declaration was ignored. The zealous Nicholas Noyes had her excommunicated from Salem church that same afternoon. She was brought from prison, in chains, to attend the ceremony in the meetinghouse. Perhaps, being "hard of hearing and full of grief," she heard few of the minister's words. But she well knew their purpose. And as a good churchwoman she understood all they implied. Excommunication, for the Puritans, meant certain damnation. Unless during her last days on earth Rebecca communed with her God by the light of a personal vision that superseded Puritan dogma, she walked to the gallows in the belief that she was going to hell.

A further bitter twist was to take place before her planned execution, however. Sir William Phipps granted Rebecca a reprieve.

Presumably he was persuaded to do so by some of those who signed her petition. However, the afflicted girls immediately "renewed their dismal outcries against her" and Phipps was prevailed on by "some Salem gentlemen" to rescind it. No doubt the "Salem gentlemen" included the stout but tireless Nicholas Noyes. The others may have been John Hathorne and Bartholomew Gedney.

Rebecca was hanged, with the other four witches tried and convicted a week earlier, on July 19. It was at the scene of execution, later dubbed "Gallows Hill," that the black depths of evil stirred by the witch-hunt were most clearly on show.

CHAPTER TWENTY-TWO

The Hanging Tree

THE site has never been established with certainty, but there is little reason to doubt that it is where tradition suggests. Gallows Hill, also called Witch Hill, is the first hill of any size on the way out of Salem in the only direction that can be traveled overland. It is reached by taking the Boston Road northward from Essex Street. In every other direction lies water. Apart from the fact that the Salemites would have had no wish to transport condemned men and women farther than necessary, there is no mention in any of the records of payments to ferrymen for the transportation of prisoners.

The first written mention of Gallows Hill as the place of execution was in 1791. A Salem doctor said in a letter that a man, almost a hundred years old, who had recently died claimed his nurse often told him that when looking after his mother in childbirth she could see through the window "those unhappy people hanging on Gallows Hill who were executed for witches by the delusion of the times." The house where the old man was born commanded a clear view over the hill. An elderly citizen told a writer on the *Salem Register* in 1800 that he had followed an ancient path to the summit of the hill and saw the oak tree that had been used as a gallows.

Neither of these stories can be relied on as proof, but they bolster the case for Gallows Hill as the most likely site. The only argument against the nearest and most accessible hill to the center of Salem being the place of execution is that the final part of the ascent was too rocky and steep for a cart. However, there is no reason why the condemned men and women should not have been made to walk the last part of their journey. Some, old and ailing, would have found it exceedingly difficult, but the marshals and constables would have felt no reluctance about driving them on.

The route to Gallows Hill today takes the visitor past the Essex Institute, the Peabody Museum, the site of the first church of Salem, the public library, and the many attractive nineteenth-century houses of Essex Street. In 1692 closely spaced houses gave way to the fields and trees of large estates. One of the few residences from that time that still stands belonged to the magistrate Jonathan Corwin. It is known as the Witch House, as much for its gables, dark wood, and altogether sinister appearance as for its association with the witch-hunt. Legend maintains that some of the accused witches were questioned here. This seems highly likely. Much of the questioning that went on before or after the formal examinations was probably not in the meetinghouse or tavern but in the magistrates' homes. The condemned prisoners would have passed Corwin's residence soon after the start of their last earthly journey. It stands at the second main intersection on Essex Street after turning out of what is now Peter Street and was then Prison Lane.

After continuing down Essex Street for three-quarters of a mile, the cart bearing the prisoners turned north onto Boston Street. Today this road is surrounded by industrial buildings, office blocks, and scruffy pizza and sandwich shops. In 1692 fields and orchards stretched, on the right of the road, to the broad expanse of the North River. On the left, marshland covered the few hundred feet to the same river where it turned abruptly southward and narrowed. Beyond marsh and water was the towering hill that was the condemned people's destination.

Before the hill, on the right, stands a much smaller rise crowned today by a square brick and glass edifice built for the sale of doughnuts. That this was the site of execution seems ruled out, but not because it is unthinkable that Salemites should buy doughnuts where their forebears hung from the gallows. There is firm evidence that the executed prisoners were buried near where they died, in crevices in the rocks. There is little space for graves and no sign of crevices on this little hill.

No marker indicates that Nicholls Street, leading off to the left, ascends to the spot where the oak or locust tree used as a gallows probably stood. Such a sign might not be welcomed by the present-day residents. Brown, blue, green, turquoise, pink, and white clapboard houses line the street, which grows ever steeper as it approaches the summit. It does not follow the path taken by the dismal procession of 1692. A more circuitous but easier ascent would have been employed for the cart laden with the condemned men and women and the crowd following in their wake.

At the very top of the hill there stands a huge oak in a garden. It is unlikely that it is the tree from which the witches hung three hundred years ago. But it might be mistaken for it by a time traveler from 1692 who once gazed up at the macabre show that was for the Puritans rare entertainment. The tradition that the condemned were hanged from a tree, not a scaffold, is upheld by the fact that the Puritans would have had no wish to use timber unless absolutely necessary. Despite the presence of vast forests beyond inhabited areas, it was scarce. Cleared land stretched for many miles in every direction from Salem. To hew trees in virgin forest was an exceedingly laborious, time-consuming task. Farther along Nicholls Street from the summit is the sheer, rocky drop where the dead are thought to have been buried.

No mercy was shown to the condemned. As they traveled their last journey, they were mocked by the afflicted girls and the rest of the huge crowd that walked and ran alongside the cart. The cart bore them, still in their chains, weeping or praying or silent, some, unable to stand, slumped on the floor, head on arms, while others held themselves upright, gazing for the last time on the fields and trees and rivers of the world they were leaving. They must also have seen in their minds dreadful images of the one they feared they were going to. None of the prisoners thought that he or she was entering oblivion. All had been taught throughout their lives that they were destined for heaven or hell. But, unlike Roman Catholics, they had never been given clear notions of what the inferno consisted of. They had simply been told it comprised suffering unimaginably more painful than anything on earth. "Worse a thousand times than whipping," Cotton Mather had said. Perhaps their hazy mental pictures included stocks and irons and dungeons. It must have been hard indeed for these prisoners to add any extra dimensions of horror to what they had already known.

But for some the terrors of eternity may have been eclipsed by the terrors of the method of getting there. Hanging is no easy death. A few may have known this from seeing people die on the scaffold. All executions for murder and other capital offenses were held publicly. Yet by and large New England was a law-abiding society, though a litigious one. Capital offenses were rare. In any case, fewer offenses carried the death penalty than in England. Earlier in the century certain sexual crimes such as sodomy, bestiality, and adultery were capital, but by 1692 this was no longer so. Only murder, rape, and sometimes persistent stealing were punished by death. Most of the condemned that July day had probably never seen anyone hang. But they would have heard all the tales of the slow deaths and other horrors of the hanging tree that formed part of English folklore. They must have known that it might take five or ten minutes to die.

The most fearful may hardly have noticed the jeering and insults from the girls and the crowd. The "trials of cruel mockings," as Nathaniel Cary calls it, continued even as the cart halted at the foot of the last, steepest part of the hill and the prisoners were forced to get out and walk. It went on even as the victims stood at the bottom of the ladder that leaned against the high branch of the tree from which hung the nooses. "To speak of [the people's] usage of the prisoners, and their inhumanity shown to them, at the time of their execution, no sober Christian could bear," writes Cary, whose own wife had so nearly suffered the same terrible fate. The mockery continued even as the condemned men and women climbed or were carried up the ladder and were placed with their heads through the noose, ready to die.

In all this cruelty was not only hatred and venom but fear. Many of the prisoners conducted themselves with dignity and grace, and all of them protested their innocence, to their very last breaths. At times they struck a chord of common humanity and raised doubts of their guilt in the crowd. The girls and their friends, and everyone actively involved in the witch-hunt, strove to keep the loathing and contempt whipped up to fever pitch.

We do not know in what order Sarah Good, Rebecca Nurse, Susannah Martin, Elizabeth Howe and Sarah Wildes were dispatched. Perhaps the most docile were sent first up the ladder. The executioner accompanied or carried the victim and, after the last words had been said, pulled the suspended noose toward him, lowered it over the prisoner's head, and pulled it tight around her neck. He then pushed her off the ladder, to fall downward and swing sideways. After that he climbed down the ladder and removed it. Unless the prisoner managed to jump upward while being pushed, to make the drop more violent so that her neck broke, she died by slow strangulation.

Rebecca Nurse was said to have gone to her death in as Christian a manner as was humanly possible. Given the effect she had had on all those who signed her petition and on the jurors at her trial, her bearing and manner as she spoke on the ladder must have swayed at least some to wonder if it was right and just that she should hang. She prayed to God, as did all the accused, to give some miraculous proof of her innocence. She also asked God to forgive those who wronged her.

Elizabeth Howe may have died the same way as Rebecca, judging by everything we know of her character. No doubt she also showed resignation and fortitude and prayed to her God to the end. One imagines Sarah Wildes also went quietly. Susannah Martin may have insisted more aggressively on her innocence and is less likely to have prayed for the souls of her murderers. But she too would have shown the dignity remarked on by several observers of the condemned persons at their deaths.

But among that first batch of witches to be hanged there was one to whom patience and resignation were as foreign in death as in life. Sarah Good, either standing at the foot of the tree or perhaps already on the ladder, was urged by the bullying Nicholas Noyes to confess. Perhaps he was trying to rally the crowd to the witch-hunt after it was set wondering and doubting. He said that Good was a witch and she knew she was a witch. She shouted, "You are a liar. I am no more a witch than you are a wizard, and if you take away my life, God will give you blood to drink." Tradition maintains that her prophecy was fulfilled. The corpulent Nicholas Noyes died some years later of an internal hemorrhage, bleeding from the mouth.

The feelings of the crowd as they watched each of the five women in turn fall from the ladder and swing from the branch in the agonies of death, must have been extraordinarily complicated as well as intense. There may have been screams of exultation and triumph as well as of horror. Once the bodies were dangling, the crowd may have stilled, their mockery silenced. At an execution in England, the crowd cheered when the prisoner appeared on the scaffold but a hush fell when he dropped. Eyewitnesses were astonished by "the sudden extinction of that joy, the . . . dead silence when they saw the object of their hatred in the act and agony of death."

Dr. Alexander Monro, professor of anatomy at Edinburgh University, told James Boswell in 1774 that "a man is suffocated by hanging in a rope just as by having his respiration stopped by having a pillow pressed on his face. . . . For some time after a man is thrown over he is sensible and is conscious that he is *hanging.*"

Another description of an English execution might have been that of any of the five women at Gallows Hill in July 1692. At the moment of dropping, "she gave a faint scream, and, for two or three minutes after she was suspended, appeared to be in great agony, moving her hands up and down frequently." Presumably her hands were left free, rather than pinioned to her sides or tied behind her back. The evidence as to what was customary in both England and America is unclear.

Often people who were hanged died in convulsions. Sometimes there were mishaps. The knot of a noose might slip to the back of the neck and delay death still further. Given the number of hangings at Salem, this probably happened more than once. When it did, it might take the prisoner ten or fifteen minutes to die.

No doubt the condemned women on Gallows Hill had hoods placed over their heads before being "turned off," as was the tradition in England. This was not to prevent their seeing the crowd but to prevent the crowd's seeing them. An English textbook of 1894 describes the effect of hanging on the features as "lividity and swelling of the face, especially of the ears and lips, which appear distorted: the eyelids swollen, and of a blueish colour; the eyes red, projecting forwards, and sometimes partially forced out of their cavities . . . a bloody froth or frothy mucus sometimes escaping from the lips and nostrils . . . the fingers are generally much contracted or firmly clenched . . . the urine and faeces are sometimes involuntarily expelled at the moment of death."

But even if Rebecca Nurse and the others were hooded, the changes to the features were not necessarily hidden. At the last public hanging in England, the condemned man's "protruding tongue and swollen distorted features [were] discernible under their thin white cotton covering."

Once all five women were dead, they were cut down from the tree and disposed of in the crevices in the rocks at the side of the hill. Such a mode of burial saved the labor of grave digging. No prayers were said. There were no marks of respect. Indeed, the dead were treated with the same contempt as when they were alive. For the relatives, such an end for their loved ones must have been exceedingly painful. One family at least could not bear it. The night after the hangings, under cover of darkness, the young men of the Nurse clan made their way up the hill to the spot where their grandmother lay in her shallow grave in the clothes she had died in. They disinterred her and bore her back down the hill. They had probably traveled by water; the Endicott, Wooleston, and North Rivers provided a convenient artery from the Nurse homestead to the foot of Gallows Hill. They could row a boat silently, whereas horses in the night might alert the men on watch or rouse the sleeping villagers. They brought Rebecca home and reburied her, perhaps saying prayers in defiance of their church over her new, though still unmarked grave. Today a memorial to her stands in the tranquil family graveyard a few hundred yards down the hill from her house, though the exact site of her bodily remains is unknown.

Ironically, a few yards from that memorial there lies under a beautiful new headstone the only remains of any of the executed witches to have been found and identified. They are those of old George Jacobs, hanged a month after Rebecca. His relatives also rescued his corpse from its common grave on Gallows Hill and buried it on their homestead. The site in time was forgotten, though marked by two sunken, weather-beaten stones, but in 1864 Jacobs's descendants, still living at the homestead, by chance unearthed the remains. They knew the legend of Jacobs's reburial and realized that this tall, lame, toothless skeleton must be that of their ancestor convicted of witchcraft. Found with it was a pin "which might have been used as a breastpin, or to hold together his ancient locks." The bones were reburied. In the 1950s, when the homestead had been abandoned by the Jacobs family after a series of fires, they were exhumed again by the town of Danvers, once Salem Village, and put into storage. In 1992 they were reburied once more, this time in the Nurse graveyard, and marked by a gray stone, decorated with angels' wings on either side of a skull. Below are inscribed the words "HERE LIES BURIED THE BODY OF GEORGE JACOBS SR, DECEASED AUGUST THE 19, 1692" and underneath is added a quotation from Jacobs himself, from the examination of May 10. Booming out over the centuries among the quiet graves are the words once declaimed above the hubbub of hatred and evil: "Well! Burn me or hang me, I will stand in the truth of Christ."

Four days after the July 19 executions, John Proctor, knowing how little hope there was of a fair trial for his fellow prisoners and himself, wrote a letter from prison to the upper echelon of the governing Puritan elite, the five senior ministers of Boston: Increase Mather, James Allen, Joshua Moody, John Willard, and John Bailey. Proctor hoped that these men would listen impartially to his arguments and intervene to have the trials moved to Boston or that they would replace Stoughton, Sewall, and the rest of the judges with others who were unprejudiced. He also pleaded that they themselves, or some of them, come to the trials. It is no surprise that he did not include Cotton Mather's name on the list. He would have been fully aware of the younger Mather's enthusiasm for convictions and hangings.

The letter lacks smoothness and eloquence but is soundly argued and forceful. Parts of it make harrowing reading. Since the accusers, judges, and jury have "condemned us already before our trials," it says, the writer is emboldened to "beg and implore your favourable assistance . . . that if it be possible our innocent blood be spared." The magistrates, ministers, and juries "and all the people in general" must be "enraged and incensed against us by the delusion of the devil" since "we know in our own consciences we are all innocent persons." Five people had recently confessed themselves to be witches and mendaciously accused "some of us of being . . . with them at a sacrament." But two of them, Martha Carrier's teenage sons, had been forced into confession by being tied neck and heels "till the blood was ready to come out of their noses."

Proctor adds, "My son William Proctor, when he was examined, because he would not confess that he was guilty when he was innocent, they tied him neck and heels till the blood gushed out of his nose, and would have kept him so 24 hours, if one more merciful than the rest had not taken pity on him and caused him to be unbound."

This letter availed Proctor nothing. Of as little use was a lengthy, closely argued petition on his and his wife's behalf signed by thirty-one neighbors. Sometimes God "may permit Satan to personate, dissemble and thereby abuse innocents and such as do in the fear of God defy the devil and all his works," the petition says. "As to what we have ever

seen or heard of [John and Elizabeth Proctor]—upon our consciences
we judge them innocent of the crime objected."

It is no accident that the neighbors who put their names to such a
boldly stated defense of the innocent should dwell in Ipswich, to the
west of Salem Village, where John Proctor had lived previously. The
inhabitants there were at the edge of, not inside, the fog of delusion.

The Proctors were brought to trial in Salem on August 5 together
with George Burroughs, John Willard, George Jacobs Senior, and
Martha Carrier. Not only was there no replacement of judges but there
was no change in the procedure or evidence. The only request of John
Proctor's that was granted, though by chance and only very partially,
was that some of the ministers of Boston be present. We know that
Increase Mather attended George Burroughs's trial. Other ministers
may also have done so. But that trial was far more important than
those of the other accused witches. Mather did not attend the trials of
Willard, the Proctors, old George Jacobs, or Martha Carrier, and it is
doubtful that any other senior ministers did so.

John Willard was a Salem Village farmer who had been arrested in
May after refusing, as constable, to arrest certain other people for
witchcraft. He fled before he was seized, but the irate Putnams had
him chased all the way to Nashawag, now Lancaster, about forty miles
from Salem. He was arrested there while hoeing. The marshal and ten
others, including six of the Putnam family and Jonathan Walcott, in a
letter to the magistrates requesting his prompt examination, claimed
that as soon as Willard was brought into the watchhouse in Salem
Village the afflicted persons were so badly tortured that the constable
had to pinion him. Presumably the afflicted had seen him escorted
through the village. The watchhouse was opposite Ingersoll's inn and
no more than a few hundred yards from the parsonage. Robert Calef
reports that the accusers could tell from forty miles away exactly when
Willard was captured. Unless these are two separate stories, they are
two accounts, one earlier, one later, of the afflicted girls' response to
Willard's capture, demonstrating how rumors grew.

A jury of inquest that included three of the Putnam family, Jonathan Walcott, and Nathaniel Ingersoll found Willard responsible for
the death of a relative, Daniel Wilkins, by witchcraft. The dead man
was discovered with "the greatest part of his back . . . pricked with an
instrument about the bigness of a small awl" and his neck and ear
were bruised to his throat and "turning the corpse over the blood run
out of his nose or mouth or both and his body not swelled, neither did
he purge elsewhere." All this seemed to the men a "diabolical act"
and they ascribed it to Willard. Among other evidence at Willard's trial
was a deposition from the eighty-one-year-old Bray Wilkins, Daniel's

grandfather and an ally of the Putnams, holding Willard responsible for a bout he had suffered recently of extremely painful bladder trouble.

Susannah Sheldon described in the gruesome detail reserved for the Putnams' worst enemies the appearance before her of four ghosts who claimed Willard had murdered them. One of them "lifted up his winding sheet and out of his left side he pulled out a pitchfork and put it in again and likewise he opened all their winding sheets and showed all their wounds."

Yet in the hierarchy of wizardry, this man was fairly insignificant.

John and Elizabeth Proctor, the ancient George Jacobs Senior, and the fiery Martha Carrier, though all thoroughgoing skeptics of the witch-hunt, were also small fry compared with George Burroughs. The minister was perceived as the spearhead of the devil's campaign to capture Salem Village and in time the whole of New England. In any case, Mather's presence at his trial, however important Proctor may have thought it, achieved nothing. Eight "confessing witches" claimed that Burroughs was the "head actor at some of their hellish rendezvouses" and "nine persons" bore witness to his "extraordinary lifting and such feats of strength as could not be done without a diabolical assistance." The girls retold their stories of Burroughs offering them the book and taking them up mountains and offering them the kingdoms of the earth, and claimed again to see the ghosts of his wives. They, of course, had spectacular fits. When these prevented them from giving their testimonies, Stoughton asked Burroughs who did he think was responsible. Burroughs said "he supposed it was the devil." Stoughton asked, "How comes the devil so loath to have any testimony born against you?" to which Burroughs had no answer. The whole trial was a performance for which the examination had been merely a dress rehearsal. Increase Mather was to say later that had he been one of the judges he could not have acquitted the prisoner. But it was the testimony of the confessing witches and witnesses to Burroughs's supposedly supernatural strength that produced this opinion. Increase had strong doubts about spectral evidence and the touch test, and had he attended any of the other trials, where confessions and testimony to supernatural gifts were absent or minor, his opinion of the guilty verdicts might well have been different.

Martha Carrier's trial is the only one of those of August 5 besides Burroughs's of which we have a full record. This is no accident. The original trial records are lost, and the five accounts written up by Cotton Mather are all of trials that depend less than the rest on spectral evidence. Mather was commissioned to write them to give the stamp of respectability to the Court of Oyer and Terminer. By that time it was under fire for its use of the afflicted girls' visions—in other words, the spectral evidence—and naturally Cotton picked trials that could be best used to counter the criticisms. However, had Increase been present even at Carrier's trial he might have wished to acquit her. Carrier was not shown, as Burroughs was, to have supernatural gifts; and the only confessing witches to accuse her were her children. What distinguished the evidence at her trial, as at Bridget Bishop's and Susannah Martin's, was that so much of it was of the kind known as "anger followed by mischief." Therefore the guilty verdict did not rely so heavily on the afflicted girls' accusations. But Increase Mather says nothing in his writing about the status of "anger followed by mischief," so presumably in his mind and others' it lay within a gray area: It carried more weight than spectral evidence but probably not enough to hang a person.

Abundant spectral evidence was brought in against Carrier, including Susannah Sheldon's having "her hands unaccountably tied together with a wheel-band, so fast that without cutting it could not be loosed." This deed was supposedly done by Carrier's specter. In a memorandum at the end of his account of the trial, Cotton Mather writes that "this rampant hag, Martha Carrier, was the person of whom the confessions of the witches and of her own children among the rest agreed that the devil had promised her she should be Queen of Hell."

As Proctor foresaw, none of the accused stood a chance. All were found guilty. Elizabeth Proctor's life was spared because she was found to be pregnant, but the rest were hanged on August 19.

Immediately after sentence was passed, the sheriff and his officers went to old George Jacobs's house and seized everything the family owned, including Jacobs's wife's wedding ring. She begged to have it back and finally prevailed, but only "with great difficulty." She was forced to *buy* back provisions from the sheriff to feed and clothe herself. They did not last long and her neighbors were obliged to come to her assistance.

As noted already, the night before the executions George Jacobs's granddaughter Margaret came to George Burroughs in prison to ask him to forgive her for giving false evidence against him. The minister not only forgave her but prayed with her and for her. No doubt he also prayed with the prisoners who were to die with him in the morning. Judging by his conduct at his execution, and theirs, his prayers gave great strength and comfort.

Everyone who was anyone was at Burroughs's execution, including Cotton Mather, John Hale, Nicholas Noyes, and Samuel Sewall.

"Mr. Burroughs was carried in a cart with the others through the streets of Salem to execution," writes Robert Calef. "When he was upon the ladder he made a speech . . . with such solemn and serious expressions as were to the admiration of all present. His prayer . . . was so well worded, and uttered with such composedness and such . . . fervency of spirit as was very affecting and drew tears from many, so that it seemed to some that the spectators would hinder the execution.''

This must have terrified the girls and the other interested parties, including Cotton Mather. What made the event all the more frightening was that after saying his own prayer Burroughs recited the Lord's Prayer without a single mistake. To ordinary people, Burroughs's speaking it accurately gave an overpowering impression of innocence. As he recited, with the unparalleled feeling of a man about to die, that plea for and promise of generosity of spirit—"Forgive us our trespasses, as we forgive those that trespass against us"—perhaps some in the crowd heard the words as they had never heard them before. They may have wondered about the all too apparent lack of forgiveness of the God they believed in and the men who represented Him. The phrase "deliver us from evil" may have set many wondering where evil truly lay. The girls shouted that they saw the black man standing next to Burroughs and dictating his words to him. The moment the ladder was removed and Burroughs hung limp, Mather, seated on his horse, declared to the crowd that Burroughs was not a properly ordained minister and that in any case the devil had often been transformed "into an angel of light." He swayed the people enough so that the executions could go on. But further reminders of the devil's powers of deception may have been necessary, since all the condemned men and women died heroically. The distinguished eyewitness Thomas Brattle writes: "They protested their innocence as in the presence of the great God, whom forthwith they were to appear before. They wished, and declared their wish, that their blood might be the last innocent blood shed upon that account. With great [emotion] they entreated Mr. Cotton Mather to pray with them: they prayed that God would discover what witchcrafts were among us; they forgave their accusers; they spake without reflection on jury and judges, for bringing them in guilty and condemning them: they prayed earnestly for pardon for all other sins, and for an interest in the precious blood of our dear Redeemer; and seemed to be very sincere, upright and sensible of their circumstances on all accounts; especially Proctor and Willard, whose whole management of themselves, from the gaol to the gallows, and whilst at the gallows, was very affecting and melting to the hearts of some considerable spectators.''

John Proctor pleaded at the last minute for a stay of execution, saying he was not ready to die, yet all the same he died nobly.

When the condemned were cut down, the sheriff and his men hurriedly disposed of the bodies, no doubt wanting the crowd to disperse as quickly as possible. George Burroughs was "dragged by the halter to a hole or grave between the rocks, about two foot deep, his shirt and breeches being pulled off and an old pair of trousers of one executed put on his lower parts." Presumably the shirt and breeches were of value and the sheriff or some of his men intended to sell them. The "old pair of trousers" must have belonged to John Willard, John Proctor, or George Jacobs. One of these must have been buried in nothing but a shift. Burroughs was pushed into the crevice along with the bodies of John Willard and Martha Carrier. "One of his hands and his chin" could be seen still sticking out. So could a foot, but whose foot, was not clear.

CHAPTER TWENTY-THREE

"I Know I Must Die"

ON September 9 six more people were tried and sentenced to death. They included that "gospel witch" Martha Cory, one of the first to have been examined. There is no knowing why her trial came later than that of many others accused after her. Some careful calculation went into the order in which prisoners were tried: It is no accident that Bridget Bishop, as the most credible "witch" with the longest history of accusations against her, was brought before the justices first. But there may have been an element of sheer chance as well in who was tried when. Perhaps Martha Cory was just lucky, if it can be considered lucky to gain a month of extra life spent in irons in the dungeons. But in any case, even after her six months in prison, Martha remained as brave and independent-minded as at her examination when she had prayed for the ministers' eyes to be opened and said, "We must not believe all these distracted creatures say."

Her courage was put to the test not only at her sentencing but soon afterward, and perhaps more severely, when Parris and Nathaniel Putnam and two deacons came to see her in prison. Their purpose was to tell her that Salem church had voted for her excommunication.

"We found her very obdurate, justifying herself, and condemning all that had done anything to [promote] her just discovery or condemnation," Parris writes. Since Martha knew she had been unjustly condemned, such obduracy seems only reasonable. Parris, of course, did not see it that way. He continues by saying that "her imperiousness would not suffer much" discourse, that is, lecturing; after some praying which she entered into reluctantly, he concluded, "the dreadful sentence of excommunication was pronounced against her." There is a certain satisfaction in his tone. So much for the "gospel woman" who had taken such pride in church membership and regarded it as a shield against accusations of witchcraft. But despite this new blow, Martha Cory continued as courageous as ever and went nobly to her death. Protesting her innocence, she "concluded her life with an eminent prayer upon the ladder."

The others tried and condemned on September 9 were Alice Parker and Ann Pudeator, Dorcas Hoar, Mary Bradbury, and Mary Easty of Topsfield. Of these five, two escaped hanging. As we saw earlier, Dorcas broke down and confessed when faced with the gallows and thus became useful to the authorities as an accuser of others. A petition for a stay of execution from John Hale and Nicholas Noyes asked only for an extra month on this earth for Dorcas, to enable her to "prepare herself for eternity." In fact, the petition saved her life. By the end of the month the hangings had stopped.

Mary Bradbury was a wealthy and eminent woman in her hometown of Salisbury, Massachusetts, who had crossed swords with George Carr, Ann Putnam's father, in 1679. As a result, Carr had spread rumors that Mary was a witch. Apparently the idea of revenge by means of accusations of witchcraft was not new in the Putnam family. Mary escaped from prison, no doubt by bribing the jailer, after a petition on her behalf signed by more than a hundred people failed to have any effect on the judges.

It is indicative of Stoughton's rigidity that not one of the many petitions put forward by friends and neighbors of accused witches, or by accused witches themselves, swayed him from his course. There is one possible but extremely unlikely exception. The two surviving sisters of Rebecca Nurse, Mary Easty and Sarah Cloyce, sent the court a joint petition from prison asking whether, since they were not allowed counsel, the judges would "please to be of counsel to us" and also asking that the pastor and church members of Topsfield, who knew them best, be allowed to testify in their favor. Mary and Sarah also requested that the accusations of the afflicted girls should not be regarded as sufficient to condemn them "without other legal evidence concurring" and that they would not be condemned "without a fair and equal hearing of what may be said for us as well as against us." They were asking, in other words, to be given a fair trial.

As far as Mary Easty was concerned, the petition had no effect at all. The judges did not advise her, nor did the pastor of Topsfield give evidence. The afflicted girls' spectral evidence was listened to as always. The only words in Mary's favor, if indeed they were heard at her trial and not left ignored in the files, merely testified to her good behavior when in prison. They came from two fellow prisoners in Ipswich jail and, independently, from the Boston prison keeper and his wife, John and Mary Arnold. Their "deportment was very sober and civil," said the prison keeper of both sisters. He explained that he testified at the request of "some of the relations. Apparently this was a brave, hopeless attempt on the part of their husbands and children to help Mary and Sarah by persuading two sets of people to bear witness to their characters. Perhaps they bribed Arnold. Or perhaps Mary Easty's truly saintly disposition had prompted a rare generosity even in someone professionally hardened to suffering.

But Sarah Cloyce was never tried. Could this have been due to her and Mary's petition? It seems extremely unlikely. Far more probable is that some quite trivial consideration, perhaps to do with sheer numbers, prevented Sarah's being taken to court with her sister that day. In the event, she remained in prison till the following January, when the grand jury dismissed the charge against her. She died in 1703 at the age of sixty-two.

If the court were ever to take notice of any petition, it would have been the second sent by Mary Easty, this time on her own, after she was sentenced. Never can a more moving plea from a prisoner to her judges have been written. Mary's concern is not for herself but for others. She accuses no one of bad faith except the afflicted girls and confessing witches and gives the judges practical advice as to how to test their honesty. She speaks what she knows to be the truth with passion, but humbly. The writing is ungrammatical and clumsy but at moments through sheer power of feeling rises to the most affecting eloquence. For its confirmation of the general view that the judges were not corrupt but deluded, as well as its moving testimony to one woman's courage and selflessness, it should be quoted at length:

". . . your poor and humble petition[er], being condemned to die, do humbly beg of you to take it into your judicious and pious considerations that your poor and humble petitioner, knowing my own innocency, blessed be the Lord for it, and seeing plainly the wiles and subtlety of my accusers . . . cannot but judge charitably of others that are going the same way [as]myself . . . I petition to your honours not for my own life for I know I must die and my appointed time is set. . . . I question not but your honours would not be guilty of innocent blood for the world but by my own innocency I know you are in the wrong way. The Lord in his infinite mercy direct you in this great work if it be his blessed will that no more innocent blood be shed. I would humbly beg of you that your honours would be pleased to examine these afflicted persons strictly and keep them apart some time and likewise to try some of these confessing witches, I being confident there is several of them has belied themselves and others as will appear if not in this world I am sure in the world to come whither I am now agoing. . . . The Lord above who is the searcher of all hearts knows that as I shall answer it at the tribunal seat that I know not the least thing of witchcraft, therefore I cannot, I dare not, bely my own soul. I beg your honours not to deny this my humble petition from a poor dying innocent person and I question not but the Lord will give a blessing to your endeavours."

Mary did indeed die at the time that had been set. It was two weeks later, on September 22. She faced death as bravely in the last moments as when she wrote her petition. "Her last farewell of her husband, children and friends was . . . as serious, religious, distinct and affectionate as could well be expressed, drawing tears from the eyes of almost all present," says Calef.

Before the date of her hanging, nine more accused witches were sentenced. Of these, four were to join Mary, Martha Cory, and the rest in the cart to the gallows. The others escaped execution by reason of confessions or pregnancy. Like Elizabeth Proctor before her, Abigail Falkner was spared because she was carrying an innocent life. Of those reprieved for confessing, one was the Ann Foster who had told John Hale she took bread and cheese in her pocket to witch meetings and who later died in prison. Another was that wild girl of the woods Abigail Hobbs. Both of these, as well as the two others reprieved, Rebecca Eames and Mary Lacy, had first said they were guilty a long time before. It seems that the magistrates had at last started bringing those confessing to witchcraft to trial. They presumably did so to scotch criticism that, though by their own admission guilty, confessors were immune to the punishment meted out to those who claimed they were innocent. To sentence the confessors to death and then reprieve them, so they could continue to give evidence against others, seems just the kind of stratagem to appeal to Hathorne and Gedney. They may well have deluded themselves about what they were doing, believing that their sole motive was to give the confessors more time to "prepare themselves for eternity."

Immediately after the second set of trials an event occurred that was as shocking as anything that had happened during the whole of the witch-hunt. Giles Cory, who had testified against his wife Martha in March and soon afterward had been arrested and examined himself, refused to be tried. He was known for his eccentricity and stubbornness, and his attitude now was fully in character. He claimed that he was innocent but that if he went to trial the same witnesses would be brought against him as at his examination and he was bound to be found guilty. He justly pointed out that no one tried by the Court of Oyer and Terminer had ever been let off. He "rather chose to undergo what death they would put him to," he declared. He may have had an additional motive. If he was never found legally guilty, his property could not be confiscated and it would pass to his relatives. But in Ipswich jail, he had already taken steps to ensure that his lands would be kept in the family by conveying by deed everything he owned to two of his sons-in-law. Sheer disinclination to continue to cooperate with a system that had tricked him into helping hang his own wife may well have been motive enough for his stubbornness.

When Cory was taken to court, either with Martha and others on September 9 or with Ann Foster and the rest on September 17, he would not speak but stood mute at the bar. On September 19 he was taken to some open space, very possibly a field near the courthouse, and made to lie on the ground while rocks were heaped on his chest. The procedure was an old English method of dealing with prisoners who refused to plead. The purpose was to force the word "guilty" or "innocent" out of them.

It must have taken him hours to die. His ribs had to crack before the breath could be squeezed from his lungs. Toward the end Cory's tongue was pressed out of his mouth and the sheriff pushed it back in again with the end of his cane. The rumor has come down through the centuries that the only words Cory would utter were "More weight, more weight." The tradition persisted into the nineteenth century that Cory's ghost walked near the spot where he died. A ballad has come down to us:

> Giles Cory was a wizard strong,
> A stubborn wretch was he,
> And fit was he to hang on high
> Upon the locust tree.
>
> So when before the magistrates
> For trial he did come,
> He would no true confession make
> But was completely dumb.
>
> "Giles Cory," said the magistrate,
> "What have thou here to plead
> To these who now accuse thy soul
> of crimes and horrid deed?"
>
> Giles Cory—he said not a word,
> No single word spoke he.
> "Giles Cory," said the magistrate,
> "We'll press it out of thee."
>
> They got them then a heavy beam,
> They laid it on his breast.
> They loaded it with heavy stones,
> And hard upon him pressed.
>
> "More weight," now said this wretched man,
> "More weight," again he cried,

And he did no confession make
But wickedly he died.

Dame Cory lived but three days more,
But three days more lived she,
For she was hanged at Gallows Hill
Upon the locust tree.

The event had an extremely unsettling effect on the populace, since pressing to death had never been practiced before in New England. (It never was again.) Thomas Putnam reacted characteristically to the fear that it might set off new opposition to the witch-hunt. The day after Cory's death he sent a letter to Judge Samuel Sewall. The content, though new in its details, is familiar in character:

"The last night my daughter Ann was grievously tormented by witches, threatening that she should be pressed to death before Giles Cory. But through the goodness of a gracious God, she had at last a little respite, whereupon there appeared unto her (she said) a man in a winding sheet, who told her that Giles Cory had murdered him by pressing him to death with his feet. . . . The apparition said, God hardened [Cory's] heart, that he should not hearken to the advice of the court and so die an easy death, because, as it said, 'It must be done to him as he has done to me.' "

Putnam continues by claiming that seventeen years before, Giles Cory had kept a servant, "almost a natural fool," who died suddenly. The jury "found the man bruised to death, and having clodders of blood about his heart." They came to the conclusion the man had been murdered "but as if some enchantment had hindered the prosecution of the matter the court proceeded not against Giles Cory, though it cost him a great deal of money to get off." Why enchantment should be needed when Cory had handed out bribes, Putnam does not explain.

It was true that Cory's servant had died and the jury had concluded he was murdered. It seems a characteristic piece of Putnam ingenuity to suggest that Cory had pressed the servant to death and thus Cory's similar death had served natural justice. It appears surprising, if not impossible, that young Ann Putnam should have known the old tale. Perhaps on this occasion, if no others, her vision was her father's invention. Putnam may have sent this letter to Judge Sewall rather than any other of the judges because, as the reasonably humane character that his diary shows him to have been, Sewall was more likely than most to deplore Cory's death.

The people condemned, but not reprieved, at the second set of trials in September were Samuel Wardwell, Margaret Scott, Wilmot

Redd, and Mary Parker. Wardwell was the only accused witch besides Margaret Jacobs to confess, recant his confession, and not go back on the recantation. He was from Andover, as were four of the others tried on September 17. By this time the Andover witch-hunt had peaked. Witches there were being arrested and examined in considerable numbers, though no new arrests were being made in Salem Village or elsewhere. Wardwell had a reputation for fortunetelling and, when examined on September 1 by John Higginson, said he was in the snare of the devil. Urged to go on, he concocted an elaborate tale of agreeing to serve Satan till he was sixty and being baptized by him in the river. He was "dipped all over," he said. But on September 13 Wardwell declared to the grand jury inquest, at which the accused were appearing before they went to their trials, that his whole confession was lies. He said "he knew he should die for it whether he owned it or no," meaning he would hang as a result of his confession whether he stuck to it or not. This seems a reasonable attitude, given that confessors were now being tried. Wardwell was not to know they would all be reprieved.

A stark reminder of the horrific effects of the imprisonments for witchcraft comes in the form of a petition about Wardwell's case from the selectmen of Andover to the Ipswich court: "Samuel Wardwell and his wife of Andover were lately apprehended and committed to prison for witchcraft, and have left several small children who are uncapable of providing for themselves and are now in a suffering condition. We have thought it necessary and convenient that they should be disposed of in some families whether there may be due care taken of them. We therefore humbly pray your honours to inform us what is our duty in this case."

Margaret Scott had been arrested at the beginning of August and examined on August 5 after she "or her appearance" repeatedly tormented a Frances Wycom "by choking and almost pressing [her] to death." Wilmot Redd of Marblehead, a married woman, had been seized in the roundup of ten witches, including Martha Carrier, in late May. At her examination at Ingersoll's tavern she had said, when asked if the afflicted girls were bewitched, "I cannot tell." On being urged further "all she could say was my opinion is they are in a sad condition." Alice Parker had been examined earlier, on May 12. Her main accuser was the reclaimed Mary Warren. After Warren's dramatic confession following three weeks in jail, ending with a torrent of bizarre allegations against Alice Parker and Ann Pudeator, "her tongue hung out of her mouth until it was black." Parker remarked acidly that "Warren's tongue would be blacker before she died."

On September 22 the cart set off from Salem prison with its heaviest load yet. The largest number of condemned men and women it had previously borne, on July 19 and on August 19, was five. Now seven women and one man were crammed into it. It is scarcely surprising that as it was going up the hill it "was for some time at a set." Perhaps it sank on its axis and a wheel stuck in a rut. The afflicted girls and others shouted that "the devil hindered it."

It seems that the afflicted girls were as afraid as ever that the condemned would win the crowd's sympathy. They seized every opportunity for new insults and mockeries. As Wardwell spoke on the ladder, protesting his innocence, tobacco smoke from the executioner's pipe wafted into his face and made him splutter and cough. The afflicted girls shouted that the devil stopped him from speaking. It seems not to have occurred to them, or anyone else, that the devil could have no possible motive for preventing a disciple from making his case.

The sense of drama at these executions must have been greatly increased by the warring feelings of hatred and sympathy within the crowd and even within individuals. The prisoners were objects of loathing and fear, but when they spoke with deep feeling of their innocence, prayed fervently, and said goodbye forever to their loved ones, they could not help but stir pity. If the accusers, ministers, and magistrates had been more confident of unwavering support, they might have warded off the danger this presented by banning the last words and prayers. It seems that these farewells were often protracted. George Burroughs's clearly were. So were Mary Easty's. But "last words" at the gallows were an old English tradition. For the audience, or that part of it not so bloodthirsty as to enjoy most the moment when the condemned was "turned off," this was the choicest part of the spectacle. The Salem authorities would not have dared deny the crowd that excitement: The concern that was growing about the justice of the trials and executions might have spread all the more quickly.

When, on September 22, the executioner's task was completed, the diehard Nicholas Noyes turned toward the bodies suspended from the tree and said "what a sad thing it is to see eight firebrands of hell hanging there." Many in the crowd must have reflected on how little like a firebrand of hell Mary Easty seemed. Perhaps it even appeared to them that none of the condemned really fit the description. Noyes's words may have had the contrary effect to what he intended, stirring opposition to the hangings.

With these September executions a turning point was reached. The crowd may have been no more restive than at George Burroughs's execution, but there was perhaps a sense, by the time the eight were "hanging there," that it had at last had its fill. Such a feeling, combined with several other developments over the next weeks, was to make these hangings the last.

CHAPTER TWENTY-FOUR

Satan's Desire

ALL through August and September Parris was beset as never before. There was no doubt now, if there ever had been, that he was surrounded by enemies. In mid-August the handwriting in his church record book, always small, becomes so tiny as almost to vanish. He describes asking the church members to stay after the rest of the congregation on Sunday, August 14. He then reports himself as saying, "Brethren, you may all have taken notice that several Sacrament days past our brother Peter Cloyce, and Sam Nurse and his wife, and John Tarbell and his wife have absented from Communion with us at the Lord's Table, yea, have very rarely (except for our brother Sam Nurse) . . . been with us in common public worship." He continues that "it is needful that the church send some persons to them to know the reason of their absence. Therefore if you be so minded, express yourselves.

"None objected," he goes on, ". . . a general or universal vote after some discourse [was] passed that Brother Nathaniel Putnam and the two deacons should join with the pastor to discourse with the said absenters about it."

This is Parris's first entry since March 27, when he so vigorously described the chastisement of Mary Sibley for giving directions for the baking of the witch cake. He had been too busy meanwhile to make entries. Not only had he recorded all the examinations after the first three, interviewed witch suspects in prison, made depositions against ten of them, held meetings with Nicholas Noyes, John Hale, and all the others involved in the witch-hunt, continued to perform his customary duties of writing sermons, conducting baptisms, marriages, and funerals, and attending sickbeds and deathbeds, but he had also had to try to maintain some sort of order in his own distraught household. With Tituba in prison, the household lacked its most useful pair of hands. It also often lacked her husband's, since John Indian was regularly called on to give evidence at the examinations and trials. Parris's wife, perhaps ailing already, had in July joined her niece in experiencing supernatural agonies, or so it seems from the confession of Richard Carrier, a son of Martha Carrier, that he afflicted "two in the Minister's house, one of them a grown person, the other a child, the grown person was the Mrs of the house." No wonder Parris had had little time to spend at his desk. Since March he had even abandoned his usual practice of copying out his sermons in his sermon book.

The plan that Nathaniel Putnam and two deacons should go with Parris to inquire of Peter Cloyce and the rest why they had been absent from communion seems disingenuous to the point of dementia. Samuel Nurse's mother, Rebecca, had been hanged for witchcraft on July 19. John Tarbell was Rebecca's son-in-law, his wife, Mary, her daughter. Peter Cloyce's wife, Sarah, was in prison. Without Parris's active involvement in the witch-hunt, Sarah would be free and Rebecca alive. It would be strange indeed if their nearest relations did not shrink from accepting the symbols of the blood and body of Christ from his hands. Later the dissenters made their objections explicit. In February 1693 they said that in the witchcraft crisis Parris "had been the great prosecutor." John Tarbell said that Parris "was guilty of idolatry, in asking the afflicted persons who they saw upon other afflicted persons." He questioned his testimony in court that "such and such, by such and such, were knocked down by their looks, and raised up by their touches." And he said in so many words that had it not been for Parris, "his mother Nurse might still have been living." Something he did not mention but cannot have forgotten is that on March 27, when Rebecca Nurse was in jail, Parris preached his notorious "Christ knows how many devils there are" sermon, saying in effect that she was guilty.

Parris's attempt to discover the reason for the Nurses' absence from communion, when it was so obvious, even suggests false innocence as a habitual psychological ploy. In reply to the objections Tarbell and the others finally stated in 1693, he said that his opinion of what was right in the circumstances "was confirmed by known and ancient experience frequent in such cases." He shows no understanding, sympathy, or even awareness of their desolation at the excommunication, death by hanging, and lack of Christian burial of their dearly loved mother.

Almost as breathtaking as Parris's disingenuousness over the Nurses' defection from communion is the Nurses' restraint. It took them seven months to tell Parris what they thought of him. The August meeting he proposed never took place because the dissidents were evasive and he himself did not press the point. He records, on August 31, "Brother Tarbell proves sick, unmeet for discourse, Brother Cloyce hard to be found at home, being often with his wife in prison at Ipswich for witchcraft, and Brother Nurse and sometimes his wife attends our public meeting, and he the Sacrament."

No doubt, while the witch-hunt still raged, the Nurses were fearful of showing open opposition to Parris and his allies. Parris too must have been reluctant to bring matters to a head. On September 11 he records, "Upon all which, we chose to wait further."

There is no mention in Parris's records of Francis Nurse, Rebecca's husband. It seems likely that he too stayed away from public worship and communion. But he was nearly eighty years old and was to die three years later. His absence may have seemed, even to Parris, excusable.

As August turned to September, Parris had ever-increasing cause to feel threatened. The vote to excommunicate Martha Cory from Salem Village church was "general," not unanimous, unlike the vote on Rebecca Nurse's excommunication from Salem church eight weeks before. Earlier in the month an eminent resident of Salisbury, Major Robert Pike, had written a vigorous letter to the magistrate Jonathan Corwin questioning the use of spectral evidence. He voiced the view, to be heard more and more as time passed, that Satan can disguise himself as an innocent person in order to afflict and tempt others. Pike was seventy-six, a member of the General Court as well as a local magistrate and judge. He claimed that the afflicted cannot know for certain whether any specter they see is merely a delusion or else the devil himself. The letter is well argued and incisive. We do not know if Jonathan Corwin ever replied to it or if it influenced his thinking. It does not appear to have. But Parris, who worked closely with Corwin, almost certainly knew of it.

Pike showed considerable courage in writing such a letter. Perhaps his age made him bold. But he had had tussles with authority before and had always survived, indeed flourished. Once he had been disenfranchised by the General Court for arguing, at a town meeting, against one of its acts. But a year later he was reinstated as a voter and then elected to the General Court. Some years afterward he took such an unorthodox view on certain ecclesiastical matters that the Salisbury church excommunicated him. But he was soon received back into the fold. Massachusetts could have done with many more men of Pike's strength of character combined with independence of outlook.

But the enemies gathering force during August and September were not merely human ones. The confessions of those arrested in Andover and examined all through the summer in Salem Village and elsewhere, at the same time as the grand jury hearings and trials were continuing in Salem, pointed to a conspiracy of witches on a scale never before dreamt of. Abigail Williams had once claimed to see forty witches at a meeting. That was the largest number spotted together at one time so far. But on August 25 Susannah Post confessed to attending a meeting numbering two hundred and said she heard there were "five hundred witches in the country." Mary Toothaker of Billerica put the total number at three hundred and five but went on to say that she had heard witches at a meeting discuss "pulling down the Kingdom of Christ and setting up the Kingdom of Satan." Ann Foster said witches planned to "ruin that place the village" and then "set up the devil's kingdom." William Barker of Andover claimed he was at a witch meeting of a hundred in Salem Village "upon a green piece of ground near the minister's house" where they met "to destroy that place by reason of the people's being divided and their differing with their ministers." He went on to say that "Satan's desire was to set up his own worship, abolish all the churches in the land, to fall next upon Salem and so go through the country." And he further ascribed to the Evil One an agenda with a tremendous subversive appeal: that "all [Satan's] people should live bravely, that all persons should be equal, that there should be no day of resurrection or judgement and neither punishment nor shame for sin." No wonder that on September 11, in his first recorded sermon since March, Parris thundered at the congregation, "The devil and his instruments will be making war with the lamb and his followers as long as they can" and "If ever there were witches, men and women in covenant with the devil, here are multitudes in New England."

Parris was equally terrified of the witches themselves and the skeptics who doubted them. If the witch-hunt was shown to be a sham, his livelihood was in jeopardy and his future at stake. But his desperate attempts to stem the tide of reason with his preaching proved futile. Though Parris was never one to give in or compromise, six weeks later he was suing for peace and reconciliation by means of a sermon on the text "Let him kiss me with the kisses of his mouth."

Reconciliation, however, was not easily achieved. Parris had a rocky road ahead of him and it was never to grow smooth, even after it led him far from Salem Village.

Meanwhile, others besides the pastor were trying to hold back the flood. On September 20 Cotton Mather wrote an urgent letter to Stephen Sewall, Judge Samuel Sewall's brother and clerk of the court as well as Betty Parris's temporary guardian, repeating a previous request for several of the trial records for the book he was writing.

"But that I may be the more capable to assist in lifting up a standard against the infernal enemy," he says, "I must renew my most importunate request, that you would please quickly to perform what you kindly promised, of giving me a narrative of the evidence given in at the trials of half a dozen, or if you please a dozen, of the principal witches that have been condemned. I know 'twill cost you some time; but, when you are sensible of the benefit that will follow, I know you will not think much of that cost."

The book Cotton was working on was *The Wonders of the Invisible World,* which had been commissioned in mid-June by Sir William Phipps. It was to be an "account of the sufferings brought upon the country by witchcraft"—in other words, a piece of witch-hunt propaganda. It seems likely that William Stoughton suggested the commission, as he had suggested all of Sir William Phipps's other actions during the course of the witchcraft crisis. Mather had already written most of the work while waiting for the trial records. One imagines him compulsively scribbling away in his study, which was filled with large volumes on theology and witchcraft, under the motto inscribed over his door consisting of the words "Be brief." That injunction speaks tomes about Mather's self-importance. Someone more safely in control of his feelings and life would not need to issue such an order, and someone less arrogant would not want to.

It is clear from Cotton's letter that he had no intention of creating a work that was anything but partial.

"Please also to [give] some of your observations about the confessors and the credibility of what they assert," he requests, "or about things evidently preternatural in the witchcrafts, and whatever else you may account an entertainment, for an inquisitive person, that entirely loves you and *Salem.* Nay, though I will never lay aside the character which I mentioned in my last words, yet I am willing, that, when you write, you should imagine me as obstinate a Sadduccee and witch-advocate as any among us: address me as one that believed nothing reasonable; and when you have knocked me down, in a spectre so unlike me, you will enable me to box it about among my neighbours till it come—I know not where at last." In other words, he says, use all the material at your disposal to try unnecessarily to persuade me, Cotton, of the reality of witchcraft and specters, so that I can use it to persuade others.

We do not know whether the selection of the five records Cotton included in his book was Sewall's or Cotton's, but they are those of the trials whose guilty verdicts are most defensible, in that they are based less fully than most on spectral evidence. Cotton at least makes no attempt to hide his bias from his readers. In his "Author's Defence" he castigates anyone who doubts the reality of witchcraft in Salem as full of "asperity, untreatableness and inconsistency." His tone throughout is defensive but boastful.

"None but the Father, who sees in secret, knows the heartbreaking exercises wherewith I have composed what is now going to be exposed, lest I should in any one thing miss of doing my designed service for his glory and for his people; but I am now somewhat comfortably assured of His favourable acceptance; and, I will not fear; what can a Satan do unto me!''

He states that the aim of his book is nothing less than "to countermine the whole plot of the devil against New England" and quotes in full a letter of approval of the manuscript from William Stoughton. This puff uses the phrase found in Cotton's letter to Stephen Sewall "lifting up a standard against the infernal enemy," which suggests that Stoughton saw the manuscript before Cotton got hold of the trial records and finished the book. Cotton must have liked the phrase and borrowed it. But Stoughton and Sewall endorse his account of the trials in a note at the end of the work, saying, "We find the matters of fact and evidence truly reported."

The rest of the *Wonders* apart from the trial narratives consists of meandering accounts of supernatural oddities befalling various "bewitched people." It includes Thomas Putnam's letter describing his daughter's vision of the man pressed to death by Giles Cory. The book also features an essay on New England as home of the saints and the devil's plot against it and excerpts from various religious authorities on rules for the detection of witches. Among the ragbag of other material, no doubt added bit by bit to fill in time as Cotton awaited the trial records, is "a narrative of an apparition which a gentleman in Boston had of his brother" and an account of outrages committed by "a knot of witches" in Sweden.

The book was finished by the early part of October and presented to Sir William Phipps on his return from his sojourn in the Eastward, where he had been fighting the Indians and French. But the book was on the losing side in the battle for the hearts and minds of the people. Nineteen men and women had been executed, one man pressed to death, one hundred fifty people languished in prison, and about two hundred more were accused. In this climate of chaos and misery, the virtues of good sense and humanity were quickly gaining ground. Ironically, the afflicted girls hastened the process. They overreached themselves in naming the richest and most powerful as witches. By now believing they were infallible, they "cried out on" Mrs. Thatcher, the mother-in-law of the magistrate Jonathan Corwin, the two sons of the distinguished former governor, Simon Bradstreet, and the wife of the Reverend John Hale of Beverly. Most rashly of all, they named Lady Phipps, wife of Sir William himself. In their frenzy of gratified, murderous vengefulness they had come to think themselves mightier than the mightiest. They were quickly proved wrong. None of these powerful people was arrested, and a huge backlash ended the witch-hunt.

The single most important element in that backlash was an essay composed by Cotton Mather's father, Increase, called *Cases of Conscience concerning Evil Spirits Personating Men*. First delivered as a sermon to a gathering of ministers in Cambridge, Massachusetts, on October 3, it casts serious doubt on the use of spectral evidence in trying accused witches and asserts, "It were better that ten suspected witches should escape, than that one innocent person should be condemned." We can never know quite why Increase and the fourteen Boston ministers who signed the introduction to the essay when it was published took so long to voice these opinions. As we have seen, the *Return* penned by Cotton Mather had expressed similar doubts but negated them with a clarion call for the prosecution of witches. The *Return* was an endorsement of the court of Oyer and Terminer; *Cases* was its death knell. It seems that the ministers' doubts increased and their caution subsided when public opinion started to turn and the name "witch" was hurled at men and women of their own class and standing. It was then that the sense and wisdom of Mather *père* gained predominance over the paranoia and bigotry of Mather *fils*.

That the view that there was dissension between father and son was aired at the time can be inferred from the postscript Increase wrote to the published version of *Cases*. First he assures the reader that he does not mean "any reflection on those worthy persons who have been concerned in the late proceedings at Salem," since "they are wise and good men, and have acted with all fidelity according to their light. . . . Pity and prayers rather than censures are their due." He goes on to state that on that account, "I am glad that there is published to the world (by my son) a breviate of the trials of some who were lately executed, whereby I hope the thinking part of mankind will be satisfied, that there was more than that which is called spectre evidence for the conviction of the persons condemned." And then he says, "Some I hear have taken up a notion, that the book newly published by my son, is contradictory to this of mine." The book he means is *The Wonders of the Invisible World*. He goes on, with a disingenuousness almost worthy of the Reverend Samuel Parris himself, "'Tis strange that such imaginations should enter into the minds of men."

It would be gratifying to go back three hundred years and retort, "Not nearly as strange as some of the other imaginations that have entered them recently." However, unchallenged, Increase continues, "I perused and approved of that book before it was printed; and nothing but my relation to him hindered me from recommending it to the world." He ignores the fact that the tone of *Wonders* is wholly different from that of *Cases:* It is credulous and biased instead of reasoned and neutral. He goes on, "But myself and son agreed unto the humble advice which twelve ministers concurringly presented before his excellency and council, respecting the present difficulties." He is now talking of the *Return*. Like any president arguing that an apparent disagreement between himself and his secretary of state is one of mere emphasis, not substance, Increase minimizes the gulf between Cotton's works and his. He would in fact have been quite right to argue that the difference was one of emphasis. But never did so much, or so many, hang on a difference of emphasis.

On October 8 another powerful weapon was directed at the witch-hunt or, to borrow Stoughton and Cotton Mather's phrase though reverse its significance, another "standard was lifted against the infernal enemy." The enemy in this case was that combination of fanaticism, ignorance, envy, and self-loathing that invokes devils and specters. A wealthy merchant and distinguished scientist named Thomas Brattle, born in Boston in 1658, educated at Harvard and elected a member of the Royal Society for his work as a mathematician and astronomer, wrote a letter to an unknown correspondent addressed merely as "Reverend Sir" that fundamentally questions the wisdom of prosecuting witches. It points out, in the wonderfully balanced cadences of a prose style smacking more of the century to come than his own, the errors of the Salem judges in relying on the "touch test," the confessions of accused witches, the visions of the afflicted girls, and the discovery of bodily "excrescences" in making convictions. It also dismisses the validity as evidence of accounts of anger followed by mischief. Brattle's luminous intelligence and forceful personality shine through all his well-reasoned arguments, strongly expressed views, light irony, and sound judgments. Never are they more in evidence than in a passage in which he addresses the issue of the accused witches' damning failure to shed tears:

"Some of the Salem Gentlemen are very forward to censure and condemn the poor prisoner at the bar, because he sheds no tears: but such betray great ignorance in the nature of passion, and as great heedlessness as to common passages of a man's life. Some there are who never shed tears; others there are that ordinarily shed tears upon light occasions, and yet for their lives cannot shed a tear when the deepest sorrow is upon their hearts; and who is there that knows not these things? Who knows not that an ecstasy of joy will sometimes fetch tears, when as the quite contrary passion will shut them close up? Why then should any be so silly and foolish as to take an argument from this appearance?"

Having disposed of the possibility of mounting a valid legal case against accused witches, Brattle goes on to question the prosecutors' good faith. He points out that they failed to issue an arrest warrant for an accused person related to one of them, that is, Mrs. Margaret

Thatcher, mother-in-law of Jonathan Corwin, and to pursue various wealthy and eminent accused witches who had used their money and influence to escape prison: Hezekiah Usher, a prominent Boston merchant, Mrs. Nathaniel Cary, Phillip English, and John Alden. In other capital offenses the accused had been chased and brought back: "Why then is it not practiced in this case, if really judged to be so heinous as is made for?"

Brattle next expresses amazement that not only "the ruder and more ignorant sort" but also "the better sort" go to the afflicted girls for advice on what ails their friends and relations. Since the girls' knowledge is obtained by "holding correspondence with specters or evil spirits," it is "sorcery and wickedness" to consult them which "the better sort" should "punish and preach down," not "allow of, encourage, yea, and practice."

But Brattle's strongest condemnation is for the credence and respect given to the afflicted girls' accusations.

"Several persons have been apprehended purely upon the complaints of these afflicted, to whom the afflicted were perfect strangers, and had not the least knowledge of imaginable, before they were apprehended." He goes on, "the afflicted do own and assert, and the Justices do grant, that the devil does inform and tell the afflicted the names of those persons that are thus unknown unto them. Now these things being duly considered, I think it will appear evident to any one, that the devil's information is the fundamental testimony that is gone upon in the apprehending of the aforesaid people." If only the accused had had Brattle as their counsel at their trials.

Brattle lists those of repute in New England who "utterly condemn" the proceedings of the court. They include Simon Bradstreet, the former governor, and Thomas Danforth, the former deputy governor. This second name seems suspect. Danforth must have had a huge change of heart since he examined Martha Cory. And he must have had another one by the time he exhorted an accused witch who had been acquitted to "repent." That was the following January. Simon Bradstreet's opposition is more believable and may explain the "crying out on" his two sons. Brattle goes on to name Increase Mather and the Reverend Samuel Willard and Nathaniel Saltonstall "who was one of the Judges, has left the court, and is very much dissatisfied with the proceedings of it." The girls had "cried out on" Nathaniel Saltonstall by now too. All the reverend gentlemen in the country are dissatisfied, Brattle says, apart from John Hale, Nicholas Noyes, and Samuel Parris. Had Brattle written his letter a little later he would have had to omit even John Hale. This enthusiastic witch hunter quickly realized his error once his own wife was cried out on.

Having demolished the credibility of the afflicted girls, Brattle turns to the confessing witches:

"For whereas there are of the said confessors 55 in number, some of them are known to be distracted, crazed women . . . ; others of them denied their guilt, and maintained their innocence for above eighteen hours, after most violent, distracting and draggooning methods had been used with them to make them confess. . . . But, finally, as to about thirty of these fifty-five confessors, they are possessed (I reckon) with the devil, and afflicted as the children are, and therefore not fit to be regarded as to any thing they say of themselves or others."

Something Brattle strangely fails to mention is that by confessing, the accused witches saved their lives.

Brattle had a special reason for composing his lengthy letter at this particular moment, as becomes clear when he says, "The court is adjourned to the first Tuesday in November, then to be kept at Salem; between this and then will be [the] great assembly, and this will be a peculiar matter of their agitation." In other words, the General Court was meeting on October 12 to discuss the Salem trials, before the next session of the court. Brattle intended his letter to be circulated among its members in the four days till then to help sway their opinions. Perhaps he also intended it to come to the eyes of Sir William Phipps. It is likely it did so, along with Increase Mather's *Cases of Conscience.*

Together they achieved their objective. On October 12 Sir William wrote to the Privy Council in London saying he had forbidden further imprisonments for witchcraft. On October 26 the General Court voted for a day of fasting and a convocation of ministers to consider how to proceed "as to the witchcrafts." This was done in such a way that the Court of Oyer and Terminer considered itself "thereby dismissed." On October 29 Sir William formally dissolved it.

CHAPTER TWENTY-FIVE

The Guilt of Innocent Blood

THERE were few new accusations of witchcraft after October. During the early part of that month some of the afflicted girls were sent for by the township of Gloucester to investigate a case of possible bewitching. As a result, four women went to prison. Salem jail was so full it could take only two of them and the other two went to Ipswich. However, after October 12, when Sir William Phipps wrote his letter to London, anyone accused was not imprisoned but bailed. Even some of those already in prison were let out on bail. Sir William later said that when he came back from the Eastward "there were at least fifty persons in prison in great misery by reason of the extreme cold and their poverty," so he "caused some of them to be let out upon bail and put the judges upon considering of a way to relieve others and prevent them from perishing in prison." He was trying to put the best possible construction on the part he had played in the discredited witch-hunt. Yet no doubt he really did take the action he claimed and a few wretches were unchained and allowed to clamber up the dank steps of their dungeons and pass through the heavy oak doors to the fresh air they had almost forgotten.

In November the afflicted girls were called to Gloucester again. A soldier thought his ailing sister was bewitched. The girls claimed they saw three specters sitting on her until she died, but though this claim was believed, the people they named were granted bail and stayed out of prison.

But an incident occurred on the way to their assignment that showed them that the days of their power and glory were numbered. As they were crossing Ipswich bridge they met an old woman and went into fits. Instead of turning on the accused witch, the passers-by merely stared or hurried past. The accusers quickly pulled themselves together and went on their way. They had at last lost credibility. They made no more accusations.

For four months everything was quiet. People tried as far as they could to resume normal lives. But a hundred and fifty or more still languished in chains in the dungeons, wondering what was to become of them. They must have felt stirrings of hope now that the Court of Oyer and Terminer was abolished, spectral evidence was discredited, and Sir William had shown a measure of mercy. But the weeks and months dragged on. Still they had no idea when they would be taken to trial. And all this time they needed financial and emotional support from their relatives. Those relatives themselves were beset, struggling to repair the neglect to their farms, take care of whatever livestock was spared them by the sheriff, and harvest such crops as they had sown in the specter-haunted spring. Meanwhile Sir William and the General Court were kept busy implementing the provisions of the charter Sir William had brought with him from London. One of the most significant of these extended the franchise from male church members to all male householders. New courts were set up and new laws enacted. The former Massachusetts measures against witchcraft were reinstated in place of the English law under which prosecutions had so far been brought. They were not significantly different since they were derived from English law, so this change in itself did not influence events. A Superior Court was created by an act of the General Court on November 25, but it was not due to have its first session in Salem till a year later and meanwhile the prisons stayed full. So on December 16 another act was passed to allow a special sitting to try the remaining accused witches.

Sir William Phipps appointed William Stoughton chief judge. This may seem strange, but no disgrace had fallen on any of the magistrates or judges of the Court of Oyer and Terminer. Almost all the doubts expressed about the trials had been concerned with the nature of the evidence admitted. Only Brattle had questioned the good faith of the prosecutors and even he had done so diplomatically. He was careful to dissociate himself from "men of a factious spirit" and expressed wonder, rather than censure, at what he believed were the judges' mistakes. The first session of the Superior Court, on January 3, included no less than four of the same judges as the Court of Oyer and Terminer. As well as William Stoughton they were Wait Winthrop, Samuel Sewall, and John Richards. The fifth judge was the former deputy governor, Thomas Danforth.

Thirty of the accused who appeared before the court were dismissed on the grounds that there was no basis for prosecution against them. Twenty-six were tried but only three found guilty. There were two main reasons for this. One was that spectral evidence was no longer admissible, on Sir William's instructions. This must have infuriated William Stoughton, but there was nothing he could do about it. When some members of the jury asked the court what weight they ought to give spectral evidence, they were told "as much as of chips in wort," in other words, less than none. The other reason for the not guilty verdicts was that juries were no longer made up only of church members. All male householders could now serve. Non–church members were far more likely to be skeptical about witches.

The three accused found guilty were Elizabeth Johnson of Andover, Mary Post of Rowley and Sarah Wardwell, wife of Samuel Wardwell, who had been hanged in September. According to Calef the first two of these women were "the most senseless and ignorant creatures that could be found." Elizabeth Johnson's grandfather was no less forthright in his view of his granddaughter's mental abilities, saying she was "simplish at the best." Johnson had made a rambling confession at her examination in August and perhaps repeated it now. Sarah Wardwell probably also repeated her former confession since her husband had been hanged as a result of going back on his. The jury concluded that if anyone was guilty of witchcraft these three were. And, after all, if no one was guilty of witchcraft, why were these trials even taking place? Stoughton signed a warrant for the three women's "speedy execution."

It is ironic that at this late date those who claimed innocence were acquitted while confessors were condemned. Clearly Stoughton had nothing on principle against sending confessing witches to their deaths. It had been a matter of expediency to save them.

Happily, however, these three did not die. Sir William reprieved them. He also reprieved five other accused witches sentenced earlier by the Court of Oyer and Terminer, having been "informed by the King's Attorney General" that the evidence against all these people was no different from that against many acquitted. When word of this was brought to the Superior Court, now sitting at Charlestown, William Stoughton was "enraged and filled with passionate anger" and walked off the bench. He shouted furiously, "We were in a way to have cleared the land. . . . who it is that obstructs the course of justice I know not; the Lord be merciful to the country."

The trials in Charlestown, to try witchcraft cases in the county of Middlesex, continued. It would be pleasing to report that in Stoughton's absence justice was done and all wrongs were righted. But though the end of the witch-hunt was swift, the reversal of its effects was exceedingly slow. Vested interests did not dissolve; closed minds did not open. None of the accused in Charlestown was found guilty but, as in Salem, this was because of the absence of spectral evidence and the change in the composition of the juries, not through any sudden enlightenment on the part of the judges. An accused witch named Sarah Dustin, between seventy and eighty years old, was found not guilty despite a reputation for witchcraft and much testimony against her of the anger followed by mischief variety. But after the verdict Judge Danforth turned to her and said, "Woman, woman, repent, there are shrewd things come in against you." Not only was she not presumed innocent till found guilty, she was presumed guilty when found innocent.

Sarah may not have cared what the judge said or did not say but must have felt bitter at being sent back to prison. This happened because she had no money for her fees. However, the jail keeper did not benefit from her stay. While still in prison, she died. Even a Puritan jail keeper could not send her bill on to heaven.

In April the Superior Court was held in Boston for the County of Suffolk. Stoughton was back again as chief judge, with Danforth, Richards, and Sewall as before. Again, everyone was let off, including the merchant John Alden who had escaped from jail some months before. He had no chance to keep "his hat on before the judges" on this occasion since he was not tried in person but acquitted by proclamation.

In May all the accused witches remaining in jail were discharged. This was on Sir William Phipps's orders. It must have seemed the logical move since there was no stronger evidence against them than against all those who had just been acquitted. There could not be. It was the type, not the amount, of evidence that had been found unsatisfactory in the recent witchcraft prosecutions. And there was no other type to be had.

About one hundred and fifty were released, but many had to stay behind bars because, like Sarah Dustin, they could not pay their prison fees. Some were let out eventually, like young Margaret Jacobs, whose bill a stranger paid out of pity. Sadly this story is less heartwarming than first appears since the man later sued Margaret for the sum. In time, she repaid him. Others, like Sarah Dustin, died in jail.

The accused witch, released at this time, who had been incarcerated longer than anyone, was of course Tituba. The other two jailed with her, over a year ago, had both died, Sarah Osborne in prison, Sarah Good by hanging. Tituba did not go back to the parsonage. Parris sold her to a new owner, using the money from the sale to pay off her prison fees.

Many families were ruined. George Jacobs Junior was left with nothing after fleeing Massachusetts to avoid being arrested. His wife was imprisoned for eleven months and his daughter Margaret for seven. Their fees to the prison officers amounted to twelve pounds, and there were other charges too. As we know, there was no money to pay Margaret's fee. George Jacobs's father, who had declared, "Burn me or hang me, I will stand in the truth of Christ," had eighty pounds' worth of property seized. The family managed to keep its homestead and stay in Salem Village, but in penury.

When Edward and Sarah Bishop were arrested, most of their household goods, cows, pigs, and sheep were taken by the sheriff. The combined number of weeks the two of them spent in prison was thirty-seven, at ten shillings a week each. Other charges and fees came to five pounds. All these costs were taken out of what was left of their estate. For a year their farm lay idle, fields unplowed, crops unharvested, the remaining animals uncared for. Twelve children were also uncared for. Presumably they survived as they could, scavenging and begging.

So it goes on, for prisoner after prisoner. The injustice of the financial burden imposed on the people unlucky enough to be seized, even those found not guilty, was staggering. Prisoners were made to pay not only for their maintenance, fuel, clothes, transportation from jail to jail, and court and prison fees but for every paper drawn up relating to their case. They even had to pay for their discharges from prison and reprieves from execution. Ann Foster's son Abraham was obliged to pay two pounds ten shillings to obtain his mother's body for burial. Even during the autumn of 1692, relatives of prisoners began petitioning the General Court for relief. On October 12 seven citizens of Andover sent a memorandum on behalf of their wives and children, asking that they be released on bail, "to remain as prisoners in their own houses, where they may be more tenderly cared for." On October 19 Thomas Hart of Lynn presented a memo stating that his mother had been in Boston jail for nearly six months despite "being ancient, and not able to undergo the hardship that is inflicted from lying in misery, and death rather to be chosen than a life in her circumstances." His father is "ancient and decrepit, and wholly unable" to act on her behalf. Thomas Barrett of Chelmsford petitioned for his daughter Martha, whose husband was a soldier in the Eastward, saying she "hath lain in prison in Boston for the space of twelve months and five days . . . your petitioner hath ever since kept two of her children, the one of five years, the other of two years old, which hath been a considerable trouble and charge to him in his poor and mean condition: besides, your petitioner hath a lame, ancient, and sick wife, who, for these five years and upwards past, hath been so afflicted as that she is altogether rendered uncapable of affording herself any help, which much augments his trouble. . . . you will please to order the releasement of his daughter from her confinement, whereby she may return home to her poor children to look after them, having nothing to pay the charge of her confinement."

After the amnesty many released prisoners and relatives of those executed began petitioning for restitution. However, the first pleas were not for financial reimbursement but reinstatement of character. In 1700 Abigail Falkner of Andover, who had been condemned and then reprieved, wrote a memo to the General Court saying that her pardon had allowed her to live "only as a malefactor" who had supposedly committed "the most heinous crimes." She asked for the "defacing of the record" on the grounds that the only testimony against her was that of spectral evidence, which had since been discredited. The court responded sympathetically, but her plea was not granted. A similar petition was presented in March 1702 by a long list of people who had been convicted, together with relatives of people who had been hanged. The latter included Mary Easty's husband and one of John Proctor's sons. In response to this plea the Massachusetts House of Representatives passed a bill forbidding the use of spectral evidence in the future and declaring that "the infamy and reproach cast on the names and posterity" of those found guilty because of it should "in some measure be rolled away." This begrudging resolution scarcely met the needs of the petitioners. A year and four months later a group of Essex County ministers sent an address to the General Court describing the afflicted girls as "young persons under diabolical molestations" and asking it to grant the petitioners' request to clear their names. Among the signatories was Joseph Green, who had in 1697 replaced Samuel Parris as pastor of Salem Village. Nicholas Noyes did not sign.

The General Court still did nothing. Six years later, on May 25, 1709, another petition was presented by some of the same people together with others. This plea asked for financial remuneration as well as the restoration of the victims' good names. A new signatory was Phillip English, who gave a detailed account of articles seized from his warehouses, wharf, and shop. He also listed the expenses incurred by him and his wife during their nine weeks in prison and in escaping from prison.

But even now, nothing was done. The next year, in September, Mary Easty's husband, Isaac, presented a memo to the General Court asking for remuneration for the loss of his "beloved wife" though, he said, "my sorrow and trouble of heart in being deprived of her in such a manner" can never truly be compensated. Relations of Elizabeth Howe, Sarah Wildes, Mary Bradbury, Edward and Sarah Bishop, George Burroughs, Giles and Martha Cory, and Rebecca Nurse all sent in petitions. At last, in October 1710, the General Court passed an act reversing the convictions of those for whom their families had pleaded. It did not extend the reversal to those who had been hanged for witchcraft but for whom no petitions were made. These included Bridget

Bishop, Susannah Martin, Alice Parker, Ann Pudeator, Wilmot Redd, and Margaret Scott.

A year later, on December 17, 1711, the sum of five hundred seventy-eight pounds twelve shillings was granted to the petitioning relatives. By far the largest amount, one hundred fifty pounds, went to the Proctors since John Proctor was the most prosperous of those hanged. The second largest, seventy-nine pounds, went to the heirs of George Jacobs Senior, and the third, fifty pounds, to those of George Burroughs. But the size of the rest of the amounts paid shows no clear rationale. The relatives of the fairly prosperous Elizabeth Howe got only twelve pounds, while William Good, husband of the destitute Sarah, got thirty pounds. Wild Abigail Hobbs was given ten pounds, despite being an accuser as well as an accused. Altogether, the relations of twenty-four people who were executed, died in prison, or spent a long time there were compensated.

But justice had still not been done. There were many others who had suffered just as badly as those compensated and who had as yet received nothing. At the end of 1738 a son of Samuel Sewall, also named Samuel, chaired a committee to obtain information relating to "the circumstances of the persons and families who suffered in the calamity of the times in and about the year 1692." The records leave unclear what the result of this action was. But not long afterward the sum of two hundred pounds was allowed to the heirs of Phillip English. It is ironic that English never knew that a part of the remuneration he had been vigorously demanding for years was finally granted. His fury at the seizure of his goods had been commensurate to his loss. No merchant had been more powerful or wealthy, none more incensed by his humbling. He had sued George Corwin for the illegal seizure of his property to the value of fifteen hundred pounds. He lost the case. But then he brought another suit; it was outstanding when, in 1697, Corwin died. English's rage against the sheriff was such that he declared his intention of seizing Corwin's body in satisfaction of the debt. The corpse had to be interred on the Corwin property, where English could not reach it, till the matter was settled.

In time other wrongs were righted. In 1703 Joseph Green, Salem Village's new minister, reversed Martha Cory's excommunication. In 1712 Salem church "erased and blotted out" the excommunications of Rebecca Nurse and Giles Cory, though they did so as a result of pressure from Samuel Nurse rather than from any remorse on the part of Nicholas Noyes.

Remorse was thin on the ground altogether in the aftermath of the witch-hunt. At no point was there clear, universal recognition that a huge wrong had been done and that the instigators of the witchcraft prosecutions were the wrongdoers. Instead there existed a mass of different individual and factional attitudes and beliefs. Certain people did indeed feel a burden of guilt and say they were sorry. The twelve men who had sat on several of the juries during the summer, including the foreman Thomas Fisk, who had asked Rebecca Nurse what she had meant by calling Dorcas Hoar "one of us" and who reversed the jury's verdict from "not guilty" to "guilty," signed a paper expressing their sorrow:

"We confess that we ourselves were not capable to understand, nor able to withstand the mysterious delusions of the powers of darkness, and prince of the air; but were for want of knowledge in ourselves, and better information from others, prevailed with to take up with such evidence against the accused, as on further consideration, and better information, we justly fear was insufficient for the touching the lives of any . . . whereby we fear we have been instrumental with others, though ignorantly and unwittingly, to bring upon ourselves, and this people of the Lord, the guilt of innocent blood. . . .

"We do heartily ask forgiveness of you all, whom we have justly offended, and do declare according to our present minds, we would none of us do such things again on such grounds for the whole world."

Someone higher up the social ladder who seems to have experienced sincere regret, though strongly mixed with fear of reprisals from God, was Judge Samuel Sewall. On January 14, 1697, he handed in a paper at the assembly of the General Court at the South Meeting House in Boston saying that he desired "to take the blame and shame" of "the opening of the late Comission of Oyer and Terminer at Salem." He asks that God "not visit the sin of him, or any other, upon himself or any of his, nor upon the land."

This assembly had been called on a day of fasting meant to atone for all New England's sins including those of the witch-hunt. The government proclamation announcing it expressed the same fear of God's anger as Sewall's confession. This is not surprising since Sewall had written it. The judge was by nature diplomatic, and the proclamation refers to "whatever mistakes on either hand have been fallen into, either by the body of this people, or any orders of men, referring to the late tragedy raised among us by Satan and his instruments." He is talking of possible mistakes both in condemning the innocent and acquitting the guilty. Insofar as there was an official government line on the witch-hunt, this was it. Innocent people may have died and guilty ones escaped; the whole thing was deeply regrettable; everyone meant well; no one was to blame.

The closest anyone in power came to casting opprobrium on any individual was when Sir William Phipps, in his letter to London of February 1693, said of William Stoughton that he "hath from the beginning hurried on these matters with great precipitancy and by his warrant hath caused the estates, goods and chattles of the executed to be seized and disposed of without my knowledge or consent." Phipps was covering his own back here. Generally speaking he, the General Court, judges, magistrates, and ministers, closed ranks.

This does not mean that the views and impulses of individuals were necessarily or even ever wholly cynical. Samuel Sewall observed a private day of fasting annually for the rest of his life. John Hale, when he wrote in his *Modest Enquiry* that he "observed in the prosecution of these affairs that there was in the justices, judges and others concerned a conscientious endeavour to do the thing that was right," no doubt meant it. And it seems likely that his observation was by and large correct, allowing for self-delusion, mixed motives, and lapses. What Hale fails to mention is that when a fanatic undertakes conscientiously to "endeavour to do the thing that is right," the results can be deadly. Hale's work is largely an honest attempt to explain how the witch-hunt got started and grew. Tituba's confession "encouraged those in authority to examine others that were suspected" and "thus was the matter driven on." The justices and judges consulted the "learned writers about witchcraft" whose precepts encouraged prosecution. But the chief spur "was the increasing of confessors till they amounted to near about fifty." Hale relates several confessions that, in their wealth of detail and correspondence with each other, were convincing at the time and astonishing still, five years later. It remained hard for him to believe they were nothing but delusions or lies. Like everyone else, except Robert Calef, he overlooked the stark fact that, by confessing, accused witches escaped death.

Hale goes on to explain how the witch-hunt was stopped. The accusations did not end with the executions, "so that those that were concerned grew amazed at the numbers and quality of the persons accused and feared that Satan by his wiles had enwrapped innocent persons under the imputation of that crime. And at last it was evidently seen that there must be a stop put, or the generation of the children of God would fall under that condemnation." The juries "generally acquitted such as were tried" and Sir William Phipps reprieved the rest. "And the confessors generally fell off from their confessions; some saying, they remembered nothing of what they said, others said they had belied themselves and others. Some broke prison and ran away, and were not strictly searched after, some acquitted, some dismissed and one way or other all that had been accused were set or left at liberty."

Had the times been calm, he goes on, there might have been a fresh inquiry into the guilt of the confessors, but "considering the combustion and confusion that matter had brought us into it was thought safer to underdo than overdo, especially in matters capital, where what is once completed cannot be retrieved. . . . Thus this matter issued [ended]somewhat abruptly."

Hale never doubts that the devil caused the witch-hunt. "When this prosecution ceased," he says, "the Lord so chained up Satan, that the afflicted grew presently well. The accused are generally quiet, and for five years since, we have no such molestations by them."

Calef's analysis of the origins and ending of the witch-hunt strikes a rather different note:

"And now to sum up all in a few words, we have seen a bigoted zeal, stirring up a blind and most bloody rage, not against enemies, or irreligious profligate persons, but . . . against as virtuous and religious as any . . . and this by the testimony of vile varlets as not only were known before, but have been further apparent since by their manifest lives, whoredoms, incest, etc. The accusations of these, from their spectral sight, being the chief evidence against those that suffered. In which accusations they were upheld by both magistrates and ministers, so long as they apprehended themselves in no danger."

But the distinction between a fanatic's "conscientious endeavour to do the thing that was right" and "bigoted zeal" is in the eye of the beholder. Hale's and Calef's analyses do not truly contradict each other. Whether one prefers Hale's respectful or Calef's cynical tone is a matter of viewpoint.

Apart from the jurors, Samuel Sewall, and John Hale, few of those implicated in the witch-hunt made apologies. Neither Hathorne nor Stoughton ever expressed the slightest regret. On the contrary, they stood by their actions. This did them no harm in their future careers. They continued as successful merchants and politicians, lived to old age, and were buried with ceremony. Hathorne lies in the "burying point," the oldest cemetery in Salem, which in the seventeenth century bordered the South River. Due to the river's narrowing, it is today north of a stretch of shore below Derby Street. The magistrate's bones rest near those of the relatives of people he committed to prison. Since 1992 they are also close to a tercentenary memorial to the twenty men and women he helped send to their deaths. This memorial takes the unusual and imaginative form of twenty stone rectangles, each engraved with a name, protruding horizontally from the inside of a low wall forming a square. Along the inside of the wall runs a path from which the names can be read, enclosing a lawn.

Hathorne's only comeuppance has been an extremely unflattering character portrayal as Judge Pyncheon in *The House of Seven Gables* by his descendant Nathaniel Hawthorne. Alas, the novel was written a hundred years after Hathorne's death, so he never saw himself vividly pictured as a cruel, rigid tyrant. Perhaps sometimes in the small hours he sweated with fear at the possibility that he had caused twenty innocent people to die. Maybe Stoughton did too. It would be pleasing to think so. But it seems far more probable that the pair of them lay awake cursing all those yellow bellies who shrank from pressing on with convictions and "clearing the land."

Cotton Mather also remained unrepentant. He spent the rest of his life as a minister, agonizing over the falling away of New England from its high Puritan ideals and his own failure to become president of Harvard, but never giving a sign that he believed he might have done wrong in the witch-hunt. He reacted with hysterical defensiveness to Robert Calef's *More Wonders of the Invisible World,* written in 1697, which criticized his part in the recent events and his subsequent lack of remorse. The title of this work is not a wry joke at Cotton's expense, lampooning his own title *Wonders of the Invisible World.* In fact, it is another work by Cotton: Calef published, without permission, the minister's account of the bewitching of a young woman named Margaret Rule, called *More Wonders of the Invisible World, or Another Brand Plucked from the Burning.* With it Calef printed a correspondence he had held with the author as well as his own narrative of the events of 1692.

Cotton's shrill defensiveness about his part in the witch-hunt is first abundantly displayed in his own text in *More Wonders.* He describes taking over the care of the bewitched Margaret in the autumn of 1693 and curing her by fasting and prayer. He stresses that he did not allow her publicly to name the specters who were torturing her, "less any good person should come to suffer any blast of reputation through the cunning malice of the great accuser; nevertheless having since privately named them to myself, I will venture to say this of them, that they are a sort of wretches who for these many years have gone under as violent presumptions of witchcraft as perhaps any creatures yet living upon earth; although I am far from thinking that the visions of this young woman were evidence enough to prove them so."

His obvious regret at not being able to name the "wretches" is made even more evident a little farther on in a most interesting paragraph. He starts by saying "that when that storm was raised at Salem" he offered to take "no less than six of the afflicted" into his own home to try to cure them by fasting and prayer. This is the only mention in any of the sources of this offer, but presumably he did actually make it. In the summer of 1692 he had taken in a young woman named Mercy Short to cure her of fits, into which she had fallen after visiting Salem prison and being begged by Sarah Good for tobacco for her pipe. Mercy threw a handful of wood shavings at the prisoner in her chains, shouting, "That's tobacco good enough for you." It hardly seems surprising that she became mentally disturbed after that. The sight and smell of the dungeons would in themselves have been enough to disturb anyone, certainly anyone vulnerable. Mercy, like so many of the afflicted girls, had a deeply troubled history. She was captured as a child by Indians who "horribly butchered" her mother, father, brother, and sister. To act cruelly toward someone helpless and in desperate misery, but at the same time possessed of supernatural powers of vengeance, must have left her in guilt-ridden terror. According to his own published account, called *A Brand Plucked from the Burning*, which preceded the narrative put out by Calef, Mather cured Mercy by fasting and prayer. He had done the same for Martha Goodwin some years earlier, as Samuel Willard had for Elizabeth Knapp.

The offer to the Salem Village afflicted does credit to Cotton's ambition and nerve. However, one wonders what his wife would have thought of having six hysterical young girls in the house. He may not have pressed the proposal. His aim, he says, was to put an end to the afflictions "without giving the civil authority the trouble of prosecuting those things which nothing but a conscientious regard unto the cries of miserable families could have overcome the reluctancies of the honourable judges to meddle with." All his sympathy and respect lies with the authorities for the *trouble* they were put to in prosecuting. There is no suggestion that prosecution was a *mistake*. Cotton goes on, "There is not that man living in this world who has been more desirous than the poor man I to shelter my neighbours from the inconveniences of spectral outcries, yea I am very jealous I have done so much that way as to sin in what I have done, such have been the cowardice and fearfulness whereunto my regard unto the dissatisfactions of other people has precipitated me." In other words, any guilt he feels lies in being pressured by others into *not* naming names.

Unlike Hathorne and Stoughton, Cotton *was* made to suffer for his sins, as the correspondence between him and Calef reproduced in *More Wonders* makes clear. In a letter to Cotton, Calef includes an eyewitness's account of Margaret Rule's behavior in her "bewitched" state. The eyewitness suggests that her chief purpose in her afflictions was to attract attention from males. Both Increase and Cotton rubbed Margaret's breast and stomach to ease her discomfort rather more than was absolutely necessary, he observes. Cotton reacted with violence. He agreed to meet Calef to discuss the matter but before the appointed time had arrived he had Calef arrested for libel. Calef's alleged crime was to take down the eyewitness's statement and talk about it to others. However, Cotton did not appear against him in court. The case was dropped and instead Mather wrote the merchant a self-pitying letter. Calef penned a reply, carefully addressing each of the points Cotton raised, which Cotton did not answer.

In June 1698 Cotton reported furiously in his diary that Calef's *More Wonders*, which unsurprisingly had found no printer in Boston, might be printed in England. In 1700 he wrote that "though I had often and often cried unto the Lord, that the cup of this man's abominable bundle of lies, written on purpose, with a quill under a special energy and management of Satan, to damnify my precious opportunities of glorifying my Lord Jesus Christ, might pass from me; yet, in this point, the Lord has denied my request; the book is printed, and the impression is this week arrived here."

Cotton's father's response was to have the book burned in Harvard College yard. He and his son prevailed on seven of their parishioners to put their names to a pamphlet defending them from its criticisms.

During his last years Cotton felt himself spurned and unappreciated by all those he had endeavored to help. Particularly ungrateful for his efforts were sailors, Negroes, women, his own relatives, the Scots, the government, and Harvard. He bemoans the thanklessness of these groups at great length in a diary entry during 1724. The effect is both unintentionally comic and sad.

1. What has a gracious Lord helped me to do for the *seafaring* tribe, in prayers for them, in sermons to them, in books bestowed upon them, and in various projections and endeavours to render the sailors a happy generation? and yet there is not a man in the world so reviled, so slandered, so cursed among sailors.

2. What has a gracious Lord given me to do for the instruction and salvation and comfort of the poor negroes? And yet some, on purpose to affront me, call their negroes by the name of COTTON MATHER, that so they may, with some shadow of truth, assert crimes as committed by one of that name, which the hearers take to be *Me*.

3. What has a gracious Lord given me to do for the profit and honour of the female sex, especially in publishing the virtuous and laudable characters of holy women? And yet where is the man whom the female sex have spit more of their venom at? I have cause to question whether there are twice ten in the town but what have, at some time or other, spoken *basely* of me.

4. What has a gracious Lord given me to do, that I may be a blessing to my relatives? I keep a catalogue of them, and not a week passes me without some good devised for some or other of them, till I have taken all of them under my cognizance. As yet where is the man who has

been so tormented with such *monstrous* relatives? Job said, *"I am a brother to dragons."*

And so he goes on.

To his credit, toward the end of his life he took the uncharacteristically enlightened action of espousing the cause of smallpox inoculation. (It may be remembered that he had trained as a doctor before entering the ministry.) The raging epidemic of 1721 had reached his own family, infecting two of his children. His opposition to the march of science and reason did not extend to a development that might save a beloved son and daughter.

However, he remained self-deluding to the end, professing utter bafflement as to why "everybody points at me, and speaks of me as by far the most afflicted minister in all New England." Anybody in the province could have told him. If there was any blame to be cast for the twenty deaths and huge, widespread misery of the witch-hunt, much of it fell squarely on Cotton.

Self-deluding as he was, he cannot but have realized that the tide had turned against his brand of Puritanism, however much he tried to convince himself that it might one day prove triumphant. He died at age sixty-six, predeceased by two wives and all but two of fifteen children.

Of all the men who helped instigate the witch-hunt, instead of merely joining in later, Samuel Parris was the only one who admitted he might have been to some small degree in the wrong. His reason for the admission was simple: to try to hold on to his job. When it became clear, in October 1692, that the tide had turned against him, he preached a sermon of a very different tone from any he had previously delivered. The rhythms and imagery are as oratorical as ever, but the purpose is conciliatory: "And so again, I beg, entreat, and beseech you, that Satan, the devil, the roaring lion, the old dragon, the enemy of all righteousness, may no longer be served by us, by our envy and strifes . . . but that all from this day forward may be covered with the mantle of love, and we may on all hands forgive each other heartily, sincerely, and thoroughly, as we do hope and pray that God, for Christ's sake, would forgive each of ourselves."

But reconciliation was not easily won. His opponents, of whom four of the most important were those "dissenting brethren" he had taken to task for not attending communion—Samuel Nurse, Peter Cloyce, John Tarbell, and Thomas Wilkins—were determined to oust him from the parish. This was by no means only because of his part in the witch-hunt. They belonged to the anti-Putnam faction led by Israel Porter which had opposed him from the start. But the witch-hunt had

made their opposition a great deal more bitter. For two years complicated maneuverings by both factions over the issues of Parris's pay, title
to the parsonage, and fitness for his job led to a series of accusations,
counteraccusations, formal and informal meetings, appeals to the governor for arbitration, and meetings with ministers in Boston, Salem,
and elsewhere. On November 26, 1694, with his back to the wall,
Parris read out in the meetinghouse a statement called "meditations
for peace," which admitted giving too much weight to spectral evidence and said that he may have spoken "unadvisedly." The tone was
highly emotional though the admissions were minimal.

The ploy did not work. Perhaps it would not have worked anyway.
But there was no chance of its doing so given the deeper issues at stake
than Parris himself, the issues of who held ultimate power in Salem
Village, the Porters or the Putnams, and what sort of place it should
be, a backward-looking enclave of old-style Puritanism or an economic
and social adjunct to the merchant-run town.

There could be no question but that the Porters would win in the
end. Sure enough, in September 1697, after a final arbitration by three
Boston ministers on back pay and the deeds to the parsonage, Parris
quit Salem Village. It must have seemed a long five and a half years
since his daughter and niece first began "getting into holes, and creeping under chairs and stools" and using "odd postures and antic
gestures." His wife had died in July 1696. Perhaps her last illness was
the final blow that made him give up the fight.

He found a position as minister in an even more remote outpost
than Salem Village, Stow, Massachusetts, a frontier community of only
twenty-eight families. This tiny hamlet had been much troubled by
warfare with the Indians, the recent departure of eight families, and a
"great diminution" of crops. Despite this, Parris pressed for more pay
than the inhabitants had offered and the title to the parsonage.
Though he had amply demonstrated already that he was not someone
to learn from experience, this repetition seems almost incredible. It
comes as no surprise to discover that relations with the people of Stow
quickly soured and he left a year later. But meanwhile, luckily for him,
he had married a woman with money. Her income saved him from
penury during his subsequent checkered career as shopkeeper, school-
master, minister again, farmer, and property speculator. He died in
1720, leaving many debts but enough assets to cover them and to leave
bequests to his children, including Betty Parris, now married.

Betty was not the only afflicted girl who eventually wed. Elizabeth
Booth, Sarah Churchill, and Mary Walcott did so too, and also Mercy
Lewis, though in her case only after having a baby. All these girls,
except possibly Elizabeth Booth, sooner or later moved from Salem

Village. No one knows what became of Abigail Williams, Elizabeth Hubbard, Susannah Sheldon, or Mary Warren. There seems a good chance that it was Abigail Williams whom Hale meant when he said that she never fully recovered her sanity but was "followed with diabolical molestation to her death."

Ann Putnam remained unmarried and stayed in Salem Village. Both her parents died in 1699. Thomas was forty-six at his death, his wife thirty-seven. They perished within two weeks of each other. It is tempting to imagine that one or both committed suicide, unable any longer to bear the guilt for more than twenty deaths and vast hardship and misery. But they may simply have died of the same infectious illness. Ann was left to bring up her nine surviving siblings. Unsurprisingly, she suffered from frequent ill health and died at age thirty-seven.

When she was twenty-six, in 1706, she made an extraordinary public statement. The occasion was her reception into the Salem Village church. Her words were read aloud in the meetinghouse by the pastor, Joseph Green, as Ann stood and the rest of the congregation remained seated. It is clear from its wording that it was primarily addressed to the Nurse family. Ann must have experienced their bitter condemnation, in looks, words, and silences, all through the past fourteen years. Samuel Nurse and the other "dissenting brethren" were no doubt present among the great crowd, listening to the words read in the agreeable tones of the benign Reverend Green, and perhaps as they did so at last feeling ease from their terrible hurt.

"I desire to be humbled before God for that sad and humbling providence that befell my father's family in the year about '92; that I, then being in my childhood, should, by such a providence of God, be made an instrument for the accusing of several persons of a grievous crime, whereby their lives were taken away from them, whom now I have just grounds and good reason to believe they were innocent persons; and that it was a great delusion of Satan that deceived me in that sad time, whereby I justly fear I have been instrumental, with others, though ignorantly and unwittingly, to bring upon myself and this land the guilt of innocent blood; though what was said or done by me against any person I can truly and uprightly say, before God and man, I did it not out of any anger, malice, or ill-will to any person, for I had no such thing against one of them; but what I did was ignorantly, being deluded by Satan. And particularly, as I was a chief instrument of accusing of Goodwife Nurse and her two sisters, I desire to lie in the dust, and to be humbled for it, in that I was a cause, with others, of so sad a calamity to them and their families; for which I desire to lie in the dust, and earnestly beg forgiveness of God, and from all those unto whom I have given just cause of sorrow and offence, whose relations were taken away or accused."

We can never know if Ann was telling the truth when she said she did nothing out of "anger, malice, or ill-will to any person." Clearly she had been accused of doing so or she would not have denied it. Her memory of the strange madness of fourteen years before, when she was twelve, must have been partial and confused. In her dreams she may have seen faces filled with terror or bodies swinging from branches or a masked man slicing through a rope with his knife. In her waking hours she must have recalled the screaming and falling and fainting. How much else remained with her cannot be guessed.

However, one imagines she must surely have remembered Rebecca. It had taken special dedication to make sure she died. When the jury pronounced her not guilty, Ann had led her friends in fits to end all fits. Perhaps she recalled feelings of hatred for the harmless old woman, inspired by her mother and father, exacerbated by Rebecca's old age and passivity. She may have told herself that such feelings were not "anger, malice, or ill-will" but mere childish dislike.

But whatever she remembered or had forgotten, she seems to have felt true regret. To help her live with herself, as well as her neighbors, she blamed the deaths of twenty innocent people not on her own human wickedness but on a "delusion of Satan."

Epilogue

A theme that has run through the whole story of the Massachusetts witch-hunt is that of disinheritance. The first accused witches had all been denied just expectations. Tituba had lost the freedom that a hundred and fifty years later was to be enshrined in the Constitution as a fundamental right. Sarah Good was denied, when her father died, the share of his riches she had every reason to think would be hers. Sarah Osborne lost her wealth and good name after marrying her servant.

Strange echoes are found in the lives of those who cried "witch." Thomas Putnam was deprived of his due as eldest son by his half-brother. Ann Putnam too was cheated of her rightful portion of patrimony. Parris received less than should have been his of his father's wealth in Barbados.

The daughters of these families, Ann Putnam and Betty Parris, suffered those losses along with their parents. For the other afflicted girls, disinheritance was even more bitter. Abigail Williams, Mary Warren, and Mercy Lewis were orphans. Elizabeth Hubbard lived as a servant with an uncle and was perhaps also an orphan. Mary Walcott had lost her mother, Susannah Sheldon her father.

The community of Salem Village, that is, its traditional, long-established section in the western part of the region, was itself disinherited. It no longer prospered as it had during the first and second generations. And with the coming of cultural change during the seventeenth century it no longer embodied the values of the wider society. Its self-respect was destroyed as it was gradually stripped of social identity and moral authority.

The theme is found in an even broader perspective. By the end of the seventeenth century Massachusetts had lost its special status as a Puritan theocracy. That portion of it that held to the aspirations of the original immigrants mourned the passing of the opportunity to build a "city on a hill," a nation of saints.

The Salem witch trials have long been seen as the last manifestation of backward-looking Puritanism. So they were. But rage, bitterness, and envy produced by deep loss, on many levels including the individual and familial as well as the social and national, had fueled and attracted the murderous hostility. When the witch-hunt was over, lives were rebuilt with the new acceptance that the fight to stop the world from changing was lost. Salem Village and Massachusetts were at last freed to bow to the inevitable economic, political, and cultural developments of the new century.

Over the next twenty years the factionalism that had so divided Salem Village was resolved. It is no accident that the pastor who replaced Samuel Parris and fostered the process was of an equable, worldly temperament. He kept a diary that described the wonders of the natural world rather than visions of angels or anguished strivings of conscience. He welcomed back into the church the "dissenting brethren" and soon had them taking communion. In 1699 he rearranged the seating in the meetinghouse so that Putnams and Nurses found themselves next to each other. This may have been made easier by the deaths of Thomas and Ann. As we have seen, in 1703 he reversed Martha Cory's excommunication and in 1706 he made Ann Putnam a church member and read out her apology.

In 1710 and 1713, two new parishes were created from the eastern parts of the village. In 1752 Salem Village at last became an independent town named Danvers. For those who had striven for village autonomy in the 1600s, this would have seemed a mockery of what they had fought for. By that time Salem Village no longer represented their values. It was no longer even in the broadest sense Puritan. The religion of their forefathers had almost ceased to exist.

But Puritanism's legacy to the new Yankee world of self-help, individualism, and personal ambition was vast. It bequeathed self-discipline, self-denial, and moral and intellectual rigor. However, it also bequeathed the tendency to separate evil from good and place evil outside the self and outside the group, in the enemy. With that tendency came another: to regard such an enemy as deserving destruction.

Such impulses lurk in us all. America's Puritan legacy gives them dangerous sanction. They can be countered only by constant reminders of our common humanity.

Key Persons Involved

BRIDGET BISHOP was the first accused witch to be hanged. The wife of a Salem sawyer, Edward Bishop, she had a long-standing reputation for witchcraft.

GEORGE BURROUGHS, noted for his physical strength despite his small stature, came to Salem Village as minister in 1680, at age twenty-eight. He was born into a well-to-do family in Suffolk, England, but was brought up by his mother in Roxbury, Massachusetts. Having graduated from Harvard in 1670, he preached in Falmouth, Maine, until an Indian attack in August 1676 forced him to flee to Massachusetts. After a period as minister in Salisbury, he came to Salem Village, where he buried his second wife and married his third. He remained in the village for less than three years, leaving after deep disagreements with Thomas Putnam and his allies. He returned to Maine but in May 1692 was brought back to Salem Village a prisoner, having been arrested for witchcraft. His unusual strength was used against him as evidence of his complicity with the devil.

GILES CORY was a prosperous eighty-year-old farmer with a reputation for eccentricity and aggression. In 1675 he was brought to court for helping cause the death of a manservant by beating him, and he paid a heavy fine. In 1692 he testified against his third wife, Martha Cory, at her examination for witchcraft, saying that her presence stopped him praying. Soon afterward he was arrested himself.

MARTHA CORY was the fourth person, and first church member, to be accused as a witch. Sixty-five years of age, respectably married to Giles Cory, and known to be pious, she nevertheless had a tainted reputation: She had once given birth to an illegitimate child, a mulatto. She was outspoken in her skepticism about the existence of witches in Salem Village.

SARAH GOOD was one of the first three people accused of witchcraft. She was born in 1653 in Wenham, daughter of a well-to-do innkeeper who committed suicide in 1672. He left a large estate to his widow, who then married a man who tried to disinherit her seven grown children. Sarah's lot worsened when she married an indentured servant who soon died, leaving huge debts. After taking legal action, she was granted a share of her father's estate but it was seized back to pay what her husband had owed. When she married again it was to a weaver and laborer who rarely had work. By 1692 she was reduced to begging for food.

DORCAS GOOD was Sarah Good's four-and-a-half-year-old daughter. She was accused of witchcraft soon after her mother, examined with Rebecca Nurse on March 24, and thrown into jail. During her eight months in the dungeons she went insane.

TITUBA and **JOHN INDIAN** were the Caribbean Indian slave couple who lived with the Reverend Samuel Parris in Salem Village in 1692. They had probably come to Boston from Barbados with him in 1680, and they moved with him to Salem Village in 1688. Tituba was the first person to be accused of witchcraft by Parris's daughter Betty and niece Abigail Williams. When examined by magistrates, she made an elaborate confession in which she described meeting the devil and invisibly pricking and pinching Betty, Abigail, and others. This confession was crucial in escalating the witch-hunt. John Indian was not accused of witchcraft, perhaps because he soon became an accuser himself.

JOHN HATHORNE was the chief magistrate in the witchcraft examinations. He was born in 1641 into one of the most powerful families in Salem. His father, William Hathorne, was the town's most important magistrate. John amassed a considerable personal fortune as a landowner and merchant and in 1684 himself became a magistrate. The manner in which he conducted the witchcraft examinations showed that he judged the accused to be guilty before they opened their mouths. His aim was not to discover if there were any cases to bring to trial but to elicit confessions.

ELIZABETH HUBBARD was one of the first four girls, with Betty Parris, Abigail Williams, and Ann Putnam, to make witchcraft accusations. She was the seventeen-year-old great-niece of Rachel Griggs, wife of Salem Village doctor William Griggs, who pronounced the afflicted girls "under an Evil Hand.'' She lived with the Griggses as their servant and was to remain one of the accusers throughout 1692.

MERCY LEWIS, seventeen, was a servant in the Putnam household and, by March 1692, had joined Betty Parris, Abigail Williams, Elizabeth Hubbard, and Ann Putnam in having fits. Together with these four and Ann Putnam Senior, she accused Martha Cory of witchcraft. She was to remain one of the chief witchcraft accusers throughout 1692. Born in Casco, Maine, she witnessed her parents' slaughter at the hands of Indians when she was fourteen. After being taken in for a time by George Burroughs and his family, she went as a servant to William Bradford in Salem and then to the family of Thomas Putnam Junior.

INCREASE and **COTTON MATHER** were the father and son who helped create the climate of fear and suspicion in which the witch-hunt took place. Increase was a leading Boston minister and politician and president of Harvard. His son tried to follow in his footsteps as a public man but only partially succeeded. However, he became an extraordinarily prolific writer. Cotton's book *Remarkable Providences,* together with Increase's *Memorable Providences,* both of which were published in the 1680s and describe supernatural occurrences, helped reinforce the superstitions that fed the witch-hunt. During the witch-hunt father and son diverged in their attitudes and influence, though both denied their differences. Increase emerged as a force for moderation and sanity while Cotton continued to promote fear and persecution.

FRANCIS and **REBECCA NURSE** had by 1692 established themselves, with their eight children, as a prosperous Salem Village family, owning three hundred acres of land despite their humble origins. Francis had been an artisan, and Rebecca was from a farming family who emigrated from England to settle in Topsfield. Rebecca was seventy-one years old, ailing and deaf, when she was accused of witchcraft in March 1692. She was well known for her goodness and piety, and her accusation aroused more protest than that of any other witch-hunt victim.

SARAH OSBORNE, with Tituba and Sarah Good, was one of the first three people to be acccused of witchcraft. Born in 1643 in Watertown, Massachusetts, in 1662 she married Robert Prince, whose sister was married to Captain John Putnam. After Prince died, she acquired an indentured servant, Alexander Osborne, and was rumored to be living in sin with him. They married in 1677. Subsequently Sarah antagonized the Putnams by trying to break the trust Robert Prince had set up for his sons. By 1692 Sarah was bedridden and possibly senile.

SAMUEL and **ELIZABETH PARRIS** were the pastor and his wife in whose house the witch-hunt started. Samuel was born in London in 1653, son of a successful merchant with business interests in Barbados. He was sent to Harvard but did not graduate. After his father's death he too became a Barbadian merchant-planter, but without much success. In 1680 he moved to Boston, working in trade till moving to Salem Village in 1688 and joining the ministry there in 1689. He married Elizabeth Eldridge in about 1680. They had three children, including the nine-year-old, Betty, who with her cousin Abigail Williams started the witch-hunt. Little is known about Elizabeth Parris. It seems she may have suffered from ill health; she died in 1696.

ELIZABETH (BETTY) PARRIS was the nine-year-old daughter of Samuel and Elizabeth Parris. She was born in Boston on November 28, 1682. With her cousin Abigail Williams and others, she started the witch-hunt by accusing Tituba, Sarah Good, and Sarah Osborne of bewitching her. Sometime in March 1692 she was sent to live with the family of Stephen Sewall in Salem Town.

ELIZABETH and **JOHN PROCTOR** were both accused of witchcraft in spring 1692, Elizabeth first, John later, when he defended his wife during her examination. John had risen dramatically in the social scale. Born in 1632, he had come to Salem Village from Ipswich, Massachusetts, in his mid-thirties, soon gaining great success not only as a farmer but also as an entrepreneur and tavern keeper. He was an outspoken critic of the witch-hunt, threatening to "thrash the devil out of" his servant Mary Warren when she joined the band of accusers.

ANN PUTNAM JUNIOR was, with Abigail Williams, one of the two most prominent of the witch accusers. The twelve-year-old daughter of Thomas and Ann Putnam, she was one of the four girls who made the first accusations against Tituba, Sarah Good, and Sarah Osborne. Some of her later spectral visions, particularly those of George Burroughs and the ghosts of his wives, were among the strangest and most gruesome described by any of the accusers. It is impossible to know to what extent she was a tool of her embittered father and disturbed mother, but at the very least she was influenced by their hatreds.

CAPTAIN JOHN PUTNAM SENIOR and **REBECCA PUTNAM** were Thomas Putnam Junior's uncle and his wife. Born in England in 1627,

John was brought to Salem Village by his parents in the 1640s. In time he became one of the wealthiest men in the area. He was an original member of the Salem Village church and a representative of Salem to the General Court for several terms. He served on the Village committee and as a selectman in Salem in 1689, 1690, and 1692. He married Rebecca Prince, sister of Sarah Osborne's first husband, in 1652. John and Rebecca took in George Burroughs and his wife as lodgers in 1680, and John sued Burroughs for debt in 1683. A close ally of his nephew Thomas, he was a strong supporter of Samuel Parris. He signed five of the legal complaints against accused witches.

THOMAS PUTNAM JUNIOR and **ANN PUTNAM** were the parents of one of the most prominent of the afflicted girls, Ann Putnam Junior. Thomas was the eldest son of the prosperous Salem Village farmer Lieutenant Thomas Putnam, and Ann was the daughter of George Carr of Salisbury, Massachusetts, a successful entrepreneur. Both were denied their economic expectations. Thomas's father remarried and left most of his estate to his new family, and Ann's mother and brothers kept her father's legacy to themselves, depriving Ann and her sisters. By 1692 the couple were losing ground economically and politically to the powerful Porter clan. They were allies and champions of Samuel Parris, the Salem Village minister, and consciously or unconsciously drove on the witch-hunt as a means of demolishing his enemies and theirs. Many of the witchcraft accusations originated with their twelve-year-old daughter Ann. Thomas Putnam signed ten of the twenty-one legal complaints against accused witches. His wife for a time was one of the band of accusers.

CAPTAIN JONATHAN WALCOTT was a farmer, captain in the Salem Village militia, and father of the afflicted seventeen-year-old Mary Walcott. His second wife, Deliverance, was Mary's stepmother and Thomas Putnam Junior's sister. The family lived a few hundred yards from the parsonage where the first girls to be afflicted, Betty Parris and Abigail Williams, lived with Reverend Samuel Parris and his wife Elizabeth. Jonathan Walcott signed two of the legal complaints against accused witches. He may have assisted his daughter Mary in a trick involving a torn coat at one of the examinations.

MARY WALCOTT was the seventeen-year-old daughter of Captain Jonathan Walcott and stepdaughter of Jonathan's second wife, Deliverance, Thomas Putnam Junior's sister. She had joined the band of afflicted girls by mid-March, when she visited Deodat Lawson in his room at Ingersoll's tavern and showed him bite marks on her wrist that she said had been caused by a witch. During the trials she, her brother Jonathan, and her father appear to have practiced deliberate fraud.

ABIGAIL WILLIAMS was the niece of Samuel Parris. In 1692 she was eleven years old and living in the Parris household. She was probably an orphan. With her cousin Betty Parris, she started the witch-hunt. Unlike Betty, who was sent away to live in Salem Town, Abigail stayed in Salem Village and remained one of the most prominent witch accusers.

Chronology

1689

Samuel Parris and family arrive in Salem Village.

NOVEMBER: Salem Village church is formed and Parris ordained as its minister.

1692

JANUARY: Parris's daughter Betty and niece Abigail Williams begin acting strangely and babbling incoherently.

FEBRUARY: Parris's Caribbean Indian slaves, Tituba and John Indian, bake a "witch cake" with the girls' urine to feed to the dog. Other girls in the neighborhood, including Ann Putnam and Elizabeth Hubbard, join Betty Parris and Abigail Williams in having fits. They accuse Tituba, Sarah Good, and Sarah Osborne of bewitching them.

MARCH 1–5: The three accused witches are examined in the Salem Village meetinghouse by magistrates John Hathorne and Jonathan Corwin. Tituba confesses to witchcraft. The three are sent to prison.

MARCH 6–19: The girls accuse Martha Cory, a respectable church member, of bewitching them. It is probably now that Betty Parris is sent to stay with the Stephen Sewall family in Salem Town.

MARCH 19: Deodat Lawson arrives in Salem Village.

MARCH 21: Martha Cory is examined and sent to prison.

MARCH 21–23: Ann Putnam's mother, Ann, joins the afflicted girls in having fits. They accuse seventy-one-year-old Rebecca Nurse of bewitching them.

MARCH 24: Rebecca Nurse and Sarah Good's four-and-a-half-year-old daughter Dorcas are examined and sent to prison.

APRIL: The accusations, examinations, and imprisonments continue. By the end of the month twenty-three more suspected witches are in jail. These include John and Elizabeth Proctor, Bridget Bishop, Giles Cory, Mary and Phillip English, and George Burroughs. Four out of the eleven legal complaints against the accused, leading to their arrests, have been made by Thomas Putnam, Ann Putnam's father.

MAY: By the end of the month at least thirty-nine more people are in jail.

MAY 14: Sir William Phipps, the new governor of Massachusetts, and Increase Mather arrive from England with the new provincial charter.

JUNE 2: Sir William appoints a Court of Oyer and Terminer to try the accused witches, with William Stoughton, the deputy governor, as chief judge. Bridget Bishop is tried, convicted of witchcraft and sentenced to death.

JUNE 10: Bridget Bishop is hanged on Gallows Hill. One of the judges, Nathaniel Saltonstall, resigns. Sir William Phipps consults the ministers of Boston, including Increase and Cotton Mather. They write the *Return of the Ministers Consulted,* which advises caution in the witchcraft proceedings but also "speed and vigour." Meanwhile, the arrests and examinations continue, now including accused in Andover, Ipswich, Gloucester, and other outlying areas rather than Salem itself.

JUNE 29: Five more accused witches are tried: Sarah Good, Rebecca Nurse, Susannah Martin, Elizabeth Howe, and Sarah Wildes. Rebecca Nurse is acquitted but the judges ask the jury to reconsider and they find her guilty. Sir William Phipps reprieves her but later withdraws the reprieve. All five are sentenced to death.

JULY 19: Sarah Good, Rebecca Nurse, Susannah Martin, Elizabeth Howe, and Sarah Wildes are hanged on Gallows Hill.

AUGUST 5: George Burroughs, John and Elizabeth Proctor, John Willard, George Jacobs, and Martha Carrier are brought to trial.

AUGUST 14: Nurse family members cease to take communion in Salem Village church.

AUGUST 19: George Burroughs, John Proctor, John Willard, George

Jacobs, and Martha Carrier are hanged. Elizabeth Proctor is spared because she is pregnant.

SEPTEMBER 9: Six more are tried and sentenced to death: Martha Cory, Mary Easty, Alice Parker, Ann Pudeator, Dorcas Hoar, and Mary Bradbury.

SEPTEMBER 17: Nine more are sentenced to death: Margaret Scott, Wilmot Redd, Samuel Wardwell, Mary Parker, Abigail Falkner, Rebecca Eames, Mary Lacy, Ann Foster, and Abigail Hobbs. The last five are spared, Abigail Falkner because of pregnancy, the others because they confess. Giles Cory refuses to stand trial.

SEPTEMBER 19: Giles Cory is pressed to death.

SEPTEMBER 22: Martha Cory, Mary Easty, Alice Parker, Mary Parker, Ann Pudeator, Margaret Scott, Wilmot Redd, and Samuel Wardwell are hanged. These are the last hangings.

OCTOBER: The afflicted girls are sent for by Andover. As a result more than fifty people are accused and many confess. The girls are then sent for by Gloucester. Four women are imprisoned. But the backlash to the witch-hunt has started. The girls have overreached themselves by naming as witches several extremely prominent people, including Lady Phipps, the wife of the governor.

OCTOBER 3: Increase Mather delivers a sermon (later published as an essay) called *Cases of Conscience concerning Evil Spirits Personating Men,* which casts serious doubt on the validity of spectral evidence—the girls' visions—and says, "It were better that ten suspected witches should escape, than that one innocent person should be condemned."

OCTOBER 8: Thomas Brattle, a merchant, mathematician, and astronomer, writes an eloquent letter criticizing the trials and convictions.

OCTOBER 12: Sir William Phipps forbids further imprisonments for witchcraft.

OCTOBER 26: The General Court votes for a day of fasting and a convocation of ministers to consider how to proceed "as to the witchcrafts."

OCTOBER 29: Sir William Phipps formally dissolves the Court of Oyer and Terminer.

NOVEMBER: The afflicted girls are sent for again by Gloucester, but when they have fits are ignored and withdraw.

1693

JANUARY 3: A newly formed Superior Court, with William Stoughton as chief judge, sits in Salem to try accused witches. Only three are found guilty. Sir William Phipps reprieves them, along with five others previously sentenced.

JANUARY 31: The Superior Court sits at Charlestown. Stoughton learns of the reprieves and walks off the bench.

APRIL 25: The Superior Court sits at Boston. None found guilty.

MAY: Sir William Phipps orders the release of all accused witches remaining in jail, on payment of their fees.

1697

Samuel Parris is ousted from Salem Village church and leaves the village.

1706

Ann Putnam makes an apology in Salem Village church for causing the deaths of innocent people and says it was due to a "great delusion of Satan."

The Salem Witch-hunt Death Toll

PERSONS HANGED FOR WITCHCRAFT DURING 1692

JUNE 10	BRIDGET BISHOP
JULY 19	SARAH GOOD
JULY 19	ELIZABETH HOWE
JULY 19	SUSANNAH MARTIN
JULY 19	REBECCA NURSE
JULY 19	SARAH WILDES
AUGUST 19	GEORGE BURROUGHS
AUGUST 19	MARTHA CARRIER
AUGUST 19	GEORGE JACOBS
AUGUST 19	JOHN PROCTOR
AUGUST 19	JOHN WILLARD
SEPTEMBER 19	GILES CORY (pressed to death)
SEPTEMBER 22	MARTHA CORY
SEPTEMBER 22	MARY EASTY
SEPTEMBER 22	ALICE PARKER
SEPTEMBER 22	MARY PARKER
SEPTEMBER 22	ANN PUDEATOR
SEPTEMBER 22	MARGARET SCOTT
SEPTEMBER 22	WILMOT REDD
SEPTEMBER 22	SAMUEL WARDWELL

PERSONS ACCUSED OF WITCHCRAFT WHO DIED IN JAIL

MAY 10, 1692	SARAH OBSORNE
JUNE 16, 1692	ROGER TOOTHAKER
DECEMBER 3, 1692	ANN FOSTER
MARCH 10, 1693	LYDIA DUSTIN

An unnamed infant of Sarah Good died prior to July 19, 1692.

Notes

The most important source for this book is Paul Boyer and Stephen Nissenbaum, eds., *The Salem Witchcraft Papers: Verbatim Transcripts of the Legal Documents of the Salem Witchcraft Outbreak of 1692* (New York, 1977). Unless stated otherwise, records of examinations, depositions, petitions, responses to petitions, the original legal accusations known as "complaints," arrest warrants, death warrants, and letters are in this work.

CHAPTER ONE
SOWING THE DRAGON'S TEETH

The primary source for information on the numbers who died and were imprisoned and the conditions of imprisonment is Calef, *More Wonders.*

For numbers hanged, pressed to death, and imprisoned: ibid., 373.

For tortures and interrogation techniques: ibid., 361, 363, 376.

For the practice of putting witch suspects in irons: ibid., 352.

Information on those dying in prison can be found in Boyer and Nissenbaum, *Salem Witchcraft Papers*, 273, 341, 609.

The plight of prisoners' relatives is described in Upham, *Salem Witchcraft*, 2:351, 380–84.

On the plight of the prisoners: ibid., 374.

On the charges for board and lodging, irons, and other expenses: Calef, *More Wonders*, 383; *Massachusetts Archives*, 135:24, quoted in Trask, *The Devil Hath Been Raised*, 281; Boyer and Nissenbaum, *Salem Witchcraft Papers*, 977–1012. A good summation is in Upham, *Salem Witchcraft*, 384n.

The dimensions and structure of the Salem Village parsonage are described in the "Salem Village Book of Record, 1672–1697," February 16, 1681, in Boyer and Nissenbaum, *Salem-Village Witchcraft*, 320. Those dimensions were confirmed by excavations begun in 1970. The parsonage foundations, at the rear of 67 Centre Street, Danvers, are on view to the public.

A detailed description of seventeenth-century New England houses can be found in Demos, *A Little Commonwealth*, 24–35.

For sizes of households in Salem Village: Trask, *The Devil Hath Been Raised*, 122–23.

Samuel Parris's character and opinions are shown by his entries in the "Salem Village Church Book of Record," in Boyer and Nissenbaum, *Salem-Village Witchcraft*, 268–312, and by his sermons, in Cooper and Minkema, eds., *Sermon Notebook*, 37–323.

For details of Parris's arrival in Salem Village: Upham, *Salem Witchcraft*, quoted in Boyer and Nissenbaum, *Salem-Village Witchcraft*, 183.

For the births of Samuel Parris's children: Gragg, *Quest for Security*, 32, 36.

Abigail Williams is mentioned by name as a member of Parris's household in Lawson, *A Brief and True Narrative*, 153.

The "Indian woman named Tituba" and her husband, "an Indian manservant," are mentioned in Hale, *A Modest Enquiry*, 413. Tituba and John Indian appear repeatedly in Boyer and Nissenbaum, *Salem Witchcraft Papers*, Tituba as an accused and confessing witch, John Indian as an accuser.

The impression of young Elizabeth Parris's character is derived from the fact that Elizabeth was sent away from home once the witch-hunt got under way, as described in Upham, *Salem Witchcraft*, 2:3; Tituba's testimony that she "would not hurt Betty, I loved Betty," in Boyer and Nissenbaum, *Salem Witchcraft Papers*, 753; and John Hale's suggestion that once Betty had confessed to the sin of fortunetelling, she was cured of her fits. See Harris et al., *John Hale*, 109. (This part of Hale's *Modest Enquiry* is not included in Burr's *Narratives*.) Though Hale does not name Betty, it seems certain that she is the "afflicted person" he refers to since the other "afflicted persons" were not cured until the witch-hunt ceased, Satan was "chained up," and "the afflicted grew presently well." See Hale, *Modest Enquiry*, 424.

On the rarity of black slaves in New England households: Morgan, *Puritan Family*, 63, and Trask, *The Devil Hath Been Raised*, 122.

On the changes in New England Puritan attitudes toward Indians from 1620 to 1700: Vaughan, *New England Frontier*, 18–20.

On the view of Indians as demonic: Cotton Mather, *Magnalia Christi Americana*, 2:566, 571, 620, 665. An excellent anthology of contemporary narratives is Vaughan and Clark, *Puritans among the Indians*.

For the normal gaps between births and family size, see Trask, *The Devil Hath Been Raised*, 123, and Demos, *Little Commonwealth*, 68.

Samuel Parris's children by his second wife, Dorothy Noyes, were Noyes (b. 1669), Dorothy (b. 1700), Samuel (b. 1702), and Mary (b. 1703): Gragg, *Quest for Security*, 179.

Elizabeth Parris's death is recorded in the *New England Historical and Genealogical Register* (April 1882), 36:189. She is buried in Wadsworth burial ground in Danvers. The verse on her headstone reads: "Sleep precious Dust, no stranger now to Rest / Thou hast thy longed wish, within Abraham's Breast / Farewell Best Wife, Choice Mother, Neighbour, Friend / We'll wail the less, for hopes of thee in the end." The lines are signed with Samuel Parris's initials; presumably he wrote them.

For the custom of placing children in families other than their own and the reasons for it: Morgan, *Puritan Family*, 38.

My conjecture about the use of rooms in the parsonage is based on general information about New England domestic arrangements: Demos, *Little Commonwealth*, 31, and Samuel Parris's remark "I told them I would go up to my study," in Boyer and Nissenbaum, *Salem-Village Witchcraft*, 283.

The home-based life of young girls in Puritan New England is described in Earle, *Child Life*, 305–7; Earle, *Home Life*, 252–80; Ulrich, *Good Wives*, 13.

The freezing indoor conditions are described in Earle, *Home Life*, 71.

On details of Puritan clothing: Demos, *Little Commonwealth*, 52–58. On the custom of family prayers, morning and evening: Morgan, *Puritan Family*, 80. On the need for candlelight in the daytime: Demos, *Little Commonwealth*, 29.

The distances between households in Salem Village are shown in the map of Salem Village on the front endpaper of Upham, *Salem Witchcraft*, vol. 1.

For the Puritans' attitude toward the pleasures of the flesh: Morgan, *Puritan Family*, 15; Peter Gay, *Loss of Mastery* (Berkeley, Calif. 1966), 49–50.

New England Puritan recipes can be found in Daly, *Recipes*.

Disapproval of disorderly behavior and sex outside marriage is shown by the range of acts punishable by imprisonment, fines, whippings, and the like: *Records and Files of the Quarterly Courts of Essex County, Mass.*, vols. 1–9.

The Anne Bradstreet quotation is from "A Letter to Her Husband, Absent upon Public Employment," in Hensley, *Works of Anne Bradstreet*, 226.

On the color of Puritan clothes: Demos, *Little Commonwealth*, 53–54.

On the Puritans' tolerance of music: Morison, *Puritan Pronaos*, 12–13.

Puritan diaries, letters and sermons include Cotton Mather, *Diary;* Sewall, *Diary;* Sewall, *Letter-Book;* Winthrop, *Winthrop Papers;* and

Cooper and Minkema, *Sermon Notebook*. A useful selection of excerpts from diaries, sermons, and other writings can be found in Heimart and Selbanco, eds., *Puritans in America*. See also Fleming, *Children and Puritanism*, 95–103, and Stannard, *Puritan Way of Death*, 44–71. There is a sad lack of the female voice in early Puritan writings, apart from that of Anne Bradstreet. On the subject of women's diaries, letters, and other writing: Earle, *Child Life*, 163–75; Ulrich, *Good Wives*, 5.

The Perkins list is quoted in Miller, *New England Mind*, 86.

On the conditions of Puritan childhood: Demos, *Little Commonwealth*, 139–42; Earle, *Child Life*, 305, 361; Morgan, *Puritan Family*, 28–61.

The quotation from Nathaniel Hawthorne: *The Scarlet Letter*, 117.

On the work expected of Samuel Sewall's daughters: Sewall, *Letter-Book*, 1:44, quoted in Morgan, *Puritan Family*, 29.

For a modern account of the lives of young women in Puritan New England: Ulrich, *Good Wives*, 43–44.

On the history and topography of Salem Town and Salem Village: Boyer and Nissenbaum, *Salem Possessed*, 37–39, 86–89.

On the population of Salem Village: Trask, *The Devil Hath Been Raised*, 122.

The layout of Salem Village is shown on the front endpaper of Upham, *Salem Witchcraft*, vol. 1.

A strong fear of Indian attacks would have been inevitable given that on January 25, 1692, York, Maine, had been attacked and fifty people killed. The messenger conveying the news to Boston passed Salem Village on the Ipswich Road: Kences, *Some Unexplained Relationships*, 190.

On the Puritans' attitude toward books: Morgan, *Puritan Family*, 248–64; Fleming, *Children and Puritanism*, 78–94; Earle, *Child Life*, 248–64.

Foremost among the "graphic accounts . . . of strange supernatural occurrences" were Increase Mather, *Remarkable Providences*, in Burr, *Narratives*, 8–37; Cotton Mather, *Memorable Providences*, in Burr, *Narratives*, 91–141.

On the clergy's conscious intention of countering rationalism and skepticism: Burr, *Narratives*, 4–6.

A discussion of literacy levels in New England can be found in Demos, *Little Commonwealth*, 22 n. 2.

On the shortage of schools: ibid., 144, 182.

On the injunctions to parents to teach their children to read: Morgan, *Puritan Family*, 45–46.

Abigail Williams's mark can be seen in Boyer and Nissenbaum, *Salem Witchcraft Papers*, 612.

On Sabbath activities and laws: Trask, *Meetinghouse at Salem Village*, 5–7; Earle, *Home Life*, 364–80; Earle, *The Sabbath in Puritan New England*, passim; Friedman, *Crime and Punishment*, 33; Fleming, *Children and Puritanism*, 18–25.

The 1647 incident in New Haven is in Fleming, *Children and Puritanism*, 21–22.

The Sewall quote is from Sewall, *Diary*, 118.

On the danger of Indian attacks: Clark, *The Eastern Frontier*, 65–68; Kences, *Witchcraft and the Indian Wars*, passim.

The political developments in New England at this time are described in Wesley Frank Craven, *Colonies in Transition*, 245. The general state of turmoil in 1692 is summarized in Hutchinson, *History of the Colony of Massachusetts Bay*, 2:9.

A good short exposition of the Calvinist theory of election can be found in Ziff, *Puritanism in America* (New York, 1973), 27–28. The major work on New England Puritanism is Perry Miller, *The New England Mind: The Seventeenth Century*, 367–97. Among the many others, one of the best is Edmund S. Morgan, *Visible Saints: The History of a Puritan Idea* (New York, 1963).

On the practice of the Puritan religion in Massachusetts: Morgan, *Puritan Family*, 90–104.

On punishments: Friedman, *Crime and Punishment*, 38; *Records and Files of the Quarterly Courts*, December 1642, February 1643, 1:44, 51.

On the punishment of Quakers: Friedman, *Crime and Punishment*, 32.

The Mather quotations are from his contributions to a book for children quoted in Fleming, *Children and Puritanism*, 85–86.

The verse is from Wrigglesworth, *Day of Doom*, 54.

On Elizabeth Sewall's weeping fits: Sewall, *Diary*, 308, 419–20.

The quotations from Parris's sermons: Cooper and Minkema, *Sermon Notebook*, 39, 50, 73, 180. For Parris's history before his arrival in Salem Village: Boyer and Nissenbaum, *Salem Possessed*, 154–56; Gragg, *Quest for Security*, 1–35.

On the candlesticks and ordination: "The Records of the Salem Village Church from November 1689 to October 1696, Kept by the Reverend Samuel Parris," in Boyer and Nissenbaum, *Salem-Village Witchcraft*, 273–74.

On the rumors of fortunetelling: Upham, *Salem Witchcraft*, 2:2–3.

On the use of "sieves and keys": Cotton Mather, *The Life of His Excellency*, 130–31. The Hale quotation is found in Harris et al., *John Hale*, 109. (This section of Hale's *Modest Enquiry* is not included in Burr, *Narratives*.)

On the afflicted girls' behavior: Calef, *More Wonders*, in Burr, *Narratives*, 341–42.

CHAPTER TWO
A WITCH CAKE

Increase's chronicles are in Increase Mather, *Remarkable Providences*, in Burr, *Narratives*, 8–38; Cotton's are in Cotton Mather, *Memorable Providences*, in Burr, *Narratives*, 93–143.

On the vogue for odd names: Earle, *Child Life*, 16–17. On Increase's name: Cotton Mather, *Parentator*, 5.

The standard basic source for the political history of the Massachusetts Bay Colony is Shurtleff, *Records of the Governor and Company*. Still readable and authoritative is Hutchinson, *History of the Colony of Massachusetts Bay*. The standard work of this century is Andrews, *The Colonial Period of American History*.

The story of Elizabeth Knapp is in Increase Mather, *Remarkable Providences*, in Burr, *Narratives*, 21–23. Samuel Willard's much longer account was in an enclosure in a letter to Mather and is printed in *The Mather Papers*, 8:555–70, and in Green, *Groton in the Witchcraft Times*, 7–21.

The standard biography of Cotton Mather is Wendell, *Cotton Mather*.

For Mather's account of the Goodwin episode see Cotton Mather, *Memorable Providences*, in Burr, *Narratives*, 99–126.

On Freud and Breuer: Breuer and Freud, *Studies on Hysteria*. A useful summary of Freud's work may be found in Storr, *Freud*.

"Theory put forward in the book": Freud, *Autobiographical Study*, 183, quoted in Breuer and Freud, *Studies on Hysteria*, 44.

The main works of Pierre Janet are *L'automatisme psychologique* and *État mental des hystériques;* of J. M. Charcot, *Leçons du mardi à la Salpêtrière*, and *L'Hystérie*. A useful interpretation of Janet's work is Mayo, *Psychology of Pierre Janet*.

An excellent study of hysteria as a predominantly female complaint is Showalter, *Female Malady*.

On skepticism about repressed memory: Crews, "The Revenge of the Repressed," and Wright, *Remembering Satan*.

Two interesting works on anorexia nervosa are Bruch, *The Golden Cage*, and Minuchin, Rosman, and Baker, *Psychosomatic Families*. The recent findings on hysteria are in Merskey, *Analysis of Hysteria*, 171, 177.

On the dancing mania in Germany and epidemics of hysteria in boarding schools: Hecker, *Epidemics of the Middle Ages*, 1–51.

CHAPTER THREE
THE HAND OF SATAN

The events of February are found in or deduced from Parris's records in Boyer and Nissenbaum, *Salem-Village Witchcraft*, 278–79; Hale, *Modest Enquiry*, in Burr, *Narratives*, 413–14; Calef, *More Wonders*, in Burr, *Narratives*, 343.

On the theory of hysterical symptoms as revealing aggression: Demos, *Entertaining Satan*, 160–64.

CHAPTER FOUR
THE NIGHTMARE OF A RELIGION

The Burr quote is in Kittridge, *Witchcraft in Old and New England*, 23–24.

The best overview of witchcraft as practiced today is Adler, *Drawing Down the Moon*, 41–176.

Adler's views on Margaret Murray are found in ibid., 46–49.

In summarizing the history of witchcraft, I have drawn chiefly on four excellent works: Kittridge, *Witchcraft in Old and New England;* Rosen, *Witchcraft;* Cohn, *Europe's Inner Demons;* and Macfarlane, *Witchcraft in Tudor and Stuart England.* Also fascinating and useful are Demos, *Entertaining Satan;* Karlsen, *Devil in the Shape of a Woman;* and Thomas, *Religion and the Decline of Magic* (New York, 1971).

For twentieth-century research on interrogation techniques: Sargant, *Battle for the Mind*, 165–96.

CHAPTER FIVE
NEW ENGLAND NIGHT-BIRDS

The events in this chapter are described in Hale, *Modest Enquiry*, in Burr, *Narratives*, 414; Calef, *More Wonders*, in Burr, *Narratives*, 343.

On the relationships within the Putnam family: Boyer and Nissenbaum, *Salem Possessed*, 134. The political and psychological links between Thomas Putnam and Samuel Parris are brilliantly explored in this work, which must be read in its entirety for full comprehension of particular references to either man.

Short profiles of Sarah Osborne and Sarah Good are found in ibid., 193, 203. The recent writer who argues a "conspiracy" theory of the Salem witch-hunt is Robinson, *Devil Discovered.*

On Mrs. Ann Putnam's history: Upham, *Salem Witchcraft*, 1:253; 2:229; Boyer and Nissenbaum, *Salem Possessed*, 135.

On Mary Walcott's history: Trask, *The Devil Hath Been Raised*, 130. On Elizabeth Hubbard's: ibid., 126. On Mercy Lewis's: ibid., 127.

For a most interesting if not completely persuasive account of the link between the fear of Indians and the witchcraft hysteria: Kences, *Witchcraft and the Indian Wars.*

On the terror inspired by the alliance of the Indians and French: Kences, *Some Unexplored Relationships,* 182–83.

"It is a solemn sight": Mary Rowlandson, "The Sovereignty and Goodness of God," in Vaughan and Clark, *Puritans among the Indians,* 35.

"A group of women emerging from church": Axtell, *The European and the Indian,* 312.

The petition of the Salem Village farmers is in the Massachusetts Archives, 112:175–77.

"Wretched remnant of a race": Wendell, *Cotton Mather,* 26.

The percentage of captives remaining with the Indians is from Axtell, *The European and the Indian,* 162–66, quoted in Kences, *Witchcraft and the Indian Wars,* 186.

Hutchinson on the Indians: Hutchinson, *History of the Colony of Massachusetts Bay,* 1:470–72. The Mather quotations are from Cotton Mather, *Memorable Providences,* in Burr, *Narratives,* 99.

CHAPTER SIX
A THING LIKE A MAN

The warrants against Sarah Good, Sarah Osborne, and Tituba specify that the accused were to be brought to Ingersoll's tavern at ten o'clock: Boyer and Nissenbaum, *Salem Witchcraft Papers,* 355, 745. But the examination was actually held in the meetinghouse: Upham, *Salem Witchcraft,* 11–12.

Sarah Good's examination: Boyer and Nissenbaum, *Salem Witchcraft Papers,* 356–67; also Upham, *Salem Witchcraft,* 12.

"Prevailed in New England for many years": Hutchinson, *History of the Colony of Massachusetts Bay,* 2:62. Deodat Lawson's description of the girls' fits: Lawson, *Narrative, Appended to His Sermon,* in Upham, *Salem Witchcraft,* 530–31.

A fascinating account of J. M. Charcot's "performing" hysterics is given in Showalter, *Female Malady,* 147–54.

CHAPTER SEVEN
BROTHER AGAINST BROTHER

On Upham's conspiracy theory regarding Tituba: Upham, *Salem Witchcraft,* 2:27–33.

The history of Salem Village and its internal disputes up to the time of the Reverend Burroughs's departure is recounted in Boyer and Nis-

senbaum, *Salem Possessed*, 37–56. I have also drawn on the records
concerning George Burroughs in Boyer and Nissenbaum, *Salem-Village Witchcraft*, 174–75.

CHAPTER EIGHT
CHURCH OF PUTNAM

On the history of Salem Village and its attempts to ordain a minister
and form a church: Boyer and Nissenbaum, *Salem Possessed*, 56–63. I
have also drawn on the records of the Salem Village church in Boyer
and Nissenbaum, *Salem-Village Witchcraft*, 268–69.

CHAPTER NINE
"AS BREATH UNTO THE WIND"

For the events of March 1 and 2: Boyer and Nissenbaum, *The Salem
Witchcraft Papers*, 370, 371, 377.

Brattle's misgivings about the afflicted girls' confused thinking on
specters are in "The Letter of Thomas Brattle, F.R.S., 1692," in Burr,
Narratives, 174–75.

The crucial documents in which Increase and Cotton Mather address the subject of specters are Cotton Mather, *The Return of Several
Ministers Consulted*, in Levin, *What Happened in Salem*, 110–11, and Increase Mather, *Cases of Conscience*, in Levin, *What Happened in Salem*,
117–26.

On the length of the proceedings: Boyer and Nissenbaum, *Salem
Witchcraft Papers*, 746.

The transportation of prisoners and magistrates is described in
Upham, *Salem Witchcraft*, 2:30, 37.

Nathaniel Ingersoll's account of expenses is in Boyer and Nissenbaum, *Salem Witchcraft Papers*, 948–49.

On Good's antics en route to prison and her appearance to William
Allen: ibid., 372.

For the continuing dramas: ibid., 753–55, 668–99.

On John Proctor: Boyer and Nissenbaum, *Salem Possessed*, 200.

The Boston jailer's account is in Boyer and Nissenbaum, *Salem
Witchcraft Papers*, 953.

On the meeting of ministers and the effect of Tituba's confessions:
Calef, *More Wonders*, in Burr, *Narratives*, 342; Hale, *Modest Enquiry*, 415.

Betty Parris's name does not appear in any of the arrest warrants or
accounts of examinations after those pertaining to Sarah Good, Sarah
Osborne, and Tituba at the beginning of March. On March 25, Betty
was at Stephen Sewall's house, though still having fits: Lawson, *Brief
and True Narrative*, in Burr, *Narratives*, 160.

For the ending of Betty's fits: Harris et al., *John Hale,* 109.

The description of the March 11 prayers is from Lawson, *Brief and True Narrative,* in Burr, *Narratives,* 342.

On the new visions: Boyer and Nissenbaum, *Salem Witchcraft Papers,* 258, 260–61, 263–66, 595, 600–605.

Lawson describes being invited to Salem Village in Lawson, *Narrative,* in Upham, *Salem Witchcraft,* 527.

On Martha Cory's arrest: Boyer and Nissenbaum, *Salem Witchcraft Papers,* 247.

On Martha Cory's history: Boyer and Nissenbaum, *Salem Possessed,* 146.

Putnam and Cheever's visit to Martha Cory is in Boyer and Nissenbaum, *Salem Witchcraft Papers,* 260–62.

The account of Martha's visit to the Putnams' is in ibid., 264–66.

Ann Putnam Senior's afflictions are in ibid., 64.

For the full exposition of the Boyer and Nissenbaum theory regarding Mary Veren: Boyer and Nissenbaum, *Salem Possessed,* 133–47.

CHAPTER TEN

THE YELLOW BIRD

The account of Lawson's meeting with Mary Walcott is based on Lawson, *Brief and True Narrative,* in Burr, *Narratives,* 152, 153.

On Lawson's being informed of the cause of death of his wife and daughter: Lawson, *Narrative,* in Upham, *Salem Witchcraft,* 527.

Subsequent events are in Lawson, *Brief and True Narrative,* in Burr, *Narratives,* 154–57, and Boyer and Nissenbaum, *Salem Witchcraft Papers,* 248–54.

The information on the Puritans' legal system is in Friedman, *Crime and Punishment,* 22–28.

The British magician is David Bridland.

CHAPTER ELEVEN

SECRET ENEMIES

The sermon quotations are from Cooper and Minkema, *Sermon Notebook,* 69, 76, 126, 193.

On Rebecca Nurse's history: Upham, *Salem Witchcraft,* 79–84. Marion Starkey follows Upham in pinpointing the Nurses' quick rise to prosperity as arousing envy and enmity: Starkey, *Devil in Massachusetts* (New York, 1949), 77.

On Francis Nurse's connection with the anti-Putnam faction, boundary disputes with Nathaniel Putnam, and Rebecca Nurse's mother being named as a witch: Boyer and Nissenbaum, *Salem Possessed*, 65, 149, 184, 187.

For the visit of Israel Porter and the others to Rebecca Nurse: Boyer and Nissenbaum, *Salem Witchcraft Papers*, 593–94.

Sarah Holton's deposition is in ibid., 600.

Lawson's account of his visit to Ann Putnam is in Lawson, *Brief and True Narrative*, 157–58.

On the torments of the previous few days: Boyer and Nissenbaum, *Salem Witchcraft Papers*, 603–5.

For the Boyer and Nissenbaum theory about Rebecca Nurse: Boyer and Nissenbaum, *Salem Possessed*, 140.

For John Tarbell's deposition: Boyer and Nissenbaum, *Salem Witchcraft Papers*, 603.

Deodat Lawson's account of Rebecca Nurse's and Dorcas Good's examination is in Lawson, *Brief and True Narrative*, in Burr, *Narratives*, 158–60.

CHAPTER TWELVE
DIABOLICAL MALICE

Seventeenth-century Massachusetts prisons are graphically described in Cahill, *Horrors of Salem's Witch Dungeon*.

For Sarah Osborne's death and Dorcas Good's removal to Boston jail: Boyer and Nissenbaum, *Salem Witchcraft Papers*, 953, 954.

For Lawson's description of Dorcas Good: Lawson, *Brief and True Narrative*, in Burr, *Narratives*, 159.

For William Good's account: Boyer and Nissenbaum, *Salem Witchcraft Papers*, 994.

For Upham's theory: Upham, *Salem Witchcraft*, 3:71.

On the psychology of groups: Penrose, *Objective Study*, 2–4; Alford, *Reparation and Civilization*.

Deodat Lawson's sermon is reproduced in full in Trask, *The Devil Hath Been Raised*, 64–106.

On Lawson's subsequent career: Boyer and Nissenbaum, *Salem Possessed*, 60.

The Rebecca Nurse petition is in Boyer and Nissenbaum, *Salem Witchcraft Papers*, 592–93.

On John Proctor's outburst: ibid., 683–84.

CHAPTER THIRTEEN
ONE OF YOU IS A DEVIL

Samuel Parris's sermon is in Cooper and Minkema, *Sermon Notebook*, 194–98.

On Sarah Cloyce's departure from the meetinghouse and the afflicted girls' accusations of her: Lawson, *Brief and True Narrative*, in Burr, *Narratives*, 161.

Samuel Barton's testimony is in Boyer and Nissenbaum, *Salem Witchcraft Papers*, 674–75.

William Rayment's testimony is in ibid., 670–71.

On the public fast day: Lawson, *Brief and True Narrative*, in Burr, *Narratives*, 160.

On the claims against Elizabeth Proctor: Boyer and Nissenbaum, *Salem Witchcraft Papers*, 667, 668, 669–71.

Nathaniel Ingersoll's character and biography are given lengthy treatment in Upham, *Salem Witchcraft*, 165–78.

Sarah Cloyce and Elizabeth Proctor's examination is described in Calef, More Wonders, in Burr, *Narratives*, 346–47.

On the characters of Simon Bradstreet and Thomas Danforth: Upham, *Salem Witchcraft*, 99–100.

Mercy Lewis's vision is in Lawson, *Brief and True Narrative*, in Burr, *Narratives*, 161.

On Puritan customs regarding breastfeeding and infant care and their long-term psychological effects: Demos, *Family Life*, 132–39; Ulrich, *Good Wives*, 141–44.

For speculations on the "Little Awakening": Boyer and Nissenbaum, *Salem Possessed*, 27–29.

CHAPTER FOURTEEN
APPARITIONS OF A HUNDRED PERSONS

Ann Putnam's accusations of murder against Rebecca Nurse are in Boyer and Nissenbaum, *Salem Witchcraft Papers*, 600–601.

Lawson's account of the torn sheet incident is in Lawson, *Narrative*, in Upham, *Salem Witchcraft*, 2:532.

Clement Coldum's deposition against Elizabeth Hubbard is in Boyer and Nissenbaum, *Salem Witchcraft Papers*, 457. Calef's remarks are in Calef, *More Wonders*, in Burr, *Narratives*, 306, 341–42.

On Mercy Lewis's giving birth to an illegitimate child, and her marriage: Robinson, *Devil Discovered*, 249.

CHAPTER FIFTEEN
A BLACK MAN WITH AN HAT

On the warrant for the arrest of Giles Cory, Mary Warren, Abigail Hobbs, and Bridget Bishop: Boyer and Nissenbaum, *Salem Witchcraft Papers*, 239.

CHAPTER SIXTEEN
INTO THE UNKNOWN

The examinations of April 21 are mentioned in Calef, *More Wonders,* in Burr, *Narratives,* 347.

The conflicts over the Topsfield boundaries are described in Upham, *Salem Witchcraft,* 238–42.

For details of Sarah Bishop's activities: Boyer and Nissenbaum, *Salem Witchcraft Papers,* 95. In "The Rev. John Hale et al. v. Bridget Bishop," read "Sarah" for "Bridget." Hale's testimony was inaccurately deposited among Bridget's papers and has been assumed until recently to refer to Bridget Bishop. But a close reading of the testimony shows that Hale must refer to Sarah. He never gives a Christian name but calls her only "Goody Bishop." Her place of residence, "in Salem bounds bordering on the abovesaid Beverly," is that of Sarah, not Bridget, Bishop. It is clear from the deposition against Sarah Bishop in Boyer and Nissenbaum, *Salem Witchcraft Papers,* 111–12, that Sarah lived in or on the edge of Beverly. Bridget lived in Salem.

The Edward Bishop incident with John Indian is described in Calef, *More Wonders,* in Burr, *Narratives,* 348.

On the deference of the afflicted girls to Israel Porter and Joseph Putnam: Boyer and Nissenbaum, *Salem Possessed,* 187–88.

On Phillip English: Bailyn, *New England Merchants,* 144–45; Philipps, *Salem in the Seventeenth Century,* 251, 284–85; Perley, *History of Salem,* 2:355, 3:70; Le Beau, "Phillip English," 1–14.

On Phillip and Mary English: Perley, *History of Salem,* 3:292–93.

On William and Eleanor Hollingsworth: ibid., 3:80–81.

On the election of Phillip English and Daniel Andrew as Salem Town selectmen: Boyer and Nissenbaum, *Salem Possessed,* 131–32.

The eight accused who were given short shrift were Mary Easty, Mary Black, Sarah Averill Wildes, Deliverance Hobbs, William Hobbs, Edward Bishop, Sarah Bishop, Mary English: Calef, *More Wonders,* in Burr, *Narratives,* 347.

CHAPTER SEVENTEEN
A WHEEL WITHIN A WHEEL

Thomas Putnam's letter is in Boyer and Nissenbaum, *Salem Witchcraft Papers,* 165–66.

For Ann Putnam's visions: ibid., 164, 166–67.

For Elizabeth Hubbard and Mercy Lewis's: ibid., 168–71.

On Susannah Sheldon: Kences, *Witchcraft and the Indian Wars,* 191. Her accusations against Burroughs are in Boyer and Nissenbaum, *Salem Witchcraft Papers,* 171.

On Burroughs's experiences in Maine: Kences, *Witchcraft and the Indian Wars,* 190.

On Lydia Dustin and Sarah Morey: Robinson, *Devil Discovered,* 344–45.

For Sarah Morey's mother's petition: Boyer and Nissenbaum, *Salem Witchcraft Papers,* 581–82.

On William Stoughton: Hutchinson, *History of the Colony of Massachusetts Bay,* 2:23; Washburn, *Sketches of Judicial History,* 140–41; Robinson, *Devil Discovered,* 24–25.

For Sewall's diary entries on the witch-hunt: Sewall, *Diary,* April 11, 1692, 358; August 19, 1692, 363.

On Burroughs's second wife: Robinson, *Devil Discovered,* 90–91.

"Contemporaries in the schools": Calef, *More Wonders,* in Burr, *Narratives,* 301.

CHAPTER EIGHTEEN
SUCH HORRID LIES

Those against whom complaints were issued during May and June were Sarah Dustin, Bethia Carter, Bethia Carter Junior, Ann Sears, George Jacobs Senior, Margaret Jacobs, John Willard, Alice Parker, Ann Pudeator, Abigail Somes, Daniel Andrew, George Jacobs Junior, Rebecca Jacobs, Sarah Buckley, Mary Whittredge, Elizabeth Hart, Thomas Farrar, Elizabeth Colson, Mehitabel Downing, Roger Toothaker, Sarah Proctor, Sarah Bassett, Susannah Roots, Benjamin Proctor, Mary De Rich, Sarah Pease, Elizabeth Cary, John Alden, John Floyd, Elizabeth Fosdick, Wilmot Redd, Sarah Rice, William Proctor, Elizabeth Howe, Arthur Abbot, Martha Carrier, Mary Toothaker, Margaret Toothaker, Elizabeth Paine, Mary Ireson, Job Tookey, Ann Dolliver, and Mary Bradbury: Boyer and Nissenbaum, *Salem Witchcraft Papers,* vols. 1–3.

On Sarah Churchill: Robinson, *Devil Discovered,* 125–26.

For Margaret Jacobs's letter to her father and recantation of her confession: Boyer and Nissenbaum, *Salem Witchcraft Papers,* 490–92.

On Margaret Jacobs: Calef, *More Wonders,* in Burr, *Narratives,* 364–66; Upham, *Salem Witchcraft,* 2:353–54; Robinson, *Devil Discovered,* 338.

For Sarah Churchill's confession and Sarah Ingersoll's deposition: Boyer and Nissenbaum, *Salem Witchcraft Papers,* 211–12.

For the warrant for the arrest of Rebecca Jacobs, Daniel Andrew, George Jacobs Junior, Sarah Buckley, and Mary Whittredge and the response from the constable, Jonathan Putnam, saying he has "made diligent search at the house of Daniel Andrew and at the house of George Jacobs for them likewise but cannot find them": ibid., 493–94.

For the story of Rebecca Jacobs's arrest: Calef, *More Wonders,* in Burr, *Narratives,* 371.

For Nathaniel Cary's account of what happened to his wife: ibid., 350–52.

On Cary's future career: ibid., 349 n. 4.

CHAPTER NINETEEN

A BOLD FELLOW WITH HIS HAT ON

On John Alden: Burr, *Narratives,* 170 n. 2, 352 n. 3; Perley, *History of Salem,* 293, 306; Robinson, *Devil Discovered,* 38–39.

For Alden's account: Calef, *More Wonders,* in Burr, *Narratives,* 353–54.

On Job Tookey: Boyer and Nissenbaum, *Salem Witchcraft Papers,* 759–64; Boyer and Nissenbaum, *Salem Possessed,* 206–8.

On Elizabeth Howe: Boyer and Nissenbaum, *Salem Witchcraft Papers,* 433–55.

For Proctor's letter from prison: ibid., 689–90.

The quotation from *The Tempest* act 1, scene 2.

For the complaint against Martha Carrier and the others: Boyer and Nissenbaum, *Salem Witchcraft Papers,* 183.

For Mary Toothaker's confession: ibid., 767–69.

On Mary and Martha Toothaker: Kences, *Witchcraft and the Indian Wars,* 180.

On the Andover witch-hunt: Calef, *More Wonders,* in Burr, *Narratives,* 371–72.

For Ann Foster's confession: Hale, *Modest Enquiry,* in Burr, *Narratives,* 418.

On Ann Foster's death: Boyer and Nissenbaum, *Salem Witchcraft Papers,* 992–93.

For the Andover witches' account of their confession: Calef, *More Wonders,* in Burr, *Narratives,* 374–75.

CHAPTER TWENTY

LOUD CRIES AND CLAMOURS

On the arrival of the charter: Calef, *More Wonders,* in Burr, *Narratives,* 348–49.

On Increase's negotiations for the charter: Craven, *Colonies in Transition,* 245.

"The time for favour has now come": Mather, *Diary,* 148.

For the history of Sir William Phipps: Cotton Mather, *Magnalia,* 278–89. For Sir William's letters, describing what he found when he arrived in Massachusetts: Burr, *Narratives,* 196–202.

For Thomas Newton's letter ordering the transportation of witches: Boyer and Nissenbaum, *Salem Witchcraft Papers,* 867–68.

On the fast of May 26: Hale, *Modest Enquiry,* in Burr, *Narratives,* 414.

On the numbers of confessors and prisoners: ibid., 416; Calef, *More Wonders,* in Burr, *Narratives,* 355.

For the petition in support of Rebecca Nurse and Nathaniel Putnam's deposition: Boyer and Nissenbaum, *Salem Witchcraft Papers,* 592–93.

For John Higginson's words: Introduction, Hale, *Modest Enquiry,* in Burr, *Narratives,* 401.

For those of Joseph Green, Samuel Parris's successor: "Diary of Rev. Joseph Green of Salem Village, Communicated by Samuel P. Fowler," Essex Institute Historical Collections 8 (1868): 220–21, quoted in Upham, *Salem Witchcraft,* 2:199.

For Cotton Mather's advice: Cotton Mather, *Letter to John Richards,* in Levin, *What Happened in Salem,* 107–9.

For Mather's account of Bridget Bishop's trial: Cotton Mather, *Wonders of the Invisible World,* 223–29.

CHAPTER TWENTY-ONE
FULL OF GRIEF

On Nathaniel Saltonstall's resignation: Brattle, "Letter," in Burr, *Narratives,* 184.

On the history of witchcraft law: Rosen, *Witchcraft,* 21–29.

For Hale's words: Hale, *Modest Enquiry,* in Burr, *Narratives,* 404, 411, 423, 427.

For Cotton's words: Mather, *Return of the Several Ministers,* in Levin, *What Happened in Salem,* 110–11.

On the reconvening of the court: Calef, *More Wonders,* in Burr, *Narratives,* 357.

On the knife trick at Sarah Good's trial: ibid., 357–58.

On the accusation of Samuel Willard: ibid., 360.

For Rebecca Nurse's acquittal and subsequent conviction: ibid., 358–59.

For the date of the executions: Boyer and Nissenbaum, *Salem Witchcraft Papers,* 377–78.

CHAPTER TWENTY-TWO
THE HANGING TREE

For the two stories about Gallows Hill: Nevins, *Witchcraft in Salem Village,* 76–77.

For the evidence for the executed prisoners being buried in crevices: Boyer and Nissenbaum, *Salem Witchcraft Papers,* 109; Calef, *More Wonders,* in Burr, *Narratives,* 361.

The mockery of the crowd is described in Calef, *More Wonders,* in Burr, *Narratives,* 352.

On capital punishment in New England: Friedman, *Crime and Punishment,* 41–44.

On English folklore about hanging: Gatrell, *Hanging Tree,* 112–19.

For the length of time it might take to die: ibid., 48.

For Cary's words: Calef, *More Wonders,* in Burr, *Narratives,* 352.

For the prisoners' protestations of innocence: Hale, *Modest Enquiry,* in Burr, *Narratives,* 423.

On the prisoners' raising doubts of their guilt in the crowd: Calef, *More Wonders,* in Burr, *Narratives,* 360–61.

The references in Calef to "the ladder" indicate that the method of hanging was the medieval one: ibid., 360.

On Rebecca Nurse's death: ibid., 360.

On Sarah Good's death: ibid., 358.

The descriptions of English executions are in Gatrell, *Hanging Tree,* 45–48, 75.

On the method of burial: Calef, *More Wonders,* in Burr, *Narratives,* 361.

On the reburial of Rebecca Nurse: Upham, *Salem Witchcraft,* 293–94.

On the reburial of George Jacobs, ibid., 320–21.

For John Proctor's letter: Calef, *More Wonders,* in Burr, *Narratives,* 362–64.

On John Willard: Robinson, *Devil Discovered,* 314–17; Calef, *More Wonders,* in Burr, *Narratives,* 361.

For the account of George Burroughs's trial: Mather, *Wonders,* in Burr, *Narratives,* 215–22.

For the account of Martha Carrier: ibid., 241–44.

On the sheriff's visit to George Jacobs's house: Calef, *More Wonders,* in Burr, *Narratives,* 364.

On Burroughs's execution: ibid., 360–61.

"They protested their innocence": Brattle, "Letter," in Burr, *Narratives,* 177.

CHAPTER TWENTY-THREE
"I KNOW I MUST DIE"

On the September 9 trials: Calef, *More Wonders,* in Burr, *Narratives,* 366.

On Martha Cory's death: ibid., 367.

On Mary Bradbury: Robinson, *Devil Discovered,* 333–35.

On Sarah Cloyce: ibid., 273–78.

On Mary Easty's death: Calef, *More Wonders*, 367–68.

On the other accused witches sentenced before September 22: ibid., 366.

On Giles Cory: ibid., 367.

On the Andover witch-hunt: ibid., 371–73.

On Wardwell's confession and recantation: ibid., 367.

On the hangings of September 22: ibid., 367–69.

CHAPTER TWENTY-FOUR
SATAN'S DESIRE

For Samuel Parris's entries in the church record book: Boyer and Nissenbaum, *Salem-Village Witchcraft*, 279.

For the dissenters' accusations and Parris's response: ibid., 282–83.

For Parris's words of August 31 and September 11: ibid., 278–79.

For the letter from Robert Pike to Jonathan Corwin: Upham, *Salem Witchcraft*, 538–44. On Robert Pike: ibid., 450–52.

For the quotations from Parris's sermons: Cooper and Minkema, *Sermon Notebook*, 200, 202, 206.

For Cotton Mather's letter to Stephen Sewall: Upham, *Salem Witchcraft*, 488; Burr, *Narratives*, 206.

On Sir William's commission: Burr, *Narratives*, 194–95.

For Cotton's "Author's Defence": Cotton Mather, *Wonders*, in Burr, *Narratives*, 210–15.

On the book's being finished by October: Burr, *Narratives*, 206.

On the numbers imprisoned and accused: Calef, *More Wonders*, 373.

On the naming of Mrs. Thatcher, the sons of Simon Bradstreet, Mrs. Hale, and Lady Phipps: Brattle, "Letter," in Burr, *Narratives*, 177–78; Calef, *More Wonders*, 369; ibid., 372; Upham, *Salem Witchcraft*, 345–47; Robinson, *Devil Discovered*, 234.

"It were better that ten suspected witches": Increase Mather, *Cases of Conscience*, in Levin, *What Happened in Salem*, 125.

"any reflection on those worthy persons": ibid., 126.

"Some of the Salem Gentlemen" and other Brattle excerpts: Brattle, "Letter," in Burr, *Narratives*, 175–76, 179, 182, 185–86, 189.

On the dissolution of the Court of Oyer and Terminer: Boyer and Nissenbaum, *Salem Possessed*, 19–20.

CHAPTER TWENTY-FIVE
THE GUILT OF INNOCENT BLOOD

On the afflicted girls' going to Gloucester: Calef, *More Wonders,* 373.

"there were at least fifty persons": Governor Phipps, "Letters," in Burr, *Narratives,* 200.

For the afflicted girls' second visit to Gloucester: Calef, *More Wonders,* 373.

On the enactment of the new witchcraft law: ibid., 381; Boyer and Nissenbaum, *Salem Witchcraft Papers,* 885–86.

On the creation of the Superior Court: ibid., 887–901.

On the hearings of the court: Calef, *More Wonders,* in Burr, *Narratives,* 382–84; Boyer and Nissenbaum, *Salem Witchcraft Papers,* 903–43.

On the discharge of prisoners: Calef, *More Wonders,* 384; Hale, *Modest Enquiry,* in Burr, *Narratives,* 422.

On Tituba being sold for her fees: Calef, *More Wonders,* 343.

On the fortunes of the Jacobs family: Upham, *Salem Witchcraft,* 353–54, 466.

On the Bishops' arrest: Calef, *More Wonders,* in Burr, *Narratives,* 370.

On the costs to the prisoners and their families: Boyer and Nissenbaum, *Salem Witchcraft Papers,* 977–1046.

On the reversals of excommunications: Upham, *Salem Witchcraft,* 507–8.

For the jurors' apology: Calef, *More Wonders,* in Burr, *Narratives,* 387–88.

On Sewall's statement and the government proclamation: ibid., 385–87.

For Phipps's letter: Phipps, "Letters," in Burr, *Narratives,* 201.

On Sewall's day of fasting: Upham, *Salem Witchcraft,* 441–42.

For Hale's quotations: Hale, *Modest Enquiry,* in Burr, *Narratives,* 415–16, 421–22, 424.

For Calef's quotations: Calef, *More Wonders,* in Burr, *Narratives,* 305–6.

On the lack of repentance and future career of William Stoughton: Sewall, *Diary,* 1:446n; Hutchinson, *History of the Colony of Massachusetts Bay,* 2:125–28.

On the future career of Cotton Mather: Upham, *Salem Witchcraft,* 503–5; Wendell, *Cotton Mather,* 124–307.

For Cotton's account of his dealings with Margaret Rule: Calef, *More Wonders,* in Burr, *Narratives,* 308–23.

For Cotton's account of his dealings with Mercy Short: *A Brand Plucked Out of the Burning,* in Burr, *Narratives,* 259–87.

For Calef's and Cotton's correspondence: Calef, *More Wonders*, in Burr, *Narratives*, 324–41.

For Cotton's diary entries and the book burning: Burr, *Narratives*, 293–94.

For Cotton's 1674 diary entry: Upham, *Salem Witchcraft*, 503–5.

For Samuel Parris's October 1692 sermon: Cooper and Minkema, *Sermon Notebook*, 206–15.

For Parris's "meditations for peace": Boyer and Nissenbaum, *Salem-Village Witchcraft*, 297–99.

On Parris's future career: Gragg, *Quest for Security*, 178–89.

Betty Parris married Benjamin Barron in Sudbury in 1710: Trask, *The Devil Hath Been Raised*, 128. Elizabeth Booth married Jonathan Pease, on October 11, 1692: Robinson, *Devil Discovered*, 123. Sarah Churchill married a weaver in Berwick, Maine, in 1709: ibid., 249. Mary Walcott married Isaac Farrer or Woburn in 1695: ibid., 249. Also in 1695 Mercy Lewis had an illegitimate child in Greenland, New Hampshire, where she was living with an aunt and uncle; later she married Charles Allen: ibid., 249.

On the future lives and deaths of Ann Putnam Senior, Ann Putnam Junior, and Thomas Putnam: Trask, *The Devil Hath Been Raised*, 129–30.

For Ann Putnam's apology: Upham, *Salem Witchcraft*, 510.

EPILOGUE

On the future of Salem Village: Boyer and Nissenbaum, *Salem Possessed*, 217–21.

Bibliography

Adler, Margot. *Drawing Down the Moon: Witches, Druids, Goddess-Worshippers, and Other Pagans in America Today.* Rev. ed. Boston, 1986.

Alford, C. Fred. *Reparation and Civilization: A Kleinian Account of the Large Group.* Free Associations 19. London, 1990.

Andrews, Charles M. *Colonial Period of American History.* 4 vols. New Haven, 1934.

Axtell, James. *The European and the Indian: Essays in the Ethnohistory of Colonial North America.* New York, 1981.

Bailyn, Bernard. *The New England Merchants in the Seventeenth Century.* Cambridge, Mass., 1955.

Boyer, Paul, and Stephen Nissenbaum. *Salem Possessed: The Social Origins of Witchcraft.* Cambridge, Mass., 1974.

———. *Salem-Village Witchcraft: A Documentary Record of Local Conflict in Colonial New England.* Belmont, Calif., 1972.

———. *The Salem Witchcraft Papers: Verbatim Transcripts of the Legal Documents of the Salem Witchcraft Outbreak of 1692.* New York, 1977.

Brattle, Thomas. "The Letters of Thomas Brattle, F.R.S., 1692." In Burr, *Narratives.*

Breuer, Josef, and Sigmund Freud. *Studies on Hysteria.* Trans. James and Alix Strachey. Ed. Angela Richards. London, 1991.

Bruch, Hilde. *The Golden Cage: The Enigma of Anorexia Nervosa.* Cambridge, Mass., 1978.

Burr, George Lincoln. *Narratives of the Witchcraft Cases, 1648–1706.* New York, 1914.

Cahill, Robert Ellis. *Horrors of Salem's Witch Dungeon.* Collectible Classics No. 9. Peabody, Mass., 1986.

Calef, Robert. *More Wonders of the Invisible World; or, The Wonders of the Invisible World Display'd in Five Parts.* London, 1700. In Burr, *Narratives.*

Charcot, J. M. *L'Hystérie.* Ed. E. Trillat. Toulouse, 1971.

———. *Leçons du mardi à la Salpêtrière, 1887–1888.* Paris, 1888.

Clark, Charles E. *The Eastern Frontier: The Settlement of Northern New England, 1610–1763.* New York, 1970.

Cohn, Norman. *Europe's Inner Demons: The Daemonization of Christians in Mediaeval Christendom.* Rev. ed. London, 1993.

Cooper, James F. Jr., and Kenneth P. Minkema. *The Sermon Notebook of Samuel Parris, 1689–1694*. Boston, 1993.

Craven, Wesley Frank. *The Colonies in Transition, 1660–1713*. New York, 1968.

Crews, Frederick. "The Revenge of the Repressed." *New York Review of Books*, November 17, 1994.

Daly, Donald R. *Recipes from a Seventeenth-Century Kitchen*. Salem, Mass., 1992.

Demos, John. *A Little Commonwealth: Family Life in Plymouth Colony*. New York, 1970.

Demos, John Putnam. *Entertaining Satan: Witchcraft and the Culture of Early New England*. New York, 1982.

Earle, Alice Morse. *Child Life in Colonial Days*. New York, 1899.

———. *Home Life in Colonial Days*. New York, 1899.

———. *The Sabbath in Puritan New England*. New York, 1892.

Fleming, Sandford. *Children and Puritanism*. New Haven, 1933.

Freud, Sigmund. *An Autobiographical Study*. London, 1991.

Friedman, Lawrence M. *Crime and Punishment in American History*. New York, 1993.

Gatrell, V. A. C. *The Hanging Tree: Execution and the English People, 1770–1868*. Oxford, 1994.

Gay, Peter. *A Loss of Mastery*. Berkeley, Calif., 1966.

Gragg, Larry. *A Quest for Security: The Life of Samuel Parris, 1653–1720*. New York, 1990.

Green, S. A. *Groton in the Witchcraft Times*. Groton, Mass., 1883.

Hale, John. *A Modest Inquiry into the Nature of Witchcraft*. Boston, 1702. In Burr, *Narratives*.

Harris, M. L., M. F. Harris, E. Spiller, and M. Carr, eds. *John Hale: A Man Beset by Witches; His Book, a Modest Inquiry into the Nature of Witchcraft*. Beverly, Mass., 1992.

Hawthorne, Nathaniel. *The Scarlet Letter*. 1850; reprint, New York: Penguin, 1986.

Hecker, I. F. C. *Epidemics of the Middle Ages*. London, 1835.

Heimart, Alan, and Andrew Selbanco. *The Puritans in America: A Narrative Anthology*. Cambridge, Mass., 1985.

Hensley, Jeannine. *The Works of Anne Bradstreet*. Cambridge, Mass., 1967.

Hutchinson, Thomas. *The History of the Colony of Massachusetts Bay*. London, 1765.

Janet, Pierre. *L'automatisme psychologique*. Paris, 1889.

———. *État mental des hystériques*. Paris, 1897.

Karlsen, Carol F. *The Devil in the Shape of a Woman: Witchcraft in Colonial New England*. New York, 1987.

Kences, James E. *Some Unexplored Relationships of Essex County Witchcraft to the Indian Wars of 1675 and 1689*. Essex Institute Historical Collections, vol. 120. July 1984.

Kittridge, George Lyman. *Witchcraft in Old New England*. New York, 1920.

Lawson, Deodat. *A Brief True Narrative of Some Remarkable Passages Relating to Sundry Persons Afflicted by Witchcraft, at Salem Village Which Happened from the Nineteenth of March to the Fifth of April 1692*. Boston, 1692. In Burr, *Narratives*.

————. *Narrative, Appended to His Sermon*. London ed., 1704; reprinted in Upham, *Salem Witchcraft*, vol. 2.

Le Beau, Bryan F. "Philip English and the Witchcraft Hysteria." *Historical Journal of Massachusetts* 15.

Levin, David, ed. *What Happened in Salem*. New York, 1960.

Macfarlane, Alan. *Witchcraft in Tudor and Stuart England: A Regional and Comparative Study*. London, 1970.

The Mather Papers. Massachusetts Historical Society Collections, 4th ser., vol. 8. Boston, 1912.

Mather, Cotton. *Diary*. Massachusetts Historical Society Collections, 7th ser., vols. 7–8. Boston, 1912.

————. *The Life of His Excellency, Sir William Phips, Knt., Late Captain General and Governor in Chief of the Province of the Massachusetts Bay, New England*. Boston, 1697; reissued, New York, 1929.

————. *Magnalia Christi Americana; or The Ecclesiastical History of New England, from Its First Planting in the Year 1620, until the Year of Our Lord 1608, in Seven Books*. Hartford, 1853.

————. *Memorable Providences relating to Witchcraft and Possessions: A Faithful Account of Many Wonderful and Surprising Things, That Have Befallen Several Bewitched and Possessed Persons in New England, Particularly a Narrative of the Marvellous Trouble and Relief Experienced by a Pious Family in Boston, Very Lately and Sadly Possessed with Evil Spirits*. Boston, 1689. Reproduced in full in Burr, *Narratives*.

————. *Parentator: Memoirs of Remarkables in the Life and Death of the Ever Memorable Dr. Increase Mather*. Boston, 1724.

————. *The Return of Several Ministers Consulted*. In Levin, What Happened in Salem.

————. *The Wonders of the Invisible World*. Boston, 1693. Excerpted in Burr, *Narratives*.

Mather, Increase. *Cases of Conscience concerning Evil Spirits Personating Men*. In Levin, What Happened in Salem.

————. *An Essay for the Recording of Illustrious Providences, Wherein an Account Is Given of Many Remarkable and Very Memorable Events, Which Have Happened in This Last Age, Especially in New-England*. Boston, 1684. Excerpted in Burr, *Narratives*. Known as *Remarkable Providences*.

Mayo, Elton. *Psychology of Pierre Janet*. London, 1951.

Merskey, Harold. *Analysis of Hysteria*. London, 1979.

Miller, Perry. *The New England Mind: The Seventeenth Century.* New York, 1939.

Minuchin, Salador, Bernice L. Rosman, and Lester Baker. *Psychosomatic Families: Anorexia Nervosa in Context.* Cambridge, Mass., 1978.

Morgan, Edmund S. *The Puritan Family: Essays on Religious and Domestic Relations in Seventeenth Century New England.* Boston, 1944.

———. *Visible Saints: The History of a Puritan Idea.* New York, 1963.

Morison, Samuel Eliot. *The Puritan Pronaos: Studies in the Intellectual Life of New England in the Seventeenth Century.* New York, 1936.

Nevins, Winfield S. *Witchcraft in Salem Village in 1692.* New York, 1961.

New England Historical and Genealogical Register.

Penrose, L. S. *On the Objective Study of Crowd Behaviour.* London, 1952.

Perley, Sidney. *The History of Salem, Massachusetts.* 3 vols. Salem, Mass., 1924–28.

Philipps, James Duncan. *Salem in the Seventeenth Century.* Cambridge, Mass., 1933.

Phipps, Governor. "Letters." In Burr, *Narratives.*

Records and Files of the Quarterly Courts of Essex County, Mass.

Robinson, Enders A. *The Devil Discovered: Salem Witchcraft, 1692.* New York, 1962.

Rosen, Barbara, ed. *Witchcraft.* London, 1969.

"Salem Village Book of Record." In Boyer and Nissenbaum, *Salem-Village Witchcraft.*

"Salem Village Church Book Record." In Boyer and Nissenbaum, *Salem-Village Witchcraft.*

Salem Witchcraft Papers. See Boyer and Nissenbaum.

Sargant, William. *Battle for the Mind.* London, 1957.

Sewall, Samuel. *Diary.* Massachusetts Historical Society Collections, 5th ser., vols. 1–3. Boston, 1918.

———. *Letter-book.* Massachusetts Historical Society Collections, 6th ser., vols. 1–2. Boston, 1886–88.

Showalter, Elaine. *The Female Malady: Women, Madness and English Cultures, 1830–1980.* New York, 1985.

Shurtleff, Nathaniel. *Records of the Governor and Company of the Massachusetts Bay.* 5 vols. Boston, 1853–54.

Stannard, David E. *Puritan Way of Death: A Study on Religion, Culture, and Social Change.* New York, 1977.

Starkey, Marion. *The Devil in Massachusetts.* New York, 1949.

Storr Anthony. *Freud.* Oxford, 1989.

Thomas, Keith. *Religion and the Decline of Magic.* New York, 1971.

Trask, Richard B. *The Devil Hath Been Raised.* Danvers, Mass., 1992.

———. *The Meetinghouse at Salem Village.* Danvers, Mass., 1992.

Ulrich, Laurel Thatcher. *Good Wives: Image and Reality in the Lives of Women in Northern New England, 1650–1750.* New York, 1980.

Upham, Charles W. *Salem Witchcraft, with an Account of Salem Village and a History of Opinions on Witchcraft and Kindred Subjects.* Boston, 1867.

Vaughan, Alden T. *New England Frontier: Puritans and Indians, 1620–1675.* Boston, 1965.

Vaughan, Alden T., and Clark, Edward W., eds. *Puritans among the Indians: Accounts of Captivity and Redemption, 1676–1724.* Cambridge, Mass., 1981.

Washburn, Emory. *Sketches of the Judicial History of Massachusetts since 1630 to the Revolution in 1775.* Boston, 1840.

Wendell, Barrett. *Cotton Mather.* New York, 1980.

Winthrop, John. *Winthrop Papers,* vols. 1–5. Boston, 1929.

Wrigglesworth, Michael. *The Day of Doom; or a Poetical Description of the Great and Last Judgement with Other Poems.* Ed. Kenneth B. Murdock. New York, 1929.

Wright, Lawrence. *Remembering Satan.* New York, 1994.

Ziff, Larzer. *Puritanism in America.* New York, 1963.

Index

Index

260

Enlightenment, x
Entertainment, 6
Envy, x, 12, 31, 99, 197
Essay for the Recording of Illustrious Providences, An (I. Mather), 16
Essex County (Massachusetts), 58, 111, 205
Essex (England), 34
Europe's Inner Demons (Cohn), 33
Evil, 2, 9, 10, 22, 31, 33, 82, 85, 97
Examinations, 1
  Alden, John, 144–46
  Bishop, Bridget, 115, 117–19
  Burroughs, Reverend George, 133–35
  Carrier, Martha, 148–49
  Cloyce, Sarah, 105–8
  Cory, Martha, 77–83, 225
  Easty, Mary, 125–26
  Good, Sarah, 41, 42–44, 46–47, 67–69
  Hoar, Dorcas, 131, 132
  Hobbs, Abigail, 105, 115–17
  Hobbs, Deliverance, 124–25
  Howe, Elizabeth, 147–48
  Indian, Tituba, 41, 42, 49–52, 67–69
  Jacobs, George, 136–37
  Jacobs, Margaret, 136–38
  leading questions, 51
  Martin, Susannah, 131, 132
  Nurse, Rebecca, 100, 225
  Osborne, Sarah, 41, 42, 47–49, 67–69
  Proctor, Elizabeth, 105–8
  purposes of, 42
  Tookey, Job, 146–47
  Toothaker, Mary, 149–50
  Warren, Mary, 111–14, 115
Excommunication, 167, 181, 191, 192, 206, 218
Exhibitionism, 20
Exorcism, 34

Falkner, Abigail, 184, 205, 227
Falmouth (Maine), 219
Familiars, 30, 76, 77, 83, 95, 117, 160, 163
Fanaticism, 11, 98, 197

Fantasy, 100
Farrar, Thomas, 244n
Fasting, 69, 104, 155, 207, 208, 210, 211
Fear
  of affection, 3
  of communists, ix, xv
  of enemies, ix
  of Indians, 38–39, 149, 234n
  of science, 16
  of sex, ix, 5
  of witchcraft, 33, 61, 84, 118
  of women, ix
Fisk, Thomas, 166, 167, 207
Fits, 11, 15, 17, 18–20, 24, 34, 36, 37, 42, 44–45, 49, 52, 69, 75, 76, 88, 89, 108, 112, 124, 225, 232n
Fletcher, Benjamin, 142
Flint, Thomas, 62
Floyd, John, 244n
Flying, witches', ix, 154
Food, 4
  stealing, 10
Fornication, 10
Fortunetelling, 13, 187, 232n
Fosdick, Elizabeth, 244n
Foster, Abraham, 204
Foster, Ann, 150, 184, 185, 193, 204, 227
Fraud, 34, 37, 44, 53, 74, 75, 76, 79, 86, 92–93, 103, 109, 110, 166, 224
French and Indian War, 144
Freud, Sigmund, 20, 21, 45

Gallows Hill (Salem Town), xvi, 168, 169–71, 226
Gedney, Bartholomew, 27, 61, 99, 145, 146, 151, 155, 168, 184
Gender
  and control, 22–23
  and education, 7
  in hysteria, 21
  and witchcraft, 31, 32–33
General Court, 15, 55, 121, 142, 155, 162, 192, 199, 201, 204, 205, 207, 208, 223, 227
Glanvill, Joseph, 163
Glorious Revolution (England), 15

About the Author

A native of London, England, where she still lives, Frances Hill has published two novels, *A Fatal Delusion* and *Out of Bounds,* both of which enjoyed great critical acclaim. She is also an accomplished journalist, with a background that ranges from writing fiction reviews for *The Times* (London) to working as a reporter in both New York and London.